LET ME CREATE A

PARADISE,

GOD SAID TO

HIMSELF

LET ME CREATE A
PARADISE,
GOD SAID TO
HIMSELF

A Journey of Conscience from
Johannesburg to Jerusalem

HIRSH GOODMAN

PublicAffairs
New York

Published in the United States by PublicAffairs™,
a member of the Perseus Books Group.

All rights reserved.
Printed in the United States of America.

Unless otherwise noted, all photos are from the author's collection.

No part of this book may be reproduced in any manner whatsoever without written
permission except in the case of brief quotations embodied in critical articles and
reviews. For information, address PublicAffairs, 250 West 57th Street, Suite 1321,
New York, NY 10107. PublicAffairs books are available at special discounts for
bulk purchases in the U.S. by corporations, institutions, and other organizations.
For more information, please contact the Special Markets Department at
the Perseus Books Group, 11 Cambridge Center, Cambridge, MA 02142,
call (617) 252-5298, or email special.markets@perseusbooks.com.

BOOK DESIGN BY JANE RAESE
Set in 12 point Bulmer

Library of Congress Cataloging-in-Publication Data
Goodman, Hirsh.
Let me create a paradise, God said to himself : a journey of conscience from
Johannesburg to Jerusalem / Hirsh Goodman.
p. cm.
ISBN 1-58648-243-2
1. Goodman, Hirsh—Childhood and youth. 2. Jews—South Africa—Biography.
3. South Africa—Social conditions—20th century. 4. Jews, South African—
Israel—Biography. 5. Israel—Social conditions—20th century.
6. Arab-Israeli conflict—Moral and ethical aspects. I. Title.
DS135.S63G654 2005
956.9405'4'092—dc22
[B]
2004060054

FIRST EDITION

2 4 6 8 10 9 7 5 3 1

For the best friend I have ever had—Isabel,
and for Shai, Maya, Gavriel and Lev

CONTENTS

CONTENTS

PART FIVE
CONQUEST AND CONSEQUENCES

ACKNOWLEDGMENTS

THIS BOOK WAS LONG IN GESTATION. It was Michael Levine, over breakfast at the King David Hotel in Jerusalem one sunny morning in April 2002, who helped me focus on the two key experiences in my life, Israel and South Africa, and combine them into one narrative. I am deeply grateful to Michael not only for that, but for agreeing to represent me and for his constant encouragement on what has been a journey like no other I have ever made.

It took a week of near solitude on the beautiful Greek island of Sifnos for the book to begin to find its voice, and the person who encouraged me to take that week off was Isabel, my wife, who has done more than anyone to make this book happen. My thanks and love run deeper than any words could express.

I would like to thank the Jaffee Center for Strategic Studies at Tel Aviv University, where I direct the Bronfman Program on Media Strategy, for making it possible for me to write this book. In particular I want to thank its Head, Dr. Shai Feldman, for his understanding and encouragement, and for his patience when a few weeks turned into a few months. With all his wisdom Shai should have known that when a South African says "just now," he or she could be speaking about days or even weeks.

I am indebted to David Kent, president and CEO of HarperCollins Publishers, Canada, and Peter Osnos, publisher of PublicAffairs, for their trust in me after reading but a few rough early chapters of the book. I appreciate their encouragement and the wonderful group of professionals they lead who have made writing this book an adventure in learning in addition to all else. They include, among many others, Iris Tupholme, VP, publisher and editor-in-chief at HarperCollins; Chris Bucci, my original editor at HarperCollins; and Jim Gifford, who replaced him. But my special thanks goes to David Patterson, without doubt one of the most brilliant editors I have had the privilege to work with in a career that has spanned many editors before him. His comments, guidance and technical skills were all much appreciated, as was his ever-present humor, even though it could do with some mild improvement.

Thanks to those who read the manuscript at various stages, Jeremy Issacharoff, Martin Indyk, Charles Bronfman, Ya'acov Kirshen, Bob Simon and Ehud Ya'ari, who provided me with valuable insights and helped me get my facts straight, and to Jonathan Cummings, who checked them. Any remaining errors are mine.

The staff over at the *Jerusalem Post* archive could not have been more helpful. In particular I would like to thank Alexander Zvielli for guiding me to the dusty boxes and yellowing files that contained my early work. I would like to express my appreciation to the *Jerusalem Post* for allowing me to use its archives at leisure and to the staff of *The Jerusalem Report* for their help.

I would like to thank Cathy Rath for her permission to use the portrait of Yitzhak Rabin on page 187 and Joel Kantor for his photograph of the destruction of Yamit on page 220. John Thomas is to be commended for his wonderful and knowledgeable copyedit of this book. My thanks to him.

And, finally, to all those who have made it possible for me to have had a career in journalism, a profession often derided but ever so critical in the preservation of democracy.

Hirsh Goodman
Jerusalem

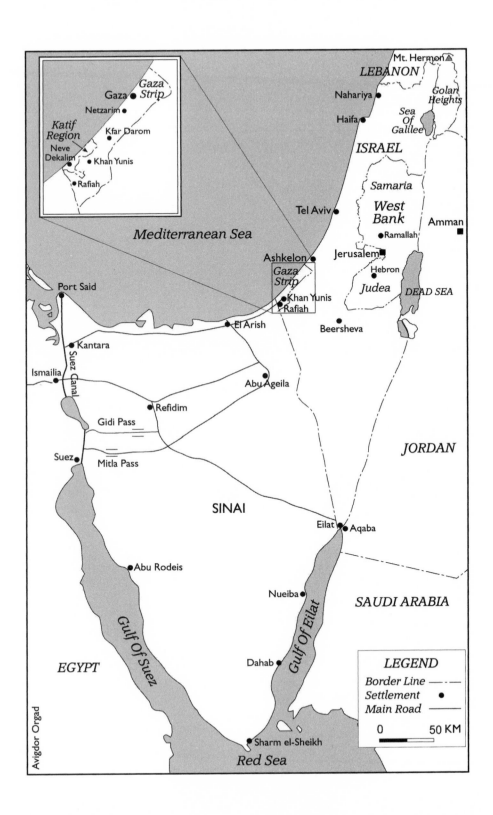

Inset map (Gaza Strip detail):

Gaza Strip
Gaza
Netzarim
Katif Region
Kfar Darom
Neve Dekalim
Khan Yunis
Rafiah

Main map labels:

Mt. Hermon
LEBANON
Nahariya
Golan Heights
Haifa
Sea Of Galilee
ISRAEL
Samara
West Bank
Amman
Tel Aviv
Ramallah
Mediterranean Sea
Ashkelon
Jerusalem
Gaza Strip
Hebron
Khan Yunis
Rafiah
Judea
DEAD SEA
Port Said
El Arish
Beersheva
Kantara
Suez Canal
Ismailia
Abu Ageila
Refidim
Gidi Pass
JORDAN
Suez
Mitla Pass
SINAI
Eilat
Aqaba
Abu Rodeis
Nueiba
SAUDI ARABIA
Gulf Of Suez
Gulf Of Eilat
EGYPT
Dahab

LEGEND
Border Line —·—·—
Settlement   ●
Main Road   ——
0   50 KM

Sharm el-Sheikh
Red Sea

Avigdor Orgad

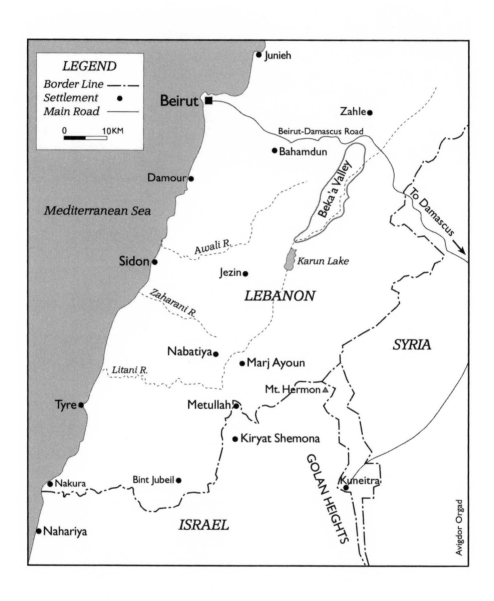

LEGEND
Border Line —·—
Settlement ●
Main Road ——

0   10KM

Junieh ●

Beirut ■

Zahle ●

Beirut-Damascus Road

Bahamdun ●

Damour ●

Mediterranean Sea

Beka'a Valley

To Damascus

Awali R.

Karun Lake

Sidon ●

Jezin ●

LEBANON

Zaharani R.

SYRIA

Nabatiya ●

Marj Ayoun ●

Litani R.

Mt. Hermon ▲

Tyre ●

Metullah ●

Kiryat Shemona ●

Nakura ●

Bint Jubeil ●

GOLAN HEIGHTS

Kuneitra ●

Nahariya ●

ISRAEL

Avigdor Orgad

PART ONE
OUT OF EVIL

1

OSMOSIS

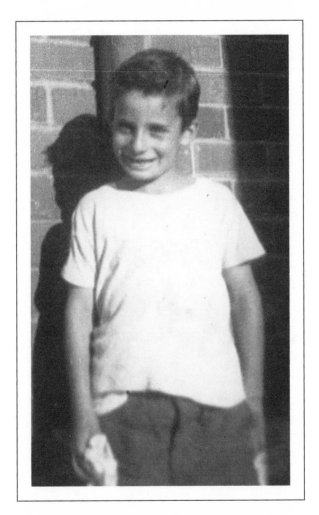

*In the backyard of 27 Yeo Street,
Johannesburg, 1956, age ten.*

I WAS BORN ON MARCH 6, 1946, in Port Elizabeth, South Africa. As Aunty Rosie recalls, my mother, Ginda, already in her late 30s, literally had to be dragged away from the card table to the maternity ward. She was playing a benefit game of bridge for the Women's Zionist League and, apparently, had a very good hand. Fearful that the Zionist cause would suffer if she left the rubber unplayed, she stuck it out, won the hand, made her donation and went off to the hospital to have me, her third child and first son.

To the best of my memory, my own devotion to the Zionist cause started at the age of six when, in the month before Passover and the month before Rosh Hashanah, the New Year, I was forced to wear clothes that were either two sizes too small for me or three sizes too big.

The entire excruciating exercise was designed to cheat the Israeli tax-man every six months when my mother would bundle off clothes to my only aunt in Israel, Feiga, and her family in Jerusalem. There was no tax on used clothes, so mom bought them new and we made them old. Dad, who was short and thin, had to wear clothes for Uncle Felix, who, of course, was tall and muscular. Mom squeezed into tight frocks destined for her petite sister and even tighter clothes bought for Aviva, our cousin. As for me, I took care of Haim and Ya'acov, our two other cousins, Ya'acov being almost two years older than me and Haim two years younger.

For three days I would wear shoes that left my toes squeezed in a geisha-like position as I made sure the virgin leather on the soles and heels of Haim's shoes were scarred and scratched enough for the tax-man. I wore trousers that stopped at the knee and shirts that choked me at the collar, leaving me gasping for air behind the knot of my compulsory school tie. And then, for the next three days, as I broke in Ya'acov's clothes, I swam about in shoes two sizes too large, pants that needed to be folded six times at the cuffs and shirts with sleeves that almost touched the ground.

At the end of the week, all the clothes were washed, washed again and then again, ironed and neatly placed in a bundle that weighed exactly 18 pounds, the postal limit, and wrapped in cheesecloth and lovingly stitched together by my mother. With an indelible pencil that was only used on these occasions, mother then divided the front of the parcel into four equal squares. In the bottom left went Aunt Feiga's address, 37 Leib Yafe Street, Arnona, Jerusalem, Israel. And, in the right top corner, ours: 27 Yeo Street, Yeoville, Johannesburg, to where we had moved from Port Elizabeth when I was two. Apparently my father's sinuses could not take the sea air.

This was not the only way I acted to foil the Israeli customs authorities. I was witness as my mother stitched the inside sleeves of my father's raincoat together and her accomplice as we stuffed salamis, tins of coffee and chocolates in them for my father to take with him on his first trip to Israel in the early '50s.

Things were so bad in the Jewish State at the time, I was told, that chicken, which I hated, was considered a treat and that, for most meals, the family ate rabbit stew, the rabbits coming directly from a hutch in the small garden behind their house. Coffee was virtually unheard of, chicory, an extract of the chicory herb, being as close as one could get, while good salami and sweets were luxuries indeed.

The plane that took my father and his Hebrew teaching colleagues on the first trip of South African educators to the fledgling Jewish State had four propellers and could have been a DC-9, I don't remember. What I do remember, however, is the Star of David on its tail and the Hebrew lettering on its side and that my dad was the only passenger with a raincoat, it being August in Israel, usually the hottest month of the year.

My parents, like almost the entire South African Jewish community, were from Latvia or Lithuania, depending where the line was at any given time. They had arrived around the turn of the century, fleeing the pogroms and lusting after the gold rush. They spoke Russian when they did not want me and my two sisters to understand, Yiddish when they were having normal conversation and English if they had to. We lived in modest circumstances in Yeoville, a suburb of Johannesburg where the grocer, the baker and the butcher were all Jewish. There were ten synagogues within a stone's throw of our house and everyone knew everyone's business.

My father Leib became a Hebrew teacher after failing as a salesman of designer shirts when he first arrived in the country. Like so many others he was a product of the Gymnasia system set up in the Pale of Settlement in Russia, an area where the Jews had been banished to by the Czar, inadvertently bringing together the worlds of religious and secular study.

All subjects in the Gymnasia were taught in Hebrew, hence my father's beautiful command of the language and his ability to move from unsuccessfully selling shirts to successfully ramming Hebrew down the throats of children who wanted nothing more than to get away from their parents' past and become real South Africans. English, he told me, he had learned by reading Tolstoy's *War and Peace* with the help of an English-Russian dictionary on the boat over to South Africa—a story I only sort-of-believed until I later came across the annotated version of the book itself, notes neatly written in pencil in the margins questioning which particular word would fit that particular sentence.

He was a workaholic. He taught at three schools, one in the early morning, the other through to midday and the third in the afternoon. When he came home at night he gave extra lessons to Hebrew strugglers, of whom there were many, and to Bar Mitzvah boys who came to learn their Torah portions at our dining room table while we were banished to silence in the kitchen or our bedrooms.

He was also a hypochondriac. True, he was already in his 40s when I was born. But my mother said he had been the same since the age of 20, his body wracked by internal ulcers for which he took white medicine from a blue bottle and high blood pressure for which he took pills, boxes and boxes of them. He was also always dying of cancer. In the end he committed suicide at the age of 96 in near perfect health claiming that anyone who had seen the Russian Revolution and the downfall of Communism in one life had seen enough.

Other than when he was around his grandchildren he was a sad man who felt that he had been given the short end of the stick. His mother had died at childbirth. His father had already run off with another woman a few months earlier, never to be heard from again. He had been brought up, but never adopted, by an uncle, Benjamin, who apparently was nothing short of a saint. He was said to have devoted his entire life to working for "charity," something I now suspect may have been a euphemism for being a beggar.

Poverty, deprivation, sacrifice, suffering and persecution—these were all themes struck by my father in any narrative about his past, particularly when comparing it to the "fleshpot of today," and never forgetting to mention that he had spent the first ten years of his life using a board balanced between two chairs for a bed. How he progressed from sleeping on a board to acquiring an education and eventually becoming very much part of the racy, absinthe-driven, cultural scene back home in Riga he described to me later in life was never quite explained.

I never spent much time on trying to trace my family roots, unlike my nephews who, in the last years of his life, systematically got my father drunk on Friday nights and then recorded their questioning him about the past. I have the tapes but have never listened to them. To do so would be like hearing a voice from the grave. I also never made much of an attempt to find out about my mother's family. Her father had also run off with another woman, leaving my mother's mother and five daughters to make ends meet by selling tea and cake to theatergoers in Riga before and after shows and during intermission.

Her oldest sister, Raya, became a fervent Communist and ran off to set up a collective settlement in the Ural Mountains. Raya then joined the merchant navy, became a purser, saw the world, became disillusioned with Communism and Russia and in the early 1970s, when the first Jews were finally able to leave the former Soviet Union for Israel, managed to slip in line and come along. It is said in the family that the Israeli immigration officer who greeted her on her arrival was the first Jewish man she had ever met. She died in 2004 at the age of 101 in an ultra-Orthodox aged home in Jerusalem.

The Zionist engine in our house was my mom. Though I never exactly understood why she was a fanatic. She had heard of Herzl, but could not quote a single sentence of the man's writings other than, perhaps, "If you will it, it is no legend," which every Jewish schoolchild knew. She had never heard of Borochov or Berdichevsky or even A. D. Gordon, the Zionist socialist ideologue at the heart of the kibbutz movement. She was no great intellect, my mom, but what a woman. She was, as was politely said, "a soldier," or a "worker" of the Women's Zionist League.

She never sought office or rank in the organization, but when it came to door-to-door collecting from the several dozen Jewish families within a few miles' radius of our home, or collecting secondhand clothes for a jumble sale, all proceeds for the Jewish State, she had no second. From Mrs. Brasque to Mrs. Cohen to old-man Myerson and Mrs. Kramer the butcher's wife, taking in a few pounds here and a couple of shillings there, all recorded in duplicate in a receipt book with a well-used sheet of carbon paper between the pages and accounted to Mrs. Harvey-Cohen, the WZO Treasurer and highly respectable wife of Mr. Harvey-Cohen, the synagogue president.

Since there were often used clothes for the next jumble sale to be dragged off from these visits, I was frequently required to accompany her to carry them back home. There was nothing I hated more than carrying bags full of musty, unwashed, long-stored, mothball-laden, old clothes through the streets of the neighborhood back to my bedroom, where they were sorted and stacked in neat piles until the next sale from over our garden fence. Then the Blacks would buy the shirts for a penny and a dress for six pence, every penny of which, of course, was destined for the Jewish State.

Shirts too small, shoes too large, bags of stinky clothes in my bedroom. By the age of six I considered myself a martyr for the Zionist cause. One ameliorating factor was the monthly cake sale that took place in the vestibule of the Yeoville Synagogue, where the fine ladies of the Jewish community would buy cakes for shillings, not pennies. The night before a sale the cakes would all be brought to our house, where a committee headed by the fabulous Mrs. Rappaport, the community beauty who had survived two rich husbands, would decide how much to price each one. One should not underestimate the politics involved. Try charging less for Mrs. Spitz's cheesecake than Mrs. Hirshbaum's chocolate torte and surviving.

Once priced, these creations would be placed in white square boxes and stacked on the spare bed in my room. Next to them, in straw baskets, sat cellophane bags of homemade sweets, all smelling delicious and tantalizingly close, but remaining secure in that one would never dream of stealing from the Zionist cause. Those bags of sweets and boxes of cake were bricks in the building of our homeland and how proud I was to be part of the effort.

Though we were not a particularly devout family in the Orthodox sense, identifying with being Jewish was everything in our lives and being Jewish and being a Zionist were, of course, the same thing. If you went to a secular school, like I did, it was understood that your afternoons would be devoted to *heider,* Hebrew school, and Saturday mornings to Children's Services, where bible stories were told and small chocolates handed out if you sat through the entire service. There must have been a dozen synagogues within a mile of our house, three of them with several hundred families belonging.

Unfortunately for me my father happened to be the principal and the person who conducted the children's services at the Hebrew school I was forced to attend. How many black eyes, curses, kicks in the shin and even gobs of spittle I had to endure from boys who hated Hebrew school, hated children's services and, apparently, hated me.

The only kid who was nice to me was Basil, the undertaker's boy, who everybody else was scared to play with, saying that his clothes had the stench of death to them. The experience was to repeat itself at my Jewish high school, King David, where again my father was a Hebrew teacher.

By that time, however, I had managed to cope with the problem simply by agreeing with my antagonists that my dad was a shit and that if I had the choice I would most definitely find myself a different father.

Most of South Africa's Jews were what one could call nonobservant Orthodox, which meant you attended Hebrew school for at least some portion of your life and went to an Orthodox synagogue, but parked a few blocks away on the Sabbath when driving was formally forbidden, so as not to offend anyone. Services were held in Hebrew, which most of the people in attendance could not fully understand, but the choir and cantor were generally magnificent in adding to the aura of seriousness and spirituality of the occasion.

Going to *shul* was a posh affair. Ours was the Berea Synagogue, a solid building with grand steps and mahogany pews and a *bimah* from where *Hazan* Mandel prayed so absolutely beautifully in unison with Mr. Balaikin's choir. The choir responded to the cantor's chants from behind a curtain above the Holy Ark, itself impressive with marble inlays and a lamp that was never allowed to go out. The women sat above in a gallery, mothers in hats carefully scanning the men below for potential matches for their daughters.

In a wooden box at the foot of the *bimah* sat the three *gabbais,* wardens, in top hats and coattails. The rabbi, Rabbi Swift, who had come to South Africa from England, was awesome, almost godly, in his robes, felt hat with a black pom-pom on top and squarely trimmed beard that just touched his impeccably white collar. When Rabbi Swift spoke from the pulpit in front of the Ark the constant buzz that pervaded services as men made their golf dates, boys discussed which girls were "giving it" and the week's gossip was exchanged came to an abrupt end. From our point of view there was absolutely no doubting that he was God's representative in Berea.

Our home, like most, was kosher. The meat brought in from Kramer's butchery was subjected to a soaking in salt to make sure that every last drop of blood had been drained. Chickens were held over a blue flame emanating from a tin filled with spirits for the purpose of burning off any blood or feathers that may have escaped the butcher's assistant, a Black man called Amos who had two fingers missing from his right hand.

We had two sets of dishes and two sets of cutlery, one for meat and the other for milk, and we had Passover dishes locked in a cupboard that was only opened once a year. One of the most remarkable things about my mom's kitchen was that the strict kosher regime was enforced by Grace, my nanny, our domestic servant and a magnificent cook, who even the most viperous of my mother's friends agreed made the best gefilte fish in Yeoville and, perhaps, even in all of Johannesburg.

Gracie had been with our family from the day we arrived in Johannesburg. When I was a baby she had carried me on her back tied in a blanket, almost like an inverse kangaroo, as she went about her daily tasks. My mom, of course, was usually off pursuing the Zionist cause, either playing cards and placing a penny in the Blue Box for every round dealt, or playing bowls at the Balfour Park Club, the Jewish country club named for Lord Balfour, the British foreign minister who in 1917 issued the declaration establishing the right for a homeland for the Jews in British Mandatory Palestine. Those were mother's morning and afternoon activities, fitted in after her daily shop, and before her evening round of the neighborhood collecting for Israel.

On Tuesday and Thursday afternoons there were WZO meetings that could never be missed, no matter what, and once a year, with great fanfare, there was the publication of the famous New International Goodwill Recipe Book, or the Yeoville Book as it is known throughout South Africa. First published in 1950, the latest 326-page edition came out in 1982, updated and metricated, with kosher recipes submitted by the ladies of Johannesburg, all of which, according to my mom, were useless. What Jewish woman, she wanted to know, would give away her most precious culinary secrets in a society where small talk was king and talk about food was almost a religious experience?

Why on earth, she wanted to know, would Goldie Fishbein want anyone to make her *teiglach* as well as her? It was not just unnatural but, worse, un-Jewish. My mom remained convinced, despite all the proof over the years to the contrary as my sisters and family churned out delicious dish after dish by going according to the book, that the contributors had added a spoon of sugar too much or missed a pinch of salt.

Our house on Yeo Street, two blocks up from Raleigh Street, the main shopping street where the trams ran, was fairly modest by South African standards. Yeoville was east of Louis Botha Avenue, a four-lane road that ran from the center of Johannesburg to Pretoria. It was our equivalent of the other side of the tracks. Yeoville was middle class and very much Jewish while west of Louis Botha was where the rich Jews lived in mansions with servants in white uniforms and swimming pools, tennis courts, billiard rooms and every luxury one could imagine.

There were, to the best of my memory, no tensions between the rich and the middle class (there were few "poor" Jews in South Africa). Rather the contrary was true. Being Jewish was the great equalizer. Those of us on the east side of the tracks enjoyed the blessings of our friends from the west and felt absolutely no embarrassment in having them over to our modest homes. Even though Apartheid South Africa was an incredibly materialistic society, to the point where in order to maintain their lifestyles 4 million Whites were prepared to use all means to subjugate 22 million Blacks, there was no class envy.

The wealth of others was almost like communal wealth. We met at Gerald's pool and had meetings at Riva's house and played tennis tournaments at the Maltz's. My folks did not have a car until my dad was 52. He was forced to buy one when his daily lift, Mr. Achron, died, but that did not prevent the Levys or the Levinrads from coming over to take us to Zoo Lake or the Wilds on a Saturday, after *shul* of course, or on Sundays, when we would venture out to Galoli's Farm, a tea resort then far outside of the city.

Though 120,000 strong and fairly widely dispersed, the South African Jewish community was very much like a family. There was no such thing as an orphan not looked after or an aged person who could not live out their life in dignity. In addition to their income taxes, many in the community paid one-seventh of their earnings to the community chest, some of which remained in South Africa to service local Jewish needs and the remainder of which went to Israel.

And though those first-generation South Africans like myself were *very* South African, with our lives centered around rugby, tennis and barbeques, at the center of it all was The Community, an all-powerful presence in the form of synagogues, schools, youth movements, sports clubs, social responsibilities, friendships, summer camps and, by osmosis, the jewel in the crown, Israel.

Israel in the home with lavishly framed reproductions of Abel Pann's illustrations from the Five Books of Moses in the lounge, brass etchings of the Wailing Wall and Rachel's Tomb in the entrance hall, portraits of Herzl and Ben-Gurion in the study and, under the glass of the dresser in my parent's bedroom, a large photograph of my father with Uncle Felix, Aunty Feiga, Aviva, Haim and Ya'acov sitting on the wall in front of Jerusalem's King David Hotel, with Ya'acov and Haim looking splendid in the shoes, shorts and shirts I had worn but a few weeks earlier.

I used to look at that picture for ages wishing I could be there with them, sitting on the wall of one of the most famous hotels in the world, the one Menachem Begin's *Etzel* underground organization had blown up prior to the War of Independence when it served as the base for the

British military occupation forces. I would imagine myself in uniform fighting for my country, for people like Felix and Feiga who had fled from Poland on foot and with Ya'acov who was about to go into the army. I loved South Africa, the physical beauty of the country, its music and people, but I was not at peace there. I was too young to understand why, and when I asked why it was that there were no White servants I was told to "shurrup" and not to speak about such things; that there were issues little boys were not supposed to understand until after their Bar Mitzvahs. That is where any discussion on the subject was usually left.

2

GRACE

*A bewildered soldier in the South African army,
soon I would become a dispatch rider in the
infantry with no motorbike.*

IN OUR HOME WE SAID GRACE after every meal except on Sunday evenings (when Grace was off). We said Grace by yelling her name from the dining room or, when guests were present, by ringing a little silver bell that had its own silver tray strategically placed at my mom's right hand. On hearing the yell or bell, Grace would waddle in with a tray, go round the table collecting the dishes and waddle off back to the scullery, the little room off the kitchen, her huge backside swaying from left to right and back again, and her bare feet sliding across the waxed floor.

The scullery room was her fiefdom. It was where she would wash and dry dishes, steam the laundry in huge vats on the potbellied stove and entertain friends who would come by and sit on a small stool in the corner and be given strong tea in an enamel cup we used to call the "postman's cup."

It was customary at the time, because postmen had to walk long distances between houses, that they be offered a cup of tea when delivering the mail. There were two postmen, however. A White one and a Black one. The Black one carried the bag, the White one, usually an illiterate Afrikaner given a state job, popped the letters into the box. The White postman would receive his tea in a cup and saucer with a small biscuit next to it and sit on the garden chair while drinking. The Black postman would be given the "postman's cup," the chipped enamel mug, and a hefty slice of white bread. He would then sit on the balcony stair, almost at his master's feet, while he loudly sipped and dipped chunks of bread into his tea and kept his eyes fixed on the ground.

Gracie lived in a small room in our backyard. It was built of the cheapest brick, had a corrugated iron roof with no insulation and lacked running water. There was a flushing toilet in an outhouse under the fig tree, but to have a bath Grace would have to lug buckets of water from our kitchen to fill the small, round, tin tub usually stored on a nail on the door of her room, and then somehow get her copious physique into it, a feat I could not hope to understand.

The room was lit by a single naked bulb hanging down from a cord in the center. Her furnishings were two wooden chairs from our old dining room set long replaced, what used to be our kitchen curtains scantily covering her window and, in the middle of the tiny room, a metal chest, a *trommel,* once used by my older sister when she went to camp. It was now covered with a white lace tablecloth, also handed down from my mother, and served as Gracie's table. Against one wall were two crates that had once contained oranges. They now displayed a few of my mom's discarded chipped china dishes, a little vase with pictures of roses that I had won at a school fair and given her as a present, and two enamel cups, as if they were prized ornaments.

On the wall above the crates were two pictures: one of me aged six and her child Maid age four, squinting into the sun from the kitchen stairs. This had been taken during one of Maid's annual monthly summer visits. The other was a copy of the one of my father, uncle, aunt and three cousins sitting on the wall of the King David Hotel in Jerusalem. She considered the picture a holy relic.

That her boss had been to the Holy Land gave Gracie standing in her church, the Church of Zion, a strange order that seemed to conglomerate Judaism and Baptist Christianity. They prayed near the rivers on Sundays, dressed in blue and white robes with the cross prominently displayed and sang in wonderful harmony, including songs that had Hebrew in them. They were known to be good, nonviolent people drawn from all the tribes.

Though members of the Church of Zion were said to have no vices, it was well known in the neighborhood that Gracie was the local *"farfie"* lady who ran the numbers racket for the "Chinaman." He used to drive up outside our house in a blue sedan with dark windows twice a day, once at noon to take the money Grace had collected from the other domestics, garden "boys," washerwomen, road laborers and flat "boys" in the area, and again at three in the afternoon when he came with the results of that day's lottery. She claimed she never won, which, by her logic, made it less of a vice.

My mother was a very caring person, but for all intents and purposes Grace was what could be called my "executive mother." She woke me up in the morning, made sure my room was warm so that I could get out of bed in comfort, ironed my school uniforms, including my underpants and socks, polished my shoes and made me breakfast. She would give me my sandwiches for school, ask me what I wanted for lunch and tell me what there would be for dinner. Just before I would hop on my bike to ride off (I had been banned from using the school bus for bad behavior) she would put her hand on my head and say: "*Tokolosh, Tokolosh, stay away, Tokolosh, Tokolosh* don't ever come back another day . . . ," and then something in her native Xhosa tongue that sounded like three clicks and a clack.

The *Tokolosh* was a three-foot-high little devil with big red ears who was constantly out to make mischief. He was the fear of all Xhosas and was the reason Gracie's bed was elevated on four one-gallon paint tins that had been filled with cement, one for each leg, which kept her out of *Tokolosh* range while she slept. Like the gambling, the *Tokolosh* was something Grace had no problem reconciling with her Christian beliefs. "We all have our Lucifers," she explained, "except ours is a midget."

Grace had a husband, Fred, a dapper man always reeking of liquor, cheap brandy or *kaffirbeer,* a homemade, vile-smelling, yeast-based brew made illegally and sold in *shabeens,* one of which was located in the "boys rooms" in the apartment building across the road from our house. Fred would often emerge from there, a little unsteady on his feet, hat tilted on his head and a smile from ear-to-ear.

Fred worked at a hotel, the Carlton, located in Hillbrow, a densely populated high-rise suburb but a few miles from our house. At the time, Hillbrow was where Johannesburg went out at night. Today the place looks like Mombasa, its once grand high-rise buildings now occupied mainly by unemployed migrants fleeing other parts of Africa for the allure of newly liberated post-Apartheid South Africa, only to find no work but that crime does pay. You do not walk through Hillbrow with a watch on even at midday and come away with it still in your possession.

Despite the proximity of our home to Fred's place of employment, Grace and Fred could have been on different planets. Under Apartheid's Pass Laws, Grace was only allowed to domicile at our home as our registered domestic; Fred could only live in the male dormitory of the Carlton Hotel, where he was registered to work. He would visit us on his day off, but by nine at night he had to be back in his dormitory, a long cold building with a brightly polished red floor and rows of bunk beds down the walls. There was a shared toilet and shower and each man had a small metal cupboard next to his bed. There was absolutely no privacy, with grown men, fathers and sometimes grandfathers, called "boys" and made to live like children in a boarding school. We saw nothing wrong in this.

It was as if Grace, my executive mother, and Fred, her husband, were not really people. When we sat and were served our meals by the servants, conversations went on as if they had no ears and could understand nothing, not even when the most intimate family matters were being discussed or, indeed, the servants themselves.

This was the case not only in our home, but in every South African home I was ever in. It was a conditioning process. When an average South African was asked in the Apartheid era what the population of a town was, they would invariably give you only the number of Whites, as if the Blacks were not there. When my brother-in-law Monty came to visit Israel in the early '70s and my friend Leo asked him about the population of Middleburg, the small Transvaal town where he lived, Monty replied 10,000. Then, as an afterthought, he added: "Oh, and about 90,000 Blacks."

Conditioning in South Africa was relatively easy. There was no television in the country, lest our Blacks ever see that their lot in life was not that of Blacks everywhere. White South Africans seldom traveled abroad, the country being isolated, air travel expensive and their living in a huge country with great holiday places and almost everything one could wish for.

The press was tightly controlled. Editors were constantly being arrested for violations of the Press Regulations. Radio was state-owned. The school curriculum was strictly monitored. In high school, for example, all were required to study from one history textbook authored by a certain Geldenhuis that taught that until Jan van Riebeek, the Dutch founder of modern South Africa, stepped foot on the soil of the Cape in 1662, South Africa was quite simply an empty country. Only after the industrious White man made the country flourish did the hoards of barbarous, heathen Blacks descend from the north causing war, death and destruction. This is what the book, and our teachers, taught us even in the Jewish day school.

There were no pornographic magazines, all films were censored for content and certain books were banned, including a children's book about a horse called "Black Beauty." No seditious materials were allowed, which, of course, included virtually everything that did not praise either the concept of Separate Development, as Apartheid was officially called, or the Dutch Reformed Church. The Church set the harsh Calvinistic rules by which all in South Africa lived their daily lives. You could not, for instance, buy an ice cream in the capital Pretoria on a Sunday, an ice cream being considered "entertainment."

The Afrikaners explained Apartheid biblically, and thus one could not argue with it, to do so would be sacrilegious. The story was simple: Ham laughed at Noah in his nakedness. God punished Ham to be Black. The Blacks were cursed on this earth and, perhaps, if one prays hard enough for them, they will have a better life in the world to come.

In the meantime Grace and Fred had to part company by nine at night. Except, that is, on the occasions when Fred was too drunk to leave at nine. Then I, even at the young age of seven, would write a note carefully copied from the text that Grace had written for me, saying: "Dear Mr. Policeman, please let Fred, husband of Grace of the Goodman home at 27 Yeo Street, telephone 433266, be out till eleven tonight because it is his auntie's birthday in Soweto and he cannot be back before then. With Thanks. Master H. Goodman."

To be found in violation of the draconian Pass Laws could mean months of prison and forced labor picking potatoes out of the red earth of the eastern Transvaal or cutting sugarcane in Natal. Second-time offenders were also sentenced to lashes, 12, 15 or 20 of them administered to the back, splitting open the skin, with a doctor in attendance. The blows came from a *shambok,* a whip made from a rhinoceros's tail and capable of inflicting unbelievable pain.

It was something we bore in mind, lashings being given not only to Blacks but also Whites guilty of crimes like smoking marijuana, car theft, rape and, God forbid, sleeping with a Black woman, which meant not only a lashing, but certain incarceration as well.

Apartheid South Africa was a cruel and violent society. The Pass Laws and domicile requirements broke down Black family structures. It is no accident that today's South Africa has the largest HIV-positive population in the world, more than five and a half million people. Over six hundred HIV-related funerals take place every day.

Next to Fred's dormitory on the roof of the Carlton was the women's dormitory, for chambermaids, kitchen help and domestics who, like Grace, had come to the city for work from the countryside, where farm help was paid in corn, sugar and cigarettes, and the poverty unbelievable. As often as Fred visited Grace's room, so would Blind John, the one-eyed garden boy, Johannes, the flat boy from 33 Yeo, and a string of others.

On the weekends the *kopjies,* the rocky hills that separated Johannesburg's sprawling suburbs, would have dozens of men sitting in circles drinking their *kaffirbeer.* As the beer went down and tempers rose, out would come the *knobkerries,* cudgels cut from thick tree branches and carved to have a big wooden knob on the end with which to pulverize one's opponent should a fight break out, which it always did.

My friends and I would walk the *kopjies,* watching the drunken Blacks fight, sometimes beating each other to death. We would see men and women copulating almost in the open, often within sight of each other. We would see tribal gatherings of Zulus and Xhosas and Basutus, each with their own culture, the Zulus being particularly warlike and violent while the Xhosas, who were herding folk, were softer and more compassionate and, therefore, preferred as domestics. The Zulus, who came from the area north of Natal, were in Johannesburg to work the mines. They lived in compounds and worked deep underground, hundreds of feet beneath the city, burrowing out the gold that made the country so incredibly wealthy, together with the diamonds, tin, copper and other generous bounty that was bestowed on Africa's southern tip.

Thus it was that we thought nothing of it when my sister, Sorrelle, who lived in a small Eastern Transvaal town called Bethal with her family, decided to build a swimming pool. One morning three trucks pulled up. Sitting in the open bins in the back were convicts with their hands on their heads. On the roof of the driver's cabin sat a White warden with a rifle and, at the tail end, a Black warden with a *shambok* always ready to inflict pain for even the slightest transgression.

There they sat, huddled together against the freezing cold, each dressed in nothing but a filthy pair of canvas shorts and a canvas shirt, no underclothes and no shoes. Singing in unison a rhythmic African chant, they dug and picked away at the earth of the south garden of the house on Mooi Street until after three days there was a hole 45 feet long, 15 feet wide and ranging from three to six feet in depth.

The Prison Service got paid two-and-sixpence for each convict per day. The pool diggers were also provided with a breakfast of *putupap*, a white maize porridge dished out by one of the convicts from a *kaffirpot* hung low over a fire, and a dinner of watery stew served at dusk, each man getting half a loaf of white bread with which to soak up the gravy.

Then, before being loaded back onto the truck, under the very-so-quick *shambok*, they were subjected to the humiliation of being body searched in full view of the entire street, each man bending down and opening up his backside to show the warders that he was not smuggling anything back into prison. We watched all of this then handed out two packs of Little Max cigarettes to the warder to share with the men.

What was especially disgraceful about it all was that these convicts were not even really criminals. The murderers and rapists, thieves and political detainees were kept behind bars or hung. These men were like Fred, arrested for breaking the Pass Law rules by being out late at night or by being in a district where they were not registered.

This did not seem to bother anyone at all. Indeed at dinner the conversation was not about innocent men being rounded up by the police for the express reason of supplying the Prison Service with income as well as to enforce the absurdity of Apartheid, but what a cost-effective exercise it had all been. Had a tractor been brought in the pool would have cost three times as much.

Everyone seemed extremely pleased with themselves, including Rex, my sister's family boy, who was serving us dressed in a white suit and white gloves, with a red sash hanging neatly across his chest. He was just pleased to be in a warm house with a fire and good food on the stove and not in prison. "You better be careful Rexie," I said dead seriously, "so they don't catch you when you're sneaking back home from doing the *humbalala jig jig* with Mary down the road, hey?"

"No way Master Hirsh," he said. Neither of us, for a minute, questioned the justice of a sentence of 90 days' slave labor for not having a pass. As with almost everything else in South Africa it was convenient not to question "why." You traveled on White-only buses and sat on White-only benches and swam at White-only beaches and went to White-only schools and never gave it a thought. It was a very convenient reality to live with if you were White, and even if you were a Jew, though one could have expected different given the Jewish experience of but a decade before and the Zionist-Socialist, egalitarian principles almost every South African Jewish child was increasingly becoming indoctrinated with.

Ultimately Jews came to lead the anti-Apartheid movement. Nearly half the people arrested when the secret police raided the African National Congress headquarters at Rivonia, a farm outside Johannesburg, in 1963, were Jewish. Issy Maisels and Helen Suzman, the Liberal politicians, were Jewish. But these people were the exception, not the rule, like everybody else. The Jews liked having Rex bring them a cola tonic down to the pool and get the fire going while the boss entertained the guests. It was considered a civilized way of life.

3
SAPLING TO SEED

Enraptured youngsters at a Habonim *camp listen to a* madrich,
a counselor, explain a map of Israel built in the sand. Leaches Bay, 1959.
(Courtesy Beulah Goodman)

WE WERE NOT TOTALLY BLIND to the absurdities that prevailed in almost every aspect of the culture we lived in, but pretty much so, even in the idealistic Zionist-Socialist youth movements we belonged to. Off I would go to my weekly meetings with my uniform recently pressed by Gracie, my shoes buffed to brilliance and all my badges and insignias perfectly in place. There we would discuss equality, egalitarianism, social justice, democracy, freedom of the press, Dialectical Materialism, the writings of A. D. Gordon extolling the virtues of labor—all within the context of Israel of course. South Africa ended where Zionist Socialism began. It all seemed perfectly normal and totally unhypocritical.

Habonim, Hebrew for "The Builders," was the name of my youth group. There were at least half a dozen others to choose from, all mirror images of the political divisions in Israel, but you usually landed up either where your friends went or in the Zionist youth movement that had the prettiest girls in your age group.

Habonim represented the mainstream Mapai faction of the Labor Party. When we joined at around age eight, we belonged to the Shtilim group, or saplings. It was the first stage of a process that would take us through Bonim (builders) and Solelim (pavers), to becoming one of the Movement's *madrichim* (leaders), responsible for passing the Word on to the next generation of wide-eyed Zionists mesmerized by the posters on the walls depicting pioneers making the desert bloom, sweat showing through their khaki shirts, as they hoed the Negev and sang *"Hava Nagila."*

Meetings were held at the Bayit, the Movement's communal home where senior *madrichim* and those who belonged to the *garin,* "the seed," the next group of Movement members on their way to Israel, lived and shared everything, including a common pot of money called a *kupa.* It was a kibbutz in the middle of Johannesburg, except mom dropped your clean laundry off once a week.

They had a governing committee, a treasurer, and a strict code of conduct and they farmed vegetables in the garden. They shared tastes in music, making sure that each person received equal time on the communal phonograph to play their records to the communal audience. This was considered reality training for the life we would choose for ourselves in Israel, yet another fostering of the illusion that life on kibbutz was nothing short of paradise. It was a place, we believed, where all people got along, where personal ambition was happily sacrificed on the altar of community need and where all would love each other's music and truly not mind not having one's own record player.

The Movement consisted further of camps and seminars and weekends on *hachshara,* a farm on the outskirts of Johannesburg where those really serious about going to Israel lived and worked communally. It was a time of shared sleeping bags and calibrated sexual discovery, with many of the kids who started dating at 14 ultimately marrying each other. It was Israeli plays acted in English about brave *Palmach* soldiers with woolen caps on their heads who had fought back the Arabs in the heroic battle of the Kastel. It was Israeli dancing and a choir that sang Israeli songs. It was about milking cows and driving tractors and dreaming of working the land of Israel.

The senior leadership spent a year in Israel preparing to be *madrichim* and a high percentage of them ultimately moved to Israel at some point in their lives. Some of them were legendary, like Luke and Benny, who were Israeli paratroopers and had actually fought in the 1956 Sinai Campaign and who had had their pictures taken with Moshe Dayan and David Ben-Gurion. And then there were the *shlichim,* the families sent from Israel for two-year stints to lead the Movement, more to guide it actually, and who had a terrific impact on our lives.

I can think of no person who had more influence over my thinking than Leib Golan, the Movement's *shaliach* in the last three years before I left for Israel. Leib was originally from Kimberley, but for the past decade or more had lived on Kibbutz Ma'ayan Baruch in the Galilee just at the point where the borders of Israel, Lebanon and Syria converge. Leib was the New Jew, a full head of pitch-black hair, white teeth, broad smile, arms as thick as trees, a black mustache, always an open-necked shirt, usually khaki, a thick, hairy chest and a broad barrel of a neck. His wife was Hermona, named after the Hermon Mountains. She was a redhead, and they had a son, Guy, later to become a fighter pilot, only to be killed in an accident one night when, for reasons never fully discovered, he landed his F-15 in a muddy field in line with but far short of the air base's runway.

Leib was pure energy and he beamed passion and love for his country. He was a Jewish pride machine. He spoke of apple orchards and the
Hazbani River and the cool waters of the Dan. He told of the land mines
along the roads, artillery battles with the Syrians, incursions from Lebanon and how the children on the kibbutz often had to sleep in air raid
shelters. But it was our country and our land. We had dried out the Hula
swamps, sold to us as worthless mosquito-breeding grounds by absen-
tee Turkish pashas, and we had turned them into wheatfields for as far as
the eye could see. We had revived a dead language and now Hebrew po-
ets, writers, journalists and academics in our own Israeli universities
were breathing further life into it.

New words approved by the Israel Academy of Language were being
added each day, each loyal to its historic biblical or medieval Hebrew
root, and brilliantly inventive in its adaptation. Leib made all this come
alive. He spoke of the challenge of creating an Israeli culture in a land
comprising new immigrants from 104 countries, of how unbelievable it
was that Israel had its own universities, already including some of the
best in the world.

And there was Yoram and his wife Ettie, both *Sabras,* native-born Israelis from Kibbutz Kinneret near the Sea of Galilee, the third oldest kibbutz in the country. He was straight out of a picture postcard a friend had
sent from Israel, suntanned and strong with an Israeli intonation in his
halting yet comprehensible English. He and Ettie were amazing singers
and created a near professional choir while they were in Johannesburg.

They brought the latest Israeli songs and dances and led us all
around late-night campfires or at regular Bayit meetings. At camp each
year, Yoram always took the lead on the four-day walks through the
wilds of the Cape, stalking ahead, maps in hand, taking occasional
squints at the sun and using a matchstick on the face of his watch to tell
him which direction we were headed. Of course we followed him
blindly. He had been an officer in the Israeli Armored Corps and it was
inconceivable that he would ever let us down.

These people and our *madrichim* introduced us to the Zionist
philosophers, to the concept of Jewish labor, to the challenges of building a country and, above all, to making sure that "It"—the Holocaust—

would never happen again. Never again would we let our people be led like sheep to the slaughter.

Eventually, as we moved up the ranks of the Movement, it began to deal with the issue of Apartheid intelligently. We were taught to be unequivocally against it and declared it abhorrent. Habonim's battles, however, were over in Israel. Those fighting Apartheid, some of its most vociferous opponents being former Movement members, were fighting a just cause. More power to them. But our home was Israel and that was where we intended to put our life on the line.

We made an issue of understanding Black culture and appreciating it, particularly the music and dance. In camp and around bonfires, Zulu and Xhosa melodies were sung with as much harmony and love as Israeli songs. We also saw and appreciated the deep respect tribal people had for their elders and the love they had for children. We were made to see that there was not one color of Black, but deep shades of it, different tribes with different customs; that the troubled urban Blacks, the people whose lives, families, communal structures, parents and children were taken away from them by the Pass Laws, were the products of our crimes, not their weaknesses.

Though we were taught social justice in the context of Israel, we had come to recognize that it had to be applied to South Africa as well. Hence on *hachshara* there was no hired labor. The campsite for hundreds of children was prepared by the seniors of the Movement who went out each year on A-Guard, or Advance Guard, to construct a watchtower out of wooden planks and rope just like the early *halutzim,* as the pioneers in Israel were called, used to do. They would pitch tent villages divided into boy and girl sections, one for each age group, and dig the plyms, holes in the ground to be used as toilets, over which a long wooden box with holes in it was placed. The value of labor was extolled, as was vigilance, so there was both kitchen duty and *shmira,* or guard duty, done by couples armed with a torch and a whistle should they see anything untoward. *Shmira,* a two-hour stint from 10 P.M. to 6 A.M., was, of course, the way boys and girls who were "going out" got two hours of privacy for smooching. Who was doing *shmira* with who was always a matter of great interest.

I never became a leader in the Movement, preferring the fooling-around-in-the-sleeping-bag routine to late-night sessions on the writings of Berdichevsky or the virtues of Dialectical Materialism. Still, I was deeply involved and the Movement was a huge part of my life. It gave me a scale of values and opened my mind to new thinking I would never have been exposed to otherwise. It gave me pride in being a Jew, in what our people were achieving in Israel, and instilled in me the importance of memory.

I was committed to their positive feeling of belonging, especially in a society where, more and more, I was beginning to realize there were many who would attempt to make me conscious, even ashamed, of being a Jew. Jerry, the drug addict in the park I had to cross on the way to school, would greet me every morning by shouting: "Hello you fucking Jew." When we went down in a scrum playing rugby against Afrikaans schools we were always called a "fokken Yood" and told that "I'm gonna make Hitler happy today Jewboy."

I needed neither Habonim nor Jerry to convince me to move to Israel. I made up my mind unequivocally one Sunday afternoon a week after my fifteenth birthday. I had gotten off the bus on the way to a soccer game at Balfour Park, when I saw two Black men fighting on the pavement. They were hitting each other, using bricks as clubs, and one man's brains were oozing out of his head. A crowd of Whites were standing by, laughing, clapping and encouraging the two men to battle until death. Four policemen sat on the bonnet of a blue van, craning their necks to watch the spectacle, laughing and clapping as hard as anyone. It was at that moment I knew I could never live in South Africa and I remember thanking God ever so deeply that I had an alternative.

As a White male I could not leave South Africa without first doing nine months of compulsory military service, something I wanted to get over with as quickly as possible. In eleventh grade, while my parents were on an extended trip to Europe, I took advantage of their absence and my ability to forge my father's signature to sign myself out of King David and into Damelin College, a cram school where I could get my matriculation out of the way in six months. They basically gave you the answers to the questions in advance.

My grades at King David were abysmal. My Latin teacher, Dr. Thomas, had told me to go sell vegetables and, of late, the sadistic headmaster, Dr. Sandler, had been caning me more than usual. It was as if he was out to get me either for being slovenly, a charge hard to refute, or for misbehaving, a relative call.

Accused and damned I would be ordered to his office, made to wait on a wooden bench in a long cold corridor with highly polished floors. One by one teachers in the staff room just across the hall would come out to see who the next victim was, giving me a knowing look: "Goodman's son—again." And then I would be called in, made to bend over as Sandler gave me two, three, four, up to six "of the best" with a rod from a quince tree or a cane from springy bamboo.

I sailed through Damelin, which left me with four months to kill before my army intake. The Movement's *hachshara* was closed for the winter, so the appropriate Movement authorities decided that it would be O.K. for me to go and work on a regular farm to get the practical, if not the ideological and spiritual, experience necessary for life on kibbutz.

My sister in Bethal, Sorrelle, knew a farmer, Mr. Stein. He agreed to take me on as a favor and assigned me to overseeing the morning and afternoon milking, running the farm store and generally being of assistance to Mr. Van Zyl, the farm's foreman, a massive Afrikaner who could neither read nor write, but could, and did, quote the Bible incessantly. The Black farmworkers and their families lived on *kraals* dotted around the farm, with the men usually doing the more skilled labor like milking or driving tractors or herding, the women tending to the *kraal* and the few sparse fields of maize they were allowed to grow near it. Battalions of convicts supplied by the Prison Service did the rest of the work.

An average day in the dairy started at 5 A.M. Then, several hundred cows were hand milked by men who would sing along in unison as they pulled at the udders, responding to the lead singer, Marias, a man who had been "chief dairy boy" for twenty years, and who now had a new boss—me.

I had never seen warm froths of fresh milk spurt out of the udder before. I loved the early morning milking, its rhythm and the wise smile of

Marias, who told me funny stories about the *Tokolosh*'s activities the previous night, all the while calling me "Master Hirsh," actually, *baasie Hishee*. A long line of little girls would stand outside the barn door, identical metal jugs balancing on their heads, waiting patiently in the early morning cold for their daily allotment of milk, often having to walk miles on this journey from home to dairy. Marias told me that the girls carried the jugs on their heads so that the *boomslang* wouldn't get them. This was a small, deadly poisonous, green snake that dropped out of trees onto the necks of its hapless victims, who would die within minutes of being bitten.

After milking I would carry a metal jug of milk to the main house, opening the door to the smell of freshly baked bread, a broad smile from Janie the cook, and a huge breakfast of fried eggs, steak and sausage. Mr. Van Zyl would wait in the outside room next to the kitchen with his coffee for Mr. Stein's daily instructions, to discuss yesterday's problems and plan for the future. Van Zyl would then grudgingly beckon me to follow him to the horses for the day's work, which could be anything from branding cattle, to castrating bulls, to overseeing the convicts as they picked their way through endless fields of corn always in fear of the *shambok* wielded by the horse-mounted wardens coming down on their backs. Van Zyl would ride between the rows of men, steering his horse so as to bump aside as many of them as possible.

From time to time he would take a cigarette out, light it, take a few puffs and then make as if to flick it away. The convicts would beg him to throw it to them, pleading "please baas, please baas," clapping their hands in front of their faces. To think that these men, like our pool diggers, were not convicts at all, but probably "guilty" of some misdemeanor like transgressing the Pass Laws, was not something Van Zyl would ponder. He felt he was being charitable, lighting up far many more cigarettes than he usually would, so as to be generous.

And so it went for three months, me preparing myself for the socialism of kibbutz life with Van Zyl as my mentor, explaining why convicts were more efficient and cheaper than combines. The combines always left ten percent on the stalk while a convict, ever fearful of the *shambok*, would never dare to leave a cob unpicked. I tried to goad him into realizing how ridiculous his beliefs were, but he always managed to find an appropriate quotation from the Old Testament to prove his point and ended every sentence with "and that was that." These Blacks had broken the law of the land "and that was that." It was not he who had made them Black, but God, "and that was that."

He had four children, two daughters always barefoot and dressed in thin cotton sacklike dresses, and two barefoot sons. These children went to the regional school dozens of miles away, from where they would probably graduate almost illiterate and destined to a life on the railways, in the post office, the army or the police.

He claimed he was not an anti-Semite, but he hated the Jews for killing Christ. He had deep admiration for the Israelis and said that they were, like the Afrikaners, a small Chosen People surrounded by a sea of enemies who had kicked the *bliksem* British out of their countries. But then again, he would add, you can't trust a Jew and they were a bunch of Shylocks and that was why he was proud to be a Brown Shirt in the "good old days when a *kaffir* was a *kaffir* and that was that."

Luckily for me my request that I serve my nine months' compulsory military service in the navy came through. I had applied to the navy because that way, I thought, I would be least likely to be in a confrontational situation with the Black people with whose struggle I identified.

I was still seventeen when I left Johannesburg aboard the steam train that would take a night and two days to reach Cape Town, chugging through the Orange Free State, past the Big Hole in Kimberley where the largest diamond in the world was found, through the Karoo desert, over the Orange River into the beautiful Cape with its wonderful mountains and mile upon mile of vineyards and bountiful fields.

I remember looking out of the window as we passed Worcester, where my family had once lived, and sped toward Cape Town, and thinking that South Africa must be an extension of God's sense of humor. Let me create a paradise, God said to himself. I will give it beauty and gold and diamonds and all the earth's treasures; I will bless it with water and good soil, with large expanses and all that is necessary to sustain life. And then I will put a few White people there and a few Blacks and let's see how they get on.

And here it was: God's sense of humor. Rows of vineyards as far as the eye could see making for a scene of beauty and tranquility. But the men who nurtured and pruned the vines and picked the grapes were paid with little more than a daily tot of brandy, their families left to live in abject misery and poverty while the White estate owners grew fat off the land and their labor.

A meeting point had been arranged for the new recruits at Cape Town's bustling station. I had only a small brown suitcase containing exactly what the navy had told me to bring: one change of civilian clothes including one set of underwear, one pair of socks and a washing kit. The clothes would be washed and put away to be returned to us in nine months, the letter had said.

I knew not a single soul when we all met under the large clock in the entrance hall. I could not pick out one clearly Jewish face in the group of forty or so young men. This was my first venture outside the cocoon of my family, friends, the Movement. I felt very lonely.

A petty officer met us, escorted us to a train where a carriage had been reserved, and within half an hour we were in Simonstown, a quaint little place with a very English feel to it that housed the navy's main port and training facilities. The whole town was navy, from the Admiral's House high on the hill overlooking the sea to the hospital and the Seaman's Bar where I got terribly drunk on rum and coke trying to impress my fellow recruits that us guys from Jo'burg were real men of the world. I have not been able to touch rum since.

The induction process began with a haircut and then a multistop tour that opened with a kit bag being thrust at you and then progressed from stop to stop where underwear, work shorts, work longs, work shirts, blue socks, white socks, peak cap, flat cap, rough blue sailor's suit with square collar, bright white sailor's formal suit with square collar were stuffed into my kit bag, together with a naval wash kit, a pair of shiny black shoes, a pair of black boots and tennis shoes. By this time the bag weighed twice as much as me. We were then taken to the tailor's for a fitting for our ceremonial whites and blues and summer and winter uniforms—all this for nine months of service. Lucky the country had gold.

We were housed in a modern and functional four-story barracks with clean showers and toilets and rows of double bunk beds arranged in perfect symmetry. The building was divided into several dormitories with twenty-four men in each. We, the newest intake, were placed on the fourth floor, which made it just that little bit harder to get to the parade ground on time, given the steps and narrow stairwells.

The traditions here were distinctly English, as if the British had forgotten to take their navy back home with them when they left South Africa. The officers almost seemed caricatures of the British seamen we knew so well from those romantic movies about the Second World War. They had trim mustaches and clipped accents and used expressions like "old chap" and "jolly good." The place was so civil that after a few days I actually began to look forward to being at sea wearing a rough woolen pullover and smoking a pipe.

I was singled out to be a Sonar operator in a submarine, which meant listening carefully to the depths outside. Because I had been selected for submarine service (which I hoped would place me even further away from the possibility of having to fight Blacks in Soweto) I was subjected to a battery of tests during which they discovered I was colorblind. There was no way I could be a submariner, they explained, even though operating Sonar depended on your ears. "We couldn't possibly have you opening a red handle instead of a green old chap," they explained.

Thus rejected from submarine service, and with all the other courses being into their second week, there was great confusion over what to do with me. Thus I was given yet another uniform, this time that of a chef with blue and white checked pants and a white jacket and white hat, and assigned to kitchen duty. The man in charge, Warrant Officer Skidmore, took one look at me on the first morning I showed up and a malicious smile curled up on his lips. "You new boy, Jewboy, there, by the stove. You fry the bacon." To this day I feel nausea when I think of the smell and the piles and piles of thin-sliced pig, enough to feed hundreds of hungry men every morning, sizzling sickeningly on the flat hot grill over which I had to preside, doing my best not to come into contact with the forbidden food.

And then, after breakfast it was washing pots with the men from the brig, the naval jail housed in a foreboding square building with 60 chimneys and no windows. It stood right in the middle of the base as a warning to men who might disobey order. Formally we were not allowed to talk, but with all the noise from the pots we did and Thomas, who was in for 30 days for drunken and disorderly behavior, told me horror stories of what it was like "inside." He also told me if I did not get him five smokes a day he would slit my throat when he got out and that if I told anyone he would pour hot water on me. Despite the ceremonial whites and blues, the shiny black shoes and white peak cap, this was definitely turning into one of the worst experiences of my life.

For a month I languished in the kitchen until being called to the commander's office. I was told that I was being transferred to the infantry, my worst nightmare. He gave me a train ticket to Bloemfontein, the judicial capital of South Africa, where a Black man or woman was in peril if they were seen outside after the 9 P.M. siren. But it was also where I had a girlfriend, Beulah, whom I had met at a Movement seminar a year before. Though we lived hundreds of miles apart, we were "going steady."

I arrived there on a Friday in my splendid Winter Blues about eight weeks into my nine months of service and counting the days. Walking into the Bloemfontein training camp from the civilized surroundings of Simonstown was a shock. It was like walking into a concentration camp. Barbed wire surrounded the facility and the barracks were long cold brick buildings with corrugated iron roofs and hard cold polished floors.

Like in the navy I arrived here when the last bunch of recruits were already halfway through their basic training. Nobody knew what to do with me but I was relieved of my navy gear, refitted as an infantry man and issued a .303 single-shot rifle. It was the first gun I had ever held, and I was totally ignorant as to how it worked.

I was assigned a bunk, thankfully near a school friend and neighbor from home, Les, who showed me the ropes. He taught me how to take my beret's rough bronze springbok badge and shine and hone it till it was as bright as a mirror. He also gave me lessons on how to wear the damn thing at just the right angle. Les taught me how to spit and polish the tips of my boots until I could comb my hair in their reflection, and how to square off my bed with the mess tins. Without his help I would have been totally lost.

The corporal in charge of our hut did not like the little Jewboy who had come from the navy in his suit. Morning after morning at the 6 A.M. parade he would find something wrong with me, be it a small crease in my pants or an unshaven hair under the tip of my nose, and he would let me have it.

"A hair you fuck, a fucken hair, what do you say?" he would scream directly into my ear. We were not allowed to flinch. If you did there would be more yelling and fifty press-ups, or he would tear the sheets off the bed and have you make it again, perfectly, in thirty seconds or more press-ups.

Beds were lined up to the last millimeter and sheets folded exactly ten fingers over the top blanket. Rifles dating back to before the Second World War had to be rust-free and uniforms pressed to perfection. Discipline was maniacal and it was a terrifying way to live. Orders were always shouted and you had to respond "Yes Sir" to everything, even when the corporal would burst into the barracks at three in the morning for a "hard-on check."

Regulations required that you sleep with your hands above the blankets and it was the corporal's job to make sure you did. He would come in, prowl around and suddenly, with a scream, pull some poor guy's blankets off and examine his private parts with a flashlight, shouting "I got it, I got the thing, I found a snake, everyone up and out and fifty press-ups now." And then he would go away, his job done.

After waiting around for orders for a week, I was fortuitously sitting one morning on the steps of our barracks, having been left behind as barracks guard while the others went off to target practice, when the camp's new commander, Kommandant Viljoen, walked by. I sprung to attention and saluted, trembling as this was the highest-ranking officer I had ever seen at such close quarters.

"You speak English?" he asked.

"Yes Sir," I shouted out in return.

"Can you make tea?"

"Yes Sir," I shouted, my arm still in stiff salute.

"Can you type?" "Yes Sir," I lied.

"Is your Afrikaans fluent?"

"Yes Sir," I lied again, "I even know Shakespeare in Afrikaans Sir," this being only very partially true having had to learn parts of Hamlet by heart for punishment in high school once.

"Come," he said. And with that my life changed dramatically.

I left the barracks and moved into the clerks' quarters, a snug room with four beds, four chairs and a table. I was assigned as the Kommandant's official translator, he having the very real problem of hardly knowing a word in English while, by law, the army officially alternated between operating one week in English and one week in Afrikaans.

Orders, menus and correspondence had to be in the language of the week, and I was the man who made it happen. That my Afrikaans was iffy at best was overcome by my ironing shirts for one of my roommates, the camp clerk, who in return would do the English to Afrikaans weeks for me and help me plod through the Afrikaans to English translations. I also made the Kommandant tea "just the way he liked it" and, after a few days, became his English-language private secretary and increasingly indispensable.

In fact Viljoen and I became such close mates he agreed to allow me to take two afternoons off a week so that I could go into town for dancing lessons. I had told him, truthfully, that I had been invited to my girlfriend's school dance but didn't know how to dance. He also allowed me to sleep out Friday nights though all the other Jewish soldiers had to be back at nine after being allowed out for synagogue services and a Friday night home-cooked meal somewhere in the local Jewish community. These nights the Kommandant always sent me out with a big wink as he told me not to "get her pregnant hey?"

But it all came to an end rather abruptly when the intake of recruits I had joined in the middle of their basic training finished their course and were dispatched to their units. I begged the Kommandant to let me stay on in Bloemfontein, working on the assumption of better the devil you know, but obviously I had not made myself indispensable enough. What the Kommandant did do, however, thinking that I could be a massive asset to the South African Army's Clerical Corps, was to have me dispatched to Dinsfakskool, the army's clerical training unit in Pretoria. The other recruits were sent off to infantry bases across the country and

South-West Africa, perhaps having to suppress another Sharpeville, the passive Black demonstration against the Pass Laws in the township south of Johannesburg in March 1960 where, almost unprovoked, the police opened fire with machine guns and pistols, killing 69 unarmed, innocent people and injuring almost 200 more.

At Dinsfakskool we were subjected to a battery of tests, at the end of which I was selected to train as a military postman. The course lasted three weeks, the pinnacle of which was a lesson on how to ride a massive Harley Davidson motorbike with a sidecar that, in a time of war, we would need for running messages from commanders to officers in the field. In the lesson, however, we were only allowed to look at the bike while a sergeant stood by and made sure no one laid a finger on it.

I can't say I graduated with flying colors, having failed the touch-typing course, but for the last four months of my service I was posted to the Lenz infantry camp not far from Johannesburg, where I was assigned to headquarters as the assistant postal clerk. My main tasks involved accompanying the camp's main postmaster, a half-wit called Van der Westhuizen, to the Lenz station, where he would watch while I received that morning's incoming mail from the stationmaster, and again in the afternoon when I delivered a bag with our mail to the stationmaster.

In between I would sort the mail into little boxes, one for each of the platoons, and then sit behind a small window for the rest of the day dishing out parcels from home to a few lucky recruits.

Unlikely as this may seem I actually landed in military prison while at Lenz. I had skipped camp one night to visit a lady at least twenty years my senior who Raymond the hairdresser had told me was known to "give it." Of course I got none, the lady, whose name was Kate, having collapsed into an alcoholic daze before I even managed to kiss her, but my absence had been noticed at roll call and I was sentenced to four days in the camp's brig for going AWOL. My shoelaces were removed and I was placed in a cell with two hairy blankets, a thin straw mattress on a hard iron bed, and a bucket and a small sink and tap in the corner. At the end of my bed was one book, the Bible in Afrikaans. In the cell next door was my friend Les, who had gone AWOL for the same reason, also having heard from Raymond. He, like I, got none. And two cells down was a young Jewish soldier, Ronald, who was being held before being transferred to the Pretoria Military Prison, where he was to be court-martialed for attacking a superior officer.

Ronald had been doing his ironing in the barracks one night when a bored Afrikaner corporal who had been giving him a hard time for weeks came in and started to taunt him. I just happened to be in the barracks at the time and remember the corporal chanting, as if a mantra, *"Kikie paitjie fucken Jewkie,"* over and over, all the time circling the ironing board, his hands moving as if executing karate blows. The corporal made the unfortunate mistake of interpreting Ronald's silence as weakness, and when he called Ronald's mother a "Jewish whore with a big cunt hole," Ronald grabbed the corporal by the neck and slowly and deliberately pressed the burning-hot iron into the corporal's face. The corporal screamed in pain and begged for mercy. Ronald was having none of it and pressed on until the corporal fainted in a blubbering heap on the ground. The smell of burning flesh permeated the room. That and the smell of sizzling bacon are two indelible memories I take away from the South African Armed Forces.

February 4, 1965, a Thursday, at around noon, a few weeks after completing the army, I left for Israel aboard an El Al Boeing 707. There were thirty-four of us in the *garin.* We were expected to start a new kibbutz or strengthen an existing one. Some members of the *garin* were my age, while others had gained degrees at university or trades at technical colleges. The plan was for us to spend six months on Kibbutz Tzora, equidistant between Jerusalem and Tel Aviv, and then to move to Gezer, a struggling kibbutz on its last legs. Our mission would be to save Gezer.

My parents, apprehensive, had tried to convince me to go to university first. My mother insisted I should become a dentist. They needed dentists in Israel, she said. My father, on the other hand, was convinced I would be back in a week and, with a typical generosity, insisted on buying me a return ticket.

There was a whirl of preparations and then it happened. The *garin* met at Jan Smuts international airport. A photographer took a group picture for the front page of the *Zionist Record,* we hugged families and friends good-bye and took off for Teheran, then to our new lives in

Israel. It was my first time in an airplane and my first time outside of South Africa. I had begun as a sapling and now I was a seed on a journey to be replanted in the soil of my own country, my own land, Israel.

PART TWO

DREAM TO REALITY

4

HOMECOMING

Aunty Feiga, Aviva, Uncle Felix, Ya'acov (lower left)
and Haim in Jerusalem around 1960. I took this
picture with me to Israel in order to be able to
identify them on arrival.

ON THE PLANE I MANAGED to get a window seat, and peering out the window I saw things from above for the first time. I had only ever seen an aerial view of anything at the cinema, or bioscope, as we called it. From up here, I thought how much I loved South Africa: the vast expanses, the wildlife, the music, food, cricket games, beaches and good times, and absolute beauty.

I loved South Africa, but when that plane took off I felt freedom for the first time. Its repressive laws affected us all, not only the Blacks. Left behind me were the 90-day and 180-day detention laws that made it legal for the security branch to arrest any opponent of Apartheid. Our neighbor's son, Hirshon the plumber's boy, was taken at two in the morning one Friday never to be heard from again. No explanations ever offered. No charges laid. After 180 days they would allow you to take one step outside the jail and then arrest you again on the spot for another 180 days, and so on endlessly. Gone were the continuous trials against alleged Communists and members of the fledgling African National Congress, Nelson Mandela's movement, with two of my former schoolteachers in the dock, the case being prosecuted by a Jew, Dr. Percy Yutar, a distinguished member of the Jewish community, universally referred to as "Dr. Persecutor."

How proud I was that we were flying in an Israeli plane. Imagine, I thought, our own plane. The pilots were stunning in their white shirts and peak caps, our pilots. Who would have thought? A Jewish pilot.

We flew north over what was then Rhodesia, Northern Rhodesia and up to Tanzania, where Kilimanjaro's snow-covered cap could be clearly seen above the clouds. We continued on to Teheran, where we stopped to refuel. I had never been so cold as when I left the aircraft for the short walk to the terminal. It was like walking into a wall.

Inside I bought a bag of pistachio nuts requested by a friend of my sister's living on Kibbutz Yizrael, paid with a one pound Sterling note my sister had given me, and went to the toilet. I had been given a few coppers change from the pistachio purchase and deposited these in the tin dish proffered me by a witchy looking lady sitting on a small stool at the entrance to the bathroom. She spat at my feet in gratitude.

It was just after two in the afternoon on Friday, February 5, 1965, when the pilot said we could see the Israeli coast on either side of the aircraft. On the left-hand side we identified Herzlia in the distance and Tel Aviv and Jaffa directly under us from the contours of the maps so familiar to us from our classrooms and Habonim clubhouses. The members of my *garin*, to my mortal embarrassment, then began singing *"Heveinu Shalom Aleichem,"* "We Bring Peace unto You," and *"Erev Shel Shoshanim,"* "Evening of Roses," which was a favorite because of the harmonies one could develop. And then, Shapshenik the loud mouth, Mr. Gung Ho, started screaming out *"Jojie Loso,"* an African war cry that had been adopted by Habonim as its own, to which, thankfully, no one responded.

The touchdown was smooth and we all clapped as the plane taxied down the runway at Lod airport outside Tel Aviv. At last a dream come true. We gathered at the bottom of the ramp that had been brought up to the plane and I gulped with pride as I saw the Israeli flag atop the semicircular control tower in the middle of the terminal building.

Some of our group, with Shapshenik in the middle of it, started dancing the *hora* and *"B' Ushaftim Mayim B'sason,"* "Gather Water in Happiness," stamping their feet in unison and simulating water by rushing in and out of the circle. I did not join the dancers. I thought they looked infantile, like yesterday's people. The Movement was behind us. We were now Israelis.

We were met inside the terminal by Foggy, a former South African now living on Kibbutz Tzora, where we were to study Hebrew, to understand the practicalities of communal life and to prepare ourselves for the challenges ahead. I had but two pieces of luggage with me: a metal *trommel,* just like Grace's, in which I had packed a few clothes—the Kibbutz, we were told, would provide us with our needs—ten of my favorite books, my collection of *Time* magazines, not one issue missed since I was given a subscription by my sister for my twelfth birthday, a few jazz records and a wash kit with spare soaps and toothpastes that we were advised to bring. The second suitcase was not mine, though I had had to wear most of the clothes neatly packed inside for the two weeks preceding my departure for Israel. It also contained a few slightly worn dresses, men and women's shoes and, wrapped in deep among the not-quite-new socks and underwear, tins of coffee and pungent salamis from Mr. Kramer the butcher on Harrow Road. This case, of course, was to be handed over to Uncle Felix, who would be waiting for me on arrival. I was petrified, I had told my mother, a veteran smuggler, that I would be stopped at customs and asked about the dresses. "Do not look suspicious," she instructed. "Be sure you are in the middle of a large group of people and do not, I repeat, do not look guilty. Just remember you are doing nothing wrong. You are helping your family in Israel and that's a *mitzvah.*"

I recognized my family immediately. In a soft but penetrating rain there was Haim wearing shoes, pants and shirt sent two parcels ago, and Aunty Feiga and cousin Aviva looking just as they did in the picture of them sitting on the wall of the King David Hotel. And, off a bit to the side, Uncle Felix, slightly reserved, very proud, a strong man with a cigarette in a plastic holder in his mouth, a legend in our family for having carried Feiga and Aviva out of Poland through storms and snow to the safety of an underground group that smuggled them to Palestine.

Felix's handshake was like a clamping iron. I gave him the second suitcase, which he slung into the sidecar of a Vespa scooter standing next to the curb and quickly covered with a raincoat. *"Polizia, polizia,"* he said, pointing to a nearby policeman as if the case contained some horrible contraband. I nodded my understanding in a conspiratorial manner. My aunt splashed my face with a rain of wet kisses and stroked my cheeks as if I were a kitten, murmuring "Hershele, Hershele," tears streaming down her face. Haim and Aviva hugged me awkwardly and told me in Hebrew that Ya'acov, my other cousin, was in the army but sends his love.

To my amazement, despite my best efforts not to have done so, I had apparently absorbed enough Hebrew at school to understand and make myself understood to my relatives. I took pictures my mother had given me out of my jacket pocket and watched as my aunt clucked and mumbled *"azei sheina,"* so good-looking, as she sorted through the images of my sisters, nieces, nephews and parents.

Uncle Felix wanted to talk about the Vespa. Not everyone in Israel had one you know, he said several times in the course of our short meeting. They also had a television at home, he said, and promised to take me to good restaurants. He was wisely establishing that while the clothes and other gifts were much appreciated, he was not a beggar. The raincoat covering the case containing the worn clothing for the family may have been my father's, but this was a proud man who had done relatively well under exceptionally difficult circumstances. Still, this was not South Africa and a tin of good Nescafe in a country where coffee was still made of chicory was a treat, as were the well-made and sturdy clothes my mom bought at a variety of outlets, which were vastly superior to anything one could buy in Israel at exorbitant prices. So what if they were worn for a day or two to make them legal.

All too soon the truck from the kibbutz was loaded and we were being called to board. Haim and Aviva kissed me shyly and left to take a bus. Felix kicked the Vespa to life, Feiga climbed on the seat behind him, and with the raincoat-covered suitcase in the sidecar, off they went in the direction of Jerusalem, not a pleasant ride in the rain. But then they had walked through war-torn Poland to get here and the Vespa with the sidecar, as I knew, was Uncle Felix's pride and joy.

I stood a while on the curb waving as they receded into the light rain. My head was spinning. I felt as if I had walked into a picture, something all these years I had only seen in frames on the walls at home, in kindergarten, Jewish day school and the Bayit. The signs were in Hebrew. The porters spoke Hebrew and the announcements from the terminal were in Hebrew. The policeman and a driver parked illegally across the street were arguing in Hebrew. And what a cacophony of people waiting outside the terminal building. Moroccans and Yemenites, Georgians with gold teeth, all Jewish, speaking in a babble of tongues, pushing and shoving and shouting to catch the attention of friends and relatives as they arrived.

All I had ever seen of my "brethren" before were Litvaks, Lithuanian Jews, and the occasional Jew of German or Polish origin, all of whom were, essentially, orderly, polite and had grown fond of golf and tennis. This was a whole new experience, like a flash scene of the Ingathering of the Exiles as performed in the plays we had put on at school each Independence Day, depicting the heroic return of the Jews from the four corners of the earth to their newly established land. Only this was real. I took in a deep breath of air, closed my eyes and felt my aunt's wet kisses still hot on my cheeks. A good, warm feeling came over me. I was intensely happy, my feet firmly planted under me, at home though I had just arrived. I was liberated.

It was misty and a light rain was still falling when the truck finally pulled out of the airport, our baggage secure on its roof and us in the back seated along four parallel wooden benches, for Kibbutz Tzora between the airport and Jerusalem and adjacent to the development town of Beit Shemesh. I had an end seat and a good view as the gear-crunching Leyland drove us through Lod, an Arab city captured by Israeli forces in the 1948 War of Independence under the command of the mythical Moshe Dayan. Dayan was now Israel's agriculture minister and had invented a new type of tomato, the Moneymaker, which never went off. It was shaped like an eggplant, and he claimed it would be the path to Israel's future.

Lod was somehow both picturesque and dreary. Its streets were narrow and, in some places, cobbled. Dominant on its skyline were the minarets of mosques and ugly Soviet-type housing projects into which new immigrants arriving mainly from North Africa were moved in the 1950s.

We drove through the town and past the Ramle prison, where Adolph Eichmann, the architect of Hitler's Final Solution for the Jews, was hanged in Israel's only ever judicial execution at two minutes to midnight on May 31, 1962. Eichmann's killing machine had eliminated one-third of the Jewish people and almost eradicated European Jewry. He had escaped to Argentina, where he lived as Ricardo Klement for fifteen untroubled years until the Mossad, Israel's legendary secret service, tracked him down, kidnapped him and brought him to justice in Jerusalem. The hangman, Shalom Nagar, a Yemenite Jew, one of twenty-four wardens in a special unit of the Prison Service that had been created to guard Eichmann twenty-four hours a day, agreed to do the job after seeing footage of the final solution in action. Eichmann's body was then cremated at 1,800 degrees centigrade in an oven 2.5 meters long and 1.5 meters high designed and built by Pinhas Zaklikowski, a concentration camp survivor who had lost his mother and four brothers in the Holocaust. Eichmann's ashes were then taken to sea and cast upon the waters by the head of the Prison Service, Arye Nir, in accordance with the biblical injunction for dispensing of an evil so evil that no trace of it should be allowed to remain on this earth.

As we drove by the stark mud-brown prison set back from the road and surrounded by several rings of guard posts and barbed-wire fences, one of the many such facilities left by the departing British to the new Jewish state, I thought of Eichmann during his trial, sitting impassively in a glass booth, only twitching ever so slightly as film footage of the carnage was shown or as witnesses broke down in the box, shattered and drained by having to remember in such great detail what they had spent over twenty years trying to forget.

Witnesses like Yehiel Dinur, known until then to the world only as Ka-Tzetnik 135633, slang for concentration camp inmate, author and chronicler of the horrors of Auschwitz, a hell he called "the planet of ashes." Until he appeared on the stand, no one, not even his own children, Daniella and Lior, knew that their father was the Ka-Tzetnik whose books, like *House of Dolls* and *Piepel,* document in careful, horrible, unbelievable detail life in the hell Eichmann created. *House of Dolls* was about women forced into prostitution to service the camp guards who, just prior to coming for their pleasure, had been marching children, women and men into gas ovens and supervising the burning of their bodies. And *Piepel* was about young Jewish men having to choose between becoming male prostitutes, also for the guards, or the gas ovens.

Ka-Tzetnik was not a pseudonym, because in Auschwitz people had no names, it was who he had been in the camp, he explained in his testimony, saying his books were written because of a pledge he had made "to those that for almost two years went from me, always leaving me behind. I can see them. They are gazing at me. I see them." He then collapsed on the stand, emotionally exhausted, and had to be hospitalized for two weeks. Ka-Tzetnik was one of the main reasons I had moved to this country. His message to me was that we had allowed ourselves to be led like lambs to the slaughter, that there are no bounds to evil and hatred and that there is nothing people will not do to survive. The countless times I read those thin volumes, the question always hammered in my head: How could we have allowed this to happen. Never again.

The truck made a left at the Ramle Junction and was soon cruising through rolling fields of green, punctuated by vineyards divided into row after row. I had not quite envisioned it this way, the neatly cultivated fields as far as the eye could see with the occasional *moshav*—a semico-operative agricultural settlement—or kibbutz dotting distant hilltops. The sun was setting to the west and the drizzle had let up. The air smelled wonderfully fresh and I was amazed at the beauty of the country. Perhaps there was more than one version of God's paradise, I thought to myself.

At the Nachshon Junction the truck turned off to refuel at a Delek petrol station. We were told that we should stretch our legs, use the toilets, visit the little zoo in the garden out back or stop by Sarah's kiosk, a must-see for the boys. I walked through the zoo quickly, hating to see animals in cages, and then on to the kiosk to buy a *gazoz*, a drink made of syrup and soda water drawn from a silver tap on the counter. The line was long but it had not formed away from the counter, but rather along it for reasons that very soon became apparent. Sarah, the lady bending over the various tubs of ice cream filling cones with scoops, had the largest breasts and the lowest-cut shirt I had ever seen.

And she knew it. We were later to learn that Sarah was a regional celebrity. Truck drivers made detours to have a peek and exchange a few naughty but playful words with Sarah of the Nachshon Junction, known universally, and now to us as well, as Sarah Parra, *parra* being a cow. "Told you this was a land of milk and honey," I said to my friend Brian, a dreadfully heavy smoker from Durban who was sitting next to me on the truck.

From Nachshon we headed north to the Shimshon Junction, starting a gentle climb through first fields and then miles and miles of forests, all hand-planted with trees paid for by the small change ladies like my mom the world over had put into the little Blue Boxes of the Jewish National Fund. These boxes graced every Jewish house I had ever entered. There was The President's Forest, named in honor of Harry Truman. It extended from the Shimshon Junction to as far southwest as Tzora and all the way east to Moshav Eshtaol and the Israel-Jordan border. From there up to Jerusalem there were over six million trees in the Martyrs' Forest alone, five million pines for the five million adults killed in the Shoah and another one million Cyprus trees, thin trees that grow up tall and straight, for the million children.

Tzora, Eshtaol, Beit Shemesh and Shimshon were all familiar to me from the Bible. Tzora and Eshtaol were Samson and Delilah's romping grounds. Beit Shemesh was burned to the ground by God after men had defied him and peeked into the Ark of the Holy Covenant en route to Jerusalem from Ashkelon. A carbon ring where the town once stood is still clearly visible. The road signs along the way said Emek Ha'Eilah, which was where David defeated Goliath, and the topography of the valley today is exactly as the Bible describes it.

And the Kibbutz Netiv Halamed Hei, named for the thirty-five young men and women killed while trying to break the siege on Jerusalem by creating an alternate route to the one through Sha'ar Hagai, which was under constant heavy Arab attack. As they were about to leave the plains for the foothills and begin their ascent to Jerusalem they came across an elderly Arab shepherd. They debated what to do with him. If they let him live there was a possibility that he could inform on them. They decided to let him go, issuing stern warnings what the punishment would be if he opened his mouth. The shepherd was obviously not impressed. By morning all thirty-five were dead, killed in an ambush by Jordanian soldiers whom he'd tipped off. It was a story we had heard many times around campfires back home.

At the Shimshon Junction we turned off to the right along a road that took us through a string of Yemenite *moshavim* with names like Isi and Noam, past a small industrial area, over a railway line and across the Kishon, referred to in the Bible as a river but now a gurgling trickle of black, polluted water covered in brown-tinged foam. At the next junction, with Beit Shemesh to the left and Tzora to the right, the truck turned toward the kibbutz, driving through wheatfields and vineyards on either side of the windy narrow road, over a precarious railway crossing that had already claimed the lives of several kibbutz members, and through the gates of what was supposed to be our new home.

We were to stay at the kibbutz for six months, studying Hebrew half the day and working the other half. It had been decided that we would not be sent to Gezer as originally planned, but would remain at Tzora, so from then on our communal plans seemed a bit unsure, with some wanting to go into the army straight away, others to another kibbutz for a while and yet others wanting to stay on at Tzora and integrate there as quickly as possible. Since our collective future would be decided anyway by the relevant hierarchies in the *garin* and the kibbutz movement in a series of endless discussions on how we could best fit into the cause of Zionist Socialism, I decided to concentrate on the here and now and found each new day more fascinating than the last.

Four of us were assigned to a wooden shack with no toilet or shower. The bathrooms were in a squat square building about 150 meters away, adjacent to the laundry. We each had a metal bed with a firm straw mattress, a bedside cupboard and one shelf above the bed with a plastic yellow clip-on light. On the bed were two white sheets, two gray blankets and a striped pillow. On the cupboard was a welcoming note, in Hebrew, and for our room a cake from the Bargais, the kibbutz family selected to be my temporary adopted family. The four of us, Brian from Durban, Michael from Cape Town and Zohar, who I knew from Johannesburg and whose mother I suspected of having had an affair with my father when we were on holiday in Muizenberg one year without my mother or his father, settled in.

We helped each other lug in our *trommels*. I placed my *Time* collection on the shelf above my bed, together with a few of my favorite books. Though not a good student I was an avid reader. Books were important to me and, next to the pile of magazines, I put out *Moby-Dick*, Durant's *Story of Philosophy*, Bury's *History of Greece*, Kazantzakis' *The Greek Passion* and *Last Temptation*, Alan Paton's *Cry the Beloved Country* and Leon Uris's *Exodus*, a book that would, a few weeks later, be relegated from shelf back to *trommel* after seeing a screening of the movie in the kibbutz dining hall one Saturday night. When about a dozen of us, age 15 or so, had gone to see the film at His Majesty's Theatre in Johannesburg soon after it was released, we left the theater as if walking on water. How proud we were. Paul Newman as Ari Ben Canaan, the *Palmach* hero, better looking than God himself, defeating the Arabs and saving the Jews, bringing them in behind the stiff backs of the British and their White Paper, returning the remains of European Jewry to safe shores, their homeland, Israel. How much I regretted that I was not in Palestine-Israel then, at Ari Ben Canaan's side, helping Ka-Tzetnik's co-survivors from the Planet of Ashes stumble ashore through the waves to a home that would ensure that neither they nor their children, nor their children's children would ever allow another Holocaust.

But seeing the movie in the kibbutz dining hall with the veteran kibbutz members bursting into laughter, literally rolling in the aisles, when Newman, with his pure American accent and blue eyes, says "I am Ari Ben Canaan and . . ." made the heroic pathetic. To the Israelis in the dining hall this was hilarious kitsch, an embarrassment. The audience would wait for the "da da da da" of the music to reach a crescendo each time old Ari Ben C was about to perform another miracle, then everyone would get up and, in unison, mimic both the deed and the music, whistling catcalls and mooing like cows.

The book came off my shelf that night. The romantic phase of my affair with Zionism and Israel was beginning to fade. Reality was about to set in.

5
RITE OF PASSAGE

*Trying so hard to look like an Israeli on a hill
overlooking the Red Canyon, south of Eilat,
winter 1965, just months after arrival. From the
hilltop one could see Egypt, Jordan and Saudi
Arabia simultaneously, something that was both
amazing and accented Israel's vulnerability.*

I MADE MY FIRST TRIP to Jerusalem about a month after we had arrived on kibbutz in an old Samson bus. It was magical. I was sitting next to my friend Jackie Metzger, who had the most wonderful bass voice I had ever heard. His father was the cantor at the Main Synagogue in Durban and Jackie had inherited his father's musical talent. The bus drove through Bab el Wad, with the wrecks of the armored cars driven by *Palmach* heroes who had tried to break the siege on Jerusalem still strewn on the side of the road, left in place as a memorial to those who had died to make this road safe for us.

And then through the village of Abu Gosh, an Israeli Arab town that had remained neutral in the 1948 war and thus remained unscathed, its population intact. Here, young Jewish *kibbutzniks* in rolled-up shorts and khaki shirts would get off the bus, heading for Ma'aleh Hahamisha or Kiryat Anavim in the hills above; Arabs in traditional garb would get on, the men wearing checked *kaffiyas* and the women silky hand-embroidered free-flowing dresses, plastic sandals on their feet. On the hills around us, as far as the eye could see, were forests of pine, all planted by the Jewish National Fund. And just a few miles to the left, where the forests abruptly stopped, was Jordan.

There was only one lane into Jerusalem at the time, with a light holding traffic or allowing it to proceed as one convoy came down and another up the final bends to the capital. It was about two on a Friday afternoon when the bus pulled into the Central Bus Station by the entrance to the city at the very top of Jaffa Road. Jackie and I collected our knapsacks, almost got trodden to death in the stampede for the bus's only exit, and looked in wonder at the buildings around us, all covered in Jerusalem stone, a stone that had no real color itself but reflected color throughout the day and with the seasons, always giving one a sense of light, intensely bright in the sunshine, pink and yellow in the dawn and a pastel orange-gold at dusk.

We walked down Jaffa Road and through Mahaneh Yehuda market with its stall owners desperate to sell off their fruits, vegetables, fresh meat and fish before the Sabbath, all screaming at the top of their voices, pleading poverty and slashing prices. Freshly slaughtered chickens, blood gushing from their necks, their little bodies still twitching, were hung upside down and, when sold, wrapped into several rolls of newspaper and handed over to the buyer. Fresh fish were scooped alive out of tanks of water, bashed on the head with a wooden rod and then scaled while not quite dead. Barrows were piled high with dates, oranges and raisins. Just walking down the market's narrow avenues, the astounding colors of the fruits and vegetables, sweets and spices, the shouting in Hebrew, the swirling and the turmoil, little boys running through the crowds with trays of tea and coffee in small cups while shoppers pushed and shoved to get a squeeze on the produce before deciding on a purchase, was like looking through a kaleidoscope.

Separated from the market by Agrippas Road was the old neighborhood of Mahaneh Yehuda, its solid stone houses built around indoor courtyards so that the outside walls could provide a defense against invaders. Between the fortress houses were dozens of little synagogues, their facades of colored glass set in metal latticework, old men already arriving for pre-Friday night services in their Shabbat best. The bustling scene was intoxicating.

Jackie and I parted on the corner of King George and Jaffa. He had a sister somewhere, and I was off to Arnona on the Number 7 bus to Uncle Felix and Aunty Feiga for my first Shabbat in Jerusalem. I had been told to tell the driver to let me off one stop before Kibbutz Ramat Rachel and to be very careful in doing so. My aunt's house was very close to the border with Jordan, as was the kibbutz. I should not walk back from the kibbutz if I missed my stop, I was told. My cousins Haim and Ya'acov once did, had gotten lost and had wandered into Jordan, causing a major international incident. They were lucky. Others had been shot for doing so.

The Rosenblatts lived in a tiny house tucked behind another home and next to Mrs. Bedil's grocery store, just a few homes away from that of Shai Agnon, Israel's Nobel Prize laureate for literature. I arrived at my aunt's about an hour before Shabbat and I very much wanted to attend synagogue. Uncle Felix insisted that I stay at home, eat the dinner my aunt had prepared and watch television. I had never seen television before and, at the time, there was no Israeli television station. Syria had a station so Uncle Felix, via a complicated aerial he had constructed on the roof, was able to pick up very snowy and erratic images from Damascus, with waves of incomprehensible Arabic coming in and out. It did not matter that Felix and family wore used clothes from Africa, that they lived in a room-and-a-half of what used to be a storeroom in someone else's yard, had only a couch, a table, four chairs and a tiny kitchen, a Vespa outside and nothing in the bank. Uncle Felix, his cigarette fixed in a plastic holder in his mouth, had "the biggest television in the Middle East, a Grundig, German, the best."

Nothing I said could persuade Uncle Felix that I would rather be in *shul*. Doing so on my first Friday night in Jerusalem was something I had long dreamed about. If it were possible I would have been at the Wailing Wall, almost within eyesight of where my relatives lived, but unreachable, being inside Jordanian-held territory. With effort one could see the golden Dome of the Rock on Temple Mount. Here I was in the center of the Jewish universe and forcibly made to sit and watch snow on Syrian television.

My aunt brought in some pre-dinner nourishment, saying I must be famished after the three-hour journey from the kibbutz. Haim came in from a tiny room Felix had fixed up for him outside in the small yard, usually occupied by Ya'acov, who was now in the army. He started to fiddle with the internal antenna Felix had rigged up to augment the one on the roof. My aunt put in front of me a plate of sandwiches of white meat I assumed to be smoked turkey, stacked thickly between two slices of black bread, which I ate with gratitude and vigor.

Like Felix, Aunt Feiga chain-smoked. She made three glasses of tea and came to sit next to me on the couch as now both Felix and Haim tried to fix the hissing television. The couch we were sitting on was also Feiga and Felix's bed, the lounge doubling as their bedroom. I said the sandwich had been delicious. What meat was it, I asked. *"Schinken,"* she replied, which I assumed was Yiddish for turkey. "Oink, oink meat," said Felix from the corner of the room, a wide grin underneath his thin mustache, his cigarette holder clamped between his teeth. "Ham. Very expensive. The best, only the best," he said.

I ran to the toilet and made it just in time. This was the first time pork had crossed my lips—twice. No matter how hard I tried I could not get the taste out of my mouth. I fell asleep that night still feeling physically ill and in dread of what I would be served for breakfast.

The six months on kibbutz passed very quickly, during which we were taken on *tiyulim,* trips, of the country from Metullah in the north to Eilat in the south, and I could not believe how in so small a country there could be such diversity from forests and mountains to arid desert all within but a few hours' travel of each other. I continued to hold everything I saw around me in awe: the technological ingenuity of the kibbutz that allowed two people to milk as many cows as a hundred rhythmic milkers back on Stein's farm in Bethal; the history, biblical and modern, that hit you at every corner; the cosmopolitan people; the fruits, vegetables, spices and shouts of the markets; the bargaining, pushing, shoving, exciting vibrant Middle Eastern rhythm; the buses chugging along with geese and chickens in boxes tied to the roof, drivers arguing with farmers who wanted to bring their goats onto the bus with them; the Hanukah candles alight in the front windows of almost every house when the festival came around in December.

I continued to see Israel in very naive terms. Even the ruined Arab villages that dotted the hills as one drove up from Sha'ar Hagai to Jerusalem evoked wonder, representing a miracle, an Israeli victory against all odds, against the better armed, better trained Arab forces. Half a million Jews, fresh from the Planet of Ashes, with virtually no prior military experience, in defiance of the British and pitched against the Palestinians backed by the combined armies of nine Arab states, had prevailed. To me those ruins did not represent the suffering of another people, not then. Clearly I was not going to use my father's return ticket. This is where I wanted to live. I felt part of a remarkable experiment and fully alive. My only regret remained that I had come to the country in 1965 and not earlier, in order to have been in the *Palmach,* or in the underground, defying the British and bringing in illegal immigrants.

Six months on the kibbutz had made me realize I did not want to be a socialist, and instead decided in early 1966 to attend a supplemental Hebrew course at the Hebrew University in Jerusalem.

It was one night at the movies in March that year when I decided I was going to be an Israeli paratrooper even though I was asthmatic, and so underweight that on the kibbutz a desperate nurse had regularly injected me with a vitamin B supplement in the hope I would fatten up before my parents came to visit, lest my mother accuse the kibbutz of starving her little boy.

The movie was a Hebrew comedy playing at the old Zion Cinema where Jaffa Street meets Ben Yehuda. A group of us from university were waiting in line to buy tickets. There was, typically, much shoving and pushing involved with people claiming that they had just hopped out of line a few minutes before to go to the toilet or meet a friend. The arguing stopped rather suddenly when two soldiers with impeccably starched, spotless white uniforms arrived and made their way to the front of the line. This was an accepted privilege of soldiers on leave. They also had the right to go to the front of any bus queue. The logic was that soldiers had but precious few hours of leave and they should be able to maximize their time.

Usually, it had seemed to me, Israeli soldiers were sloppy. Their shirts were often out of their seldom-ironed uniforms, their shoes far from the spit and polish of my army days in South Africa. But these two were different. Their hair had been cropped, on their heads they wore white caps, their black shoes were shining and, on their left breast, they wore the crossed batwings that singled them out as members of the whispered about Shayetet 13, Israel's elite frogman unit. Their wings were set against a green background, which meant they had been on an advanced training course and had probably been operating deep behind enemy lines. On their right breast, silver paratroop wings on a white background meant they had done over a hundred jumps.

One of the requirements to even get into the course, or so it was rumored, was a full-uniform, full-pack, alternate march and swim from Ashdod to Haifa, about a 100 kilometers along Israel's Mediterranean coast. Only those who have ever tried to run carrying a weapon and full pack dressed in drenched camouflage combat uniforms made of canvas (called leopard skins, purchased from the French and originally intended for desert warfare) can begin to comprehend what these men must have been through to earn those wings. Color-blind, asthmatic and underweight, I was going to be an Israeli paratrooper no matter what to get those silver wings, brown boots and red beret.

Still a member of the *garin* while at university, I moved back to Tzora when my classes ended. This would be my home while in the army; the place I would come back to on leave, where my mail would be sent and from where, every third week, I would receive a small parcel of chocolate, shoe polish, a cake and some sweets, mailed by my foster parents, the Bargays, Uri the regional vet and Ella a teacher on the kibbutz.

As for my own parents, I decided, as with Damelin College, it was better to let them know after the fact. As far as they were concerned I was safely enrolled at the Hebrew University, poised to study Economics and History, sharing a room in a civilized dormitory with a "nice" boy from Argentina and just a short bus ride away from Aunty Feiga who could always be trusted to look after me.

On the kibbutz we were allocated rooms in a long hut parallel to the top road and far from the smell of the cowsheds. Brian and I shared a room, which was convenient as he had a record player and I had records, we liked the same books and were both somewhat distant from the *hora*-dancing, hard-core ideological kernel of the *garin* who seemed to have remained in Habonim back in Johannesburg, having the same debates on the same subjects, and missed that they had been in Israel for over a year now. In retrospect it was terrific of the kibbutz to provide us with a home while we went in for three years of military service. Our rooms were kept for us even when we were away for months on end, and the parcels kept coming. But, overall, I had found kibbutz a disappointing experience. Socialism seemed to stop at the front gate. The swimming pool and four floodlit tennis courts were for kibbutz members and their guests exclusively, almost like the Royal Golf Club in Johannesburg that did not admit Jews. The thought of inviting kids from Beit Shemesh across the road where there were no sports facilities, or from one of the impoverished collective farms in the neighborhood, was never entertained. The kibbutz also owned a bike-manufacturing factory in Beit Shemesh that employed local workers to do the work while the kibbutz provided the management. At the end of the day the workers were paid the minimum wage while the kibbutz collected healthy subsidies for providing work in a development town. The workers returned to their dingy jerry-built apartments in Beit Shemesh while "management" drove home to the kibbutz just in time for a late afternoon swim or a few sets of tennis before dinner. For me, the kibbutz was a model of Israel's past, not its future.

Yet I was not so sure that riding on the bus down from the Jerusalem induction center to the Tel Hashomer military intake base was such a great place to be either that cold August morning in 1966. After arrival we had our teeth X-rayed for identification purposes should we be killed in the line of duty. Then we were fingerprinted and forms were filled out and placed in a brown envelope with a number on it, which we were told to carry at all times and warned of dire consequences if it were lost.

The number on mine was 983438 and the form inside gave me a "Profile," an aggregate of one's state of health, of 89, eight points subtracted because of my color-blindness. (They didn't catch the asthma.) The highest one could score was 97, 100 being impossible because no person was perfect and, or so the story went, because everyone was circumcised.

Carrying one suitcase of personal belongings and our brown envelopes we were marched onto a bus by a sergeant from the induction center. There were about thirty of us in all, eight from our *garin*, all silent as the bus pulled out of Jerusalem to a world unknown.

"Look around you," the sergeant yelled at the top of his voice as the bus got under way. "One out of ten of you will be dead by the end of your service. That's the statistic and that's not even in time of war. But then again, by the time we finish with you you're all going to wish you were dead," he and the driver cracked up in laughter, obviously having been through this routine many times before.

Since those of us from our *garin* had enlisted jointly and were expected jointly to remain in the kibbutz movement, we were automatically assigned to the Nahal Brigade, a quasi-military unit that gave recruits basic training and then dispatched them to establish a new settlement somewhere, or to enhance an existing one.

But that was not why I had joined the army, and being a fighter-farmer was not part of my dream. Being a paratrooper was. I wanted to walk into Mr. Sandler's office in my brown boots, my silver wings pinned on the left breast of the special khaki uniform with slits at the back that only paratroops wore, bend down and say: "Cane me now you bastard." Or meet Jerry the druggie in the park and dare him to call me a "fucking Jew."

Earning that red beret would be like a second Bar Mitzvah, a passage into manhood and independence, a test of dedication and self-discipline, the growth of a commitment into a blood bond. It would mean graduating from being a bright-eyed Zionist into an Israeli, and with that earning the right to question and ask, doubt and criticize on an equal footing with the rest of the country, certainly with my two cousins, Haim and Ya'acov, who had both spent time in military prisons, Ya'acov for going AWOL for three months and Haim for selling military uniforms on the open market while he served as an Israeli Defense Forces storeman. Uncle Felix was actually proud of them, saying that only *"freiyerim"* went into units where you could get killed. No place safer than prison, he said.

There was a way out of having to go through the Nahal kibbutz process. At the end of basic training, instead of going off to a settlement, outstanding graduates could be selected for training as noncommissioned officers, and those who were particularly fit could volunteer for Nahal's paratroop battalion, the 50th. This is what I planned to do.

The induction process at Tel Hashomer was a blur, uniforms, underwear, socks, boots, towels, mess tins, sleeping bags, all stuffed into duffel bags as we moved down a line, ending with inoculations administered by young women soldiers telling us to be brave. We were then trucked out to Camp 80 between Hadera and Afula, inland from the coast about halfway between Tel Aviv and Haifa.

Our *garin* was placed in C Platoon and assigned a tent with eight iron beds, each with hard straw mattresses and two gray-brown prickly blankets. There were no sheets as we were expected to sleep in our khaki sleeping bags with their canvas shell and a coarse inner blanket that smelled of generations of sweat and wet socks. We were told to put our civilian suitcases under our beds, forget about them and to take them home on our first leave if we ever got one.

We marched to the barber, were shorn of our hair and were ordered into heavy canvas leopard-spotted work fatigues, which included a floppy canvas hat that kept falling over my eyes. Wearing the hat was compulsory. We were shown how to make our beds and how we were expected to prepare for early morning inspection, including a close shave with cold water each day except for Shabbat. We were each issued a .303 single-bolt rifle, sold to Israel by Czechoslovakia during the War of Independence, and were told never to let it out of our sight, and even to sleep with it at night. You even had to take it to the bathroom with you.

The toilets were horrible affairs called Carousels that led me to a week of self-enforced constipation until I could take it no longer. They were circular wooden huts in the center of which was a circular wooden platform. This was divided into ten cubicles separated by thin wooden walls, each cubicle with a hole in the platform over which one crouched, virtually back-to-back with nine others, and did your business into a huge earthen hole, throwing white disinfectant powder down it after you finished. It was a disgusting experience.

It was also frightening having to take one's rifle into the Carousel and holding it while wiping your bottom and in a crouch. Word had it that in the last intake a Yemenite boy by the name of Amrani had lost his rifle when it slid between his legs into the hole beneath, and that he had been forced to climb down on a rope and retrieve it. He had sat in the shower and scrubbed himself for two solid days and still could not get rid of the smell, they said.

The corporals in boot camp were tough and took delight in making us feel as humiliated and inadequate as possible, but unlike the South African army, which just seemed stupid and cruel, here I felt they were doing this to me for my own good. We were being challenged to prepare us for the inevitable fight. Israel was under constant attack at the time. In the north there were exchanges of fire with the Syrians over water rights that threatened to erupt into full-scale war, and terrorism by Palestinian *fedayeen* operating out of Jordan was almost a daily occurrence. In Egypt, Nasser made no secret of the fact that he was preparing for war with Israel.

The platoon sergeant would come screaming into our tent at two in the morning yelling that you had thirty seconds to be outside in full battle dress, an impossible task. But defending Israel was an impossible task if normative measures were applied. It was hammered into you time and time again that the impossible must be made possible. We managed this by going to sleep in full battle dress, learning to tie our boots in ten seconds and be lined up outside in three straight rows in another twenty.

By the end of a week getting outside in thirty seconds was pie. By the end of the second week we were out there disassembling and assembling our rifles in the dark in one minute, and running around the parade ground, rifles held high in the air, not stopping until ordered to do so. There were so many times you came to the point where you could not possibly continue, when your arms felt like lead and the rifle above your head like a ten-ton block, when the ache in your back and legs was so intense that moving even one more inch seemed an impossibility, but you did it. You were constantly being pushed to new limits in a sustained and brutal way, often wet for days on end, going to sleep in damp clothes, crawling out of a warm sleeping bag in the early hours of the morning to do a two-hour stint of guard duty, maybe getting another hour of sleep before another relentless day. And this was just basic training.

I began to feel my body growing hard as a rock. After a month or so, shaving in cold water and visiting the Carousel were about the most pleasant parts of the day. We were taught basic weapons systems, taking them to pieces and putting them back again blindfolded and against a ticking clock, over and over again. We were on the physical obstacle course with full pack for hours each day and on long route marches through the beautiful orange orchards of Pardes Hanna, sometimes to the Mediterranean near the miserable development town of Olga.

In addition to the physical regimen designed to show us that there were no limits to what could be done, we were lectured incessantly to respect the enemy. We were taught enemy weapons systems, given lectures on their army, especially their special units, shown films of Syrian officers skinning live snakes and Fatah terrorists jumping through hoops of fire in Jordanian training camps. There were clips of the Egyptian and Iraqi air forces with modern fighters and of column after column of Egyptian tanks rolling off to war in Yemen.

We were also shown the effects of Egyptian chemical warfare against the Yemeni army. Never take your enemy for granted, never underestimate him, we were told. To be complacent is to summon defeat. Always expect the worst and plan for it. Nothing is impossible. Never take chances. Be ingenious. Those were the key messages driven into us during basic training, and that there is no higher value than human life. Do nothing that will risk your life or the lives of others. Be brave but always careful. As an officer or noncommissioned officer never ask your men to do anything you would not do yourself. "After me," was the call of leadership.

Leaving a comrade in the field, even if dead, was heresy, worse than cowardice, unforgivable. You knew that you could always trust your comrades completely to look after you, and that you would always look after them. The bond was intractable. Respect the enemy, respect human life, respect each other and respect your officers, each one of whom has done everything they are asking of you. It was a very intense three months.

On the final day, a Thursday at five in the afternoon, we marched out, platoon after platoon, onto the camp's parade ground. At the far end a temporary stand had been set up where several hundred parents were seated to watch their children graduate from their initiation into the Israeli army. A military orchestra pumped out martial music to the beat set by a jumpy little man in full military uniform as we marched past the camp's commander and other dignitaries, some from the kibbutz movement seated in the VIP box, smartly presenting arms.

I had no parents in the stands, and my loneliness was intense as I accepted a Bible with a khaki plastic cover from my platoon commander, was given a slap on the back and told that I had done well. I was off to the 50th Paratroop Battalion. I was a step closer to my dream, to seeing red, to being an Israeli paratrooper. I was very proud.

6

SEEING RED

Finally, an Israeli paratrooper, February 1967,
a dream come true that would soon produce
many a nightmare.

WE HAD TRAINED FOR THIS MOMENT for months. Running down a narrow trench, a dozen of us, one behind the other, first man in the row shooting and, when his magazine was empty, kneeling down to let the others pass, the next in line taking over the shooting immediately so that there would be no break in the fire. And, coming just as determinedly against you, the enemy, the two sides running at each other like caged gladiators.

Bang, bang, bang bang bang. The shots reverberated in the trench, clumps of brown sand falling on our heads as we ran like wild men, adding to the mayhem by throwing hand grenades around each corner.

Then it was my turn. *"Finie,"* barked Pinhas, my best friend with whom I had spent nine months in a pup tent shivering in the winter, sweating and caked with dust in the summer. He had emptied his magazine and was now kneeling like in the textbooks waiting for me to take over the lead. I tapped him three times on his helmet to signal that I was passing him and he should not fire unless he wanted to shoot me in the back. I pulled the loading mechanism of the Uzi, released the safety catch and, as I had been taught, shot in bursts of three seconds. Each magazine had thirty-two bullets, and each of us had two magazines taped together. It took only a few seconds to change them, as for months we had been woken up at night, blindfolded, and made to do the maneuver.

All-in-all one's turn at the front of the line, running down the deep sand trench, the enemy armed with superb Kalashnikov semiautomatics running against you, head to head, him firing, you firing, lasted but a few seconds. But the horror felt like it would be the rest of your life. Groans, moans, shouts, falling clumps of sand, dust in eyes and mouth, explosions, acrid smoke, screams of agony. Hell.

And then I saw him fall. A little fellow directly in front of me in a khaki uniform with brass buttons and a greenish metal helmet held in place with a thin leather strap, lying there in a pool of blood quickly staining the sand under him. I had killed my first man. This was what I had been trained for. My Uzi was better than his Kalashnikov, my training better than his, my reflexes faster.

I kneeled to the ground, Moyal now passing me, tapping me three times on my helmet, and running on. I waited until the last man passed and then joined the line again, running, reloading my Uzi and simultaneously trying to adjust the webbing belt that held my spare magazines, two water bottles and collapsible spade, the sharp tip of which was digging deeper and deeper into my back.

It was midmorning on Monday, June 5, 1967. We were fighting in Sheikh Zuweid, where the Egyptians had their main defenses in the northern Sinai, pawns in a drama that was to change the face of the Arab-Israeli conflict: the Six Day War.

The Israeli Defense Forces had been placed on high alert in mid-May after the Egyptians blockaded the Strait of Tiran, preventing oil supplies from the Shah's Iran from reaching Israel's southern port of Eilat, and ordered UN peacekeeping forces out of the Sinai. This amounted to a declaration of war. In the third week of May, the 50th Paratroop Battalion had moved to a eucalyptus forest near the Israeli Negev settlement of Kerem Shalom, a few kilometers from the Egyptian border where the Sinai meets the Gaza Strip at Rafiah. Initially our battalion was scheduled to parachute into El Arish on the Mediterranean Sinai coast, but it was discovered that the Egyptians had laid massive minefields and peppered these with sharp stakes at all possible jump sites, so the idea was dropped. We were devastated, having dreamed about a combat jump and getting a red background behind our wings.

As the days turned into weeks in that forest, we became like horses chomping at the bit, raring to go and not understanding why the Israeli cabinet was procrastinating. The country's prime minister was Levy Eshkol, a man so indecisive that a joke making the rounds had him being offered tea or coffee with his breakfast and him answering *"katei"*—or half-and-half. We listened to the radio incessantly, mainly to the calming, almost poetic analysis by Chaim Herzog, twice head of Israeli Military Intelligence and destined to become Israel's sixth president.

Herzog left one feeling confident and with a deep sense of national unity. We were all in this together. The way he explained it, this was not a war of our choosing. Nasser had openly sworn to destroy the Jews just weeks before in a speech to the Egyptian parliament and there was not a day the Syrians weren't shelling towns and settlements in the north. The UN had withdrawn from the entire Sinai without a murmur, the French had declared an arms embargo on Israel, the Soviets were being openly hostile, the Arab world was firmly behind Nasser and the Americans were distant and noncommittal. Israel was totally alone. Two million people, 200 aircraft, under 1,000 tanks, an armed force of 275,000, virtually no navy and hostile borders on four fronts—Lebanon, Syria, Jordan and Egypt.

In the 1948 war, 6,000 Israeli men and women, one percent of the Israeli population, had been killed in the fighting. Who knew what the price would be now with Syria, Jordan and Egypt armed to the hilt with American, European and Soviet weapons? Israel's borders were long, convoluted, porous and vulnerable. The Egyptians had been piling divisions into the Sinai, and were poised at Kuntilla to dart across the Negev, cut Israel in half and forge a corridor to Jordan.

Despite all this there was a feeling of destiny, pride, determination, a need to survive—and fear. We all knew the country was fragile, that this was not a war over a piece of territory, not a retaliatory raid for some terrorist incursion into Israel, not even heavy fighting like that over water rights in the north, which had been my baptism under fire in 1966, but an existential war of survival.

And then the order came. Just before midnight on Sunday, June 4th, we carefully packed our half-tracks, mounted a 0.5 mm machine gun facing forward over the head of the driver and two .303 mm machine guns facing outward on each of the flanks. We didn't go to sleep. At around six in the morning we left in formation, positioning ourselves at the edge of the forest and then charging into the desert over dunes, the dust of the tanks ahead of us thick in our eyes and above us a flight of Fouga Magister trainer jets rigged out as attack aircraft. Into battle. Canisters of smoke were released to hide our positions from the enemy, leaving our eyes smarting and a horrible and indelible taste in our mouths. All around us was firing and the sound of incoming shells. Before long we had our first casualty.

Our officer, Kussion, a red-haired hysterical type, let out a scream. Blood started pouring through his shirt, and his arm was hanging by the skin of his elbow. Baruch, the medic, stopped the flow of blood from the chest wound and managed to bind the arm in a sling, but relief was temporary and the bleeding started again. Kussion's life seemed to be ebbing away. Then, through the smoke, like a miracle, an ambulance half-track arrived, having responded to our radio call, and took him off to a nearby field hospital. Kussion survived and came back to the battalion several months later, as hysterical and grumpy as ever. Baruch was killed two days later in the El Arish railway station attending a wounded soldier on the side of the road.

At last the trench originally dug by the Egyptians came to an end. We emerged cautiously to the most incredible sight I had ever seen: thousands of abandoned pairs of boots dotting the dunes, cast off by fleeing Egyptian soldiers who wanted to be as unencumbered as possible as they ran through the soft sand. We negotiated our way through a minefield, traversed a barbed-wire fence and entered an Egyptian company encampment of several khaki tents and two wooden huts. The guard posts on the camp's perimeter had been abandoned, as had two intact and still loaded cannons. Several corpses lay in the yard, victims of an air force strafing, probably by the Fougas we had seen earlier that morning.

Then four men came out of one of the huts, their hands in the air, the lead soldier holding a white cloth in one hand and a picture of his wife and two children in the other. The man behind him held two bottles of rose jam as a gift, pleading for mercy. God knows, I remember thinking, what these people must be feeling right now. For years they had been indoctrinated with anti-Semitic propaganda, having studied the Protocols of the Elders of Zion in high school and been made to believe that Jews drank the blood of gentile babies on Passover. Little did they know that they were dealing with Hirshie Goodman recently of 27 Yeo Street, Yeoville; Pinhas, the sweetest boy I had ever met, who would go on to be a pediatrician; Reuven, a dashing playboy, the darling of every woman on the base; Yossie, a kibbutznik from Shoval, where socialism ran so deep that its members shared all their clothes apart from underwear and socks; Moyal, a tough little Moroccan from the mixed Arab-Jewish town of Lod, who had been saved from a family of drug addicts, placed on a kibbutz and, against all his instincts, volunteered for the paratroops, grumbling all the time, but one of the best friends any man could want; and our company sergeant, Nehemia Tamari, who came from a long line of distinguished soldiers, went on to command Sayeret Matkal, the army's most elite ranger unit, and eventually became a general in charge of the Central Command before being killed in a helicopter crash one windy night in 1992.

Moyal, who spoke Arabic, calmed the prisoners down, asking them if they had any weapons. "No," they answered, and then pointing to parched lips begged *"Maya, maya"*—water, water.

The four sat in an unhappy huddle in the middle of the parade ground near a flagpole where a forlorn and tattered Egyptian flag hung limply. Some of our company secured the camp while four of us were given a map and a jeep and told to deliver the prisoners to Rafiah Junction. Two of the Egyptians, an officer and a sergeant, were jammed in the back with Moyal and myself, while the other two were ordered to sit on the bonnet with their hands on their heads, something that caused them excruciating pain as the jeep's engine heated up while we traveled through the desert.

The junction was sheer mayhem when we arrived. We had no idea what to do or where to go and there was no one to tell us. It was then that the eight of us embarked on a journey reminiscent of Alice's through the looking glass. We quickly came upon the attempted lynching of an Egyptian soldier by some raving cooks and drivers from a rear auxiliary brigade. He had stumbled onto the convoy in his flight from the front line and they were just about to put a rope around his neck when a lieutenant colonel by the name of Pichotka came roaring by on his half-track and started firing in the air. A hero of the 1956 war, Pichotka had parachuted into the Mitla Pass together with our brigade commander, Rafael Eitan. We were told to take the terrified man together with our other four prisoners north to a central POW depot by the abandoned UN observer camp near Khan Yunis.

Off we went with the fifth man now also on the boiling bonnet of the jeep, none of us great experts in navigation, an unending stream of trucks and half-tracks going in the other direction and night beginning to fall. Finally we saw a blue UN flag and the white barracks that were the hallmark of all UN camps. Until recently it had been occupied by the Sikh Brigade of the Indian delegation to the observer force that had patrolled the Israel-Gaza border since the 1956 cease-fire agreements. We drove in to find it totally deserted.

Two of us remained with our prisoners while Moyal and I looked around, I somewhat nervously, Moyal with the skill of an accomplished thief. We found nothing except, in a room adjacent to the commanding officer's office, dozens and dozens of cartons of tinned pineapples, food I had not seen since I left South Africa and that Moyal had never encountered. We brought out two cases, each containing twelve tins, put them on the ground and formed a circle, Israelis and Egyptians, captives and capturers together. We opened the tins, first drinking the juice and then, with filthy fingers thick with the grime of battle, plucking at the elusive slices and greedily eating them up. Sated, we loaded five more cartons onto the jeep, retook our positions and bounced off into the fading light to look for the POW depot.

The road became narrower and narrower and suddenly there seemed to be no Israeli vehicles around. Panic began to rise and we stopped to consult our map and debate whether to turn around or forge on into uncertain territory. It was then that Pichotka again roared by, came to a screeching halt, reversed to our position, asked us whether we were crazy, stupid or both, pointed us in the opposite direction to which we had been going, and roared off again, leaving us with our cargo of five prisoners who were becoming increasingly restive as the engine got hotter and our confidence seemed to lag.

Eventually we found the POW depot, a long convoy of open trucks in which dozens of Egyptian prisoners had been jammed and forced to sit on the floor, their eyes blindfolded with flannelette, the gauze material one uses to clean the barrel of a weapon. On top of the driver's cabin were two armed soldiers who made sure that the prisoners observed total silence and kept their hands firmly on their heads. I had no idea how many hours these men had been made to sit like this.

The scene was so pitiful I almost revolted in handing our five prisoners over and suggested that we keep them with us until a better solution could be found. Amazingly, the little guy who had almost been hanged joined our conversation in accented but good Hebrew. (It turned out his military task had been to monitor Israeli wireless communications.) He said that anything was preferable to sitting on the boiling bonnet of the jeep and that while he admired our good intentions, they should join their shoeless, blindfolded and desolate colleagues in the back of the trucks. At least that way, he said, they knew they would be safe.

We left our Egyptian prisoners behind and rejoined our unit in time for an almost all-night drive along the highway to El Arish, the largest Egyptian town in the Sinai and an important railway junction. The scene was surreal as we advanced, driving in total silence, lights off, the road illuminated by a silver moon. To the right, beautiful groves of stately palm trees standing tall in pristine white sand, swaying gently in the Mediterranean breeze, the sea calm and effervescent, phosphorous bubbles coming off the waves lapping at the beach; and to the left, pillars of black smoke as far as the eye could see, destroyed Egyptian tanks, trucks, jeeps, armored personnel carriers, bodies strewn on the hills surrounding the breeched Egyptian defenses, some having become entangled in barbed wire while desperately running from aerial attack.

Mile after mile of horror and destruction, with silent groups of prisoners held by the side of the road waiting to be interrogated. It was critical, we had been told, to find out whether the Egyptians had chemical weapons deployed deeper in the Sinai. They had used them a short while before in the war against Yemen and we feared they would use them again if we came close to crossing the crucial Mitla and Gidi Passes on the way to Cairo. We were not yet equipped to defend ourselves against chemical weapons. The gas masks, from Germany of all places, would arrive only later in the war.

We arrived in El Arish at dawn and our company was bivouacked in a half-built mosque at a juncture guarding the entrance to the railway station and a crossroads that led south to Kantara on the Suez Canal and inland through the heart of Sinai to Sharm el Sheikh, Sinai's most southern tip on the Red Sea, where it enters the Gulf of Suez. We weren't there for long, just long enough to take turns sleeping on the hard cement floor, but doing so blissfully, and to eat our first "hot" meal in two days of sardines fried in a half-open sardine can over a chemical burner and weak, lukewarm tea.

We were replaced at the mosque by a Druze company from the Druze Battalion, famed for its tracking skills. The Druze were scattered throughout the Levant, mainly in Syria and Lebanon as well as Israel.

They spoke Arabic but had a secret religion with the Prophet Jethro at its center. The men walked around in baggy pants and, in Israel, they lived mainly on the Carmel ridge in the vicinity of Haifa, their villages a great attraction for Israelis on Saturdays, their food spectacular. While fiercely loyal to each other, they were also loyal to the countries in which they lived, and though they lived among Muslims they had a deep hatred for them. Just how deep was demonstrated when the first thing the six or eight of them did as they came in to replace us was drop their pants and defecate and urinate on the floor and wall of the mosque, looking us defiantly in the eye as they did so. We quickly learned that our replacements were interrogators who specialized in gleaning information from reticent prisoners. Later in the war I was to see them in action when an Egyptian air force officer captured at the Officer's Club on El Arish beach, where I was stationed as a guard, was proving difficult.

He was being interrogated in the billiard room, held face down on the green billiard table, and was refusing to give anything more than his name, rank and number. Then, quick as lightning, one of the Druze interrogators whipped off the officer's pants, pulled down his underpants, inserted the tip of a billiard cue into his anus and gently began to push. The officer began to speak. Quickly, uncontrollably, sobbing, dehumanized and humiliated, he told all he knew, which, it turned out, was little indeed given that he was no more than the mess captain in charge of the Officer's Club canteen.

From El Arish we had been ordered to backtrack and join up with other paratroop units near Khan Yunis in the Gaza Strip. Some paratroop units had been sped from the Sinai to Jerusalem, where fierce fighting was taking place against determined British-trained Jordanian legionnaires on Ammunition Hill, a heavily fortified position cutting between Jewish West Jerusalem and the Jordanian-controlled East. The Syrians had also heavily shelled the Galilee overnight, from Rosh Pina in the north to Ein Gev on the eastern shore of the Kinneret.

Day was blending into night and night into day. Sleep was had only fitfully in the back of the half-track as it bounced along the road, darting out of the way of oncoming vehicles, passing truck after truck of prisoners being taken back in the direction of Israel, our ears glued to the radio, dependent on the calm voice of Chaim Herzog to give us perspective.

When we arrived in Khan Yunis, Rafael Eitan, or Raful as he was called, had just ordered a Sherman tank to ride its left tread over fourteen Mercedes-Benz taxis that had been lined up on the narrow road hedged with old, thick-trunked eucalyptus trees, smashing the cars and rendering them absolutely useless. Apparently an Israeli soldier had walked into a local barber shop that morning and demanded a shave from the "conquered" barber. The barber complied, but not fully. After shaving the left side of the soldier's face he then cut his throat from ear to ear. The taxis, it seemed, were Raful's revenge.

It was now Wednesday morning, June 7th, just after 10:30 A.M. While we were still taking in the scene the radio reported that Motta Gur's reserve paratroop battalion had entered the Old City of Jerusalem and taken Temple Mount. The broadcaster was breathless as he reported the event and then the radio played Gur's scratchy radio message to his commanders: *"Har Ha'bayit be'yadeinu,"* he said. "Temple Mount is in our hands."

It was as if the Messiah had arrived, the dream of a united Jerusalem come true. How often had I climbed the roof of the monastery opposite the walls of the Old City and peered in, praying that one day I would be able to see and touch the Wall, sometimes being sniped at by Jordanian troops stationed in the 700-year-old Ottoman-built battlements. I had even gone to the YMCA office in November 1965 and lied that I was half Christian, confused about my religious affiliation, and very much needed to touch base with my Christianity by visiting the Church of the Holy Sepulcher in Jerusalem's Old City, and Bethlehem, for Christmas. I had hoped that the man at the YMCA, who had the power to do so, would sign the permit for me to pass through the Mandelbaum Gate. He replied that he would be very happy to meet me for services at the Scottish Church down the road the following Sunday, and each Sunday after that until I had sorted myself out. But a permit was out of the question.

We had little time to ponder the implications of a liberated Jerusalem, having been ordered to leave Khan Yunis and press with lightning speed back along the coastal road toward the Suez Canal for the second phase of Operation Nachshon. Israel's three-pronged thrust into the Sinai was named for Nachshon Ben Aminadav, the first Hebrew to set foot in the Red Sea when God parted it for the Israelites on their way out of bondage to the Promised Land.

We reached Kantara, a major ferry crossing point about halfway down the Suez Canal and close to the city of Ismailia on the opposite bank. The town was neat and had a port feel to it with its now abandoned ferry station, trees lining the wide streets and quaint shop fronts, all boarded up. It was hard for us to believe that we were actually at the Suez Canal, and eerie to see the ships scuttled by the Egyptians to block the waterway against an Israeli amphibious attack.

This time we were bivouacked in a private house that must have belonged to a pharmacist given the diplomas on the wall of a small study off the veranda. We were given strict instructions not to touch a thing, but were told that we could use, with care, the toilets and showers and that we should sleep in a small courtyard facing the canal. There were three outside rooms, one a storeroom, another an outdoor kitchen where a brass pot of beans, still hot, stood on a small coal stove, and a maid's room. We were told to take turns at guard duty and rest, but instead we cooked a communal meal for the eight of us of sardines, halva, tinned meat fried in sardine oil, crackers, fresh mangoes from a tree in the courtyard and canned pineapple for desert, eaten on plates borrowed from the kitchen while sitting on the ornate balcony of the house overlooking the Suez Canal.

Five days into the war and the Israeli army had conquered the whole Sinai Peninsula and, other than the northern entrance at Port Said, was in control of the Suez Canal; all of the West Bank from the Jordan River, including the eastern half of Jerusalem, Bethlehem, Nablus, and Hebron, all the way down to Jericho. In the north, Israeli armored units had routed the Syrians, who had fled their positions, other than those soldiers who had been left chained to their posts, and was about to take Hermon Mountain and the city of Kuneitra, the largest Syrian city on the Golan Heights. The air forces of Egypt, Jordan, Syria and even faraway Iraq had been destroyed. Egypt's land forces were left decimated in the sands of the Sinai, hundreds of men having died and hundreds of tanks destroyed in the Mitla Pass, a site of carnage so powerful that even months later passing through it was like visiting a museum of death, with mangled tanks and armored vehicles charred black, monuments to defeat. Israel seemed invincible.

Late Thursday night, a week into the war, Yoram Yair, or Yaya as he was known to all, our company commander also destined to become a general in later years, called us together and told us we had done a great job. We were being given weekend leave before reporting back to the Officer's Club in El Arish on Sunday, where we would be stationed for several months to come. Early that morning we climbed into our half-tracks and drove north along the coastal highway, again stunned by the beauty of the palm groves before and after El Arish, through the Gaza Strip to the Ashkelon–Tel Aviv highway. From there the road was lined with thousands of people, mainly women and children who threw sweets and cookies at us, warbling in the way Moroccan women do at weddings, all the way to our base at Bilu near the orchard town of Rehovot, where we put away our gear, showered and had an inspection. By two in the afternoon I was on the road again, hitching home to the kibbutz for thirty-six hours of warmth and normalcy.

Rides were easy to come by. People were shoving their children out of cars to give soldiers lifts. We were treated as the saviors of the country. With my wings, red beret and brown boots, there was no mistaking who I was and what I represented. I was now as much an Israeli as the two commandos at the Zion Cinema that night so many months before. I had had to beg the doctor who did the medicals for entry into the paratroops to pass me as fit despite my asthma. A letter of waiver was needed from my parents, but that was no problem given my expertise in forging my father's signature. More importantly, the doctor was a former South African, Ronnie Schneerweis, also a graduate of Habonim, who knew that keeping me out would have been tantamount to leaving a comrade in the field.

A truck dropped me off at the junction to the kibbutz, from where I had about 2 kilometers to walk. It was almost nine at night and I could not wait to surprise my new kibbutz girlfriend. Unfortunately she surprised me by being in bed with a member of my *garin* who had dropped out of the 50th early on and had been sent back to the kibbutz until the army decided what to do with him.

I was too exhausted to care. I flopped into bed, put on the radio and slept and slept and slept well into the next afternoon. That night, Saturday, alone in my room, thinking of going back to the war zone the next morning, I listened absently to the radio as I chose a couple of books to take with me. Then David Ben-Gurion came on with his chirpy little voice, his sentences clipped and hard.

Israel, he said, better rid itself of the territories and their Arab populations as soon as possible. If it did not Israel would soon become an Apartheid State. Demography, he said, was a greater danger than not having the territorial depth the right wing was always claiming Israel needed to defend itself.

That phrase, "Israel will become an Apartheid State," resonated with me. In a flash I understood what he was saying. I had seen the results of war and the beginnings of occupation with men hunched in trucks, hands on their heads, humiliated; taxis crushed mercilessly; people's livelihoods taken away in an instant; homes taken over and billiard cues used to extract the truth. The taking of the biblical towns of the West Bank, the peak of the Golan, Jerusalem and the Suez Canal in six days with 776 soldiers killed, when thousands of casualties had been expected, was a miracle. Israel's victory was tremendous and the song "Jerusalem of Gold," which had won the annual national song festival the year before, almost replaced the national anthem. But Ben Gurion's warning would return to me incessantly as we settled into our base in El Arish for what seemed to be a long time to come.

Toward the end of my three-year stint I was called into an interview with Yaya. He asked me if I wanted to attend the officers' course and make the army my career. I told him I would love to but that I had decided to get married instead. He told me I was insane and I replied that while he was probably right about the wedding, frankly, I was more than happy to be getting out of uniform. It had been an adventure, I said, but I could not see it as a profession.

In August 1969 I returned to South Africa to get married to Beulah, a girl I had known since the age of 16, had emigrated to Israel with as members of the same *garin* and had gone out with intermittently ever since. We were young, but in those days in Israel if you weren't married by the age of 23 there was something wrong with you. We both knew we were making a mistake from the outset. We had changed and developed differently since we were kids and by now had very little in common, but the cake was bought, the function hall readied, the menu decided upon, the flowers ordered, Beulah's dress fitted, bridesmaids chosen, a ring purchased and the entire Bloemfontein Jewish community was expecting a wedding; there was just no way out. "Don't do it," my oldest sister Sorrelle warned. But I had spent my teens growing up in Beulah's house, just could not hurt her parents, and neither could she. It was unthinkable.

The whole trip, from wedding through honeymoon, was a disaster. I found that my high school friends and I had drifted apart. We had no shared values and vastly different lifestyles. I resented how they remained blind to Apartheid. I couldn't relax around the pool being waited on by Black servants with white gloves.

For the wedding itself I was forced to slip back into the mould. I had been wearing nothing but kibbutz blue working clothes, other than on Shabbat, and an army uniform for almost five years, and made a point of being an Israeli and not a South African, which meant wearing sandals in winter. Now I was forced into a shiny green-brown suit and, to my everlasting humiliation, a brown Homburg hat.

And then, as if a sign of things to come, on the Sunday morning before the synagogue service complete with cantor, choir and all, when getting out of bed in a hurry to open a locked door, I got my weenie caught in the zipper of my pants. I went through incredible agony detaching myself and ended up in bandages for the first few days of our honeymoon. Then after moaning and groaning my way through Kruger National Park on the way back from our honeymoon, I jumped a stop sign and caused a car accident, in which I totaled the new Zephyr my brother-in-law, Eric, had lent me for the holiday. I also caused serious damage to the vehicle I hit, injuring the wives of the mayor, magistrate and a big-time banker of Nigel, a small town in the Eastern Transvaal.

I was incredibly nervous as the trial date approached, fully expecting to be sentenced to ten lashes at the very least. In the two weeks between the accident and the trial I lived in absolute dread of falling into the country's system of "justice." I was petrified of the police and the power of the Afrikaner mayor, the magistrate and the banker over them. I would wake up at night imagining that they would nab me for having left the country and not having reported for reserve duty, or would arrest me for being a Communist because I was living on a kibbutz, or hang me for treason for having served in a foreign army. And then there was the issue of my having burned my South African passport in an anti-Apartheid demonstration on campus at the Hebrew University earlier that year. But luck was with me. Hymie Goldberg from Bethal, Sorelle's town in the Eastern Transvaal, was my lawyer. He proved beyond any doubt that I could not have seen the oncoming car given the placement of the stop sign, which happened to be true. He also happened to be very friendly with the mayor, the magistrate and the banker and we quietly agreed to out of court compensation and a fine.

I found South Africa stifling and was deeply relieved when I could hang up my green-brown suit in my mom's closet never to be worn again. The Homburg was left behind in Bloemfontein together with several wedding presents that were not going to be useful in Israel, like the seven little silver bells we received from various uncles and aunts who did not realize that there were no servants to be summoned on the kibbutz.

Back in Israel we moved to Jerusalem, where Beulah got a job teaching English and I returned to university. Having decided that kibbutz living was not for me, I came to feel the same about university pretty quickly, especially after a seminar paper I wrote on the Cuban Missile Crisis was failed for being "too journalistic."

This led me to take a bus into town one day and head for the offices of the *Jerusalem Post* on Havatselet Street in the center of town. The *Post* was still in the same building that had been partially blown up by Palestinians on February 1, 1948, because they felt that the paper had become too effective in espousing the Zionist cause. They left five tons of explosives parked in a truck next to the big plate-glass windows of the street-level press room. The blast rocked buildings within a mile radius. The *Post* came out the next day, having been produced in temporary offices, and on its front page David Courtney's famous comment: "Truth is louder than TNT and burns brighter than the flames of arson."

I remember having a strong sense of history as I entered the building for the first time. The *Post* was a thin but influential paper with a monopoly on the English-language press. Being the first paper read by diplomats and the foreign journalists based in Israel made it an important channel for the government to get its message out. It was well known, for example, that a special taxi took early copies off the press down to the Allenby Bridge, where King Hussein's driver would be waiting for the paper in order to rush it to the palace in Amman so that the good King could read it with his breakfast.

As I walked up the two flights of stairs to the paper's editorial offices I could hear the hum of the printing press in the basement and got a whiff of that wonderful newspaper smell, a cocktail of fresh ink and molten lead, as the swinging door to the composition room opened and closed. Section editors, copy boys and proofreaders ran up and down the stairs in a frenzy of activity. I knew instantly that I wanted to be part of this world.

At the top of the landing there was a counter and a telephone exchange being operated by an elderly woman with thick glasses that gave her eyes an owl-like effect. She was wildly pulling and punching cords and plugs from one socket to another while simultaneously knitting and eating an apple.

After several minutes of being oblivious to my presence she looked up and asked me what I wanted. When I said a job in the editorial department she let out a sigh and then, at the top of her voice, screeched "Ronnie."

Another wait of several minutes, another bone-chilling screech from Ahuva, that was her name, before a thin, dark, youngish man who looked like a harried version of Mahatma Gandhi came out of a side room where, I assumed, he was working as an editor. He looked down his nose at me and asked me what qualifications I had. I replied that I had none other than English, Hebrew, good writing skills, a high work ethic and low salary expectations. He told me there was not a chance in hell of me getting a job in the editorial department and that I should try the advertising department where they were looking for a bilingual translator and clerk. He said I should ask for Yuki.

Yuki was John Wosner, who had been on Kibbutz Yisrael in the Jezreel Valley with a lot of former South Africans before moving to Jerusalem, where he was now deputy manager of the *Post*'s advertising department. As soon as I opened my mouth he immediately started to mimic my accent, repeating everything I said and thinking he was very funny.

He took me in to see Avraham Levine, the manager, who asked me about myself and then pushed over a copy of that morning's *Davar*, the Labor Party daily. On the bottom quarter of the front page was a government-sponsored ad showing a drawing of an El Al plane landing at Lod Airport and a string of new immigrants climbing down the gangway, some drawn as Yemenites, others as Russians with furry Cossack hats and others as Europeans. Under the ad was the Hebrew phrase *"Mi Oleh le'Oleh Kocheinu Ole,"* which when translated literally means that from immigrant to immigrant the country is strengthened.

"How would you translate that?" he asked.

"Immigration Strengthens the Nation," I said without a moment's hesitation and got the job, much to the delight of Yuki, who now had someone to mimic all day in what was to become an extremely irritating habit. That aside, I was delighted with the job. I had my foot in the door and I knew it would be only a matter of time before I moved over to editorial. In the meantime there was much to be learned about production, synergy between departments and how a newspaper worked in general.

And so I did, first by coming in on Saturdays to "tear" the wires, which meant taking reams and reams of wire copy that had come in from AP and Reuters over the weekend and organizing it into local, foreign, sports and economic news. I picked up work as a casual translator from Hebrew to English on Saturday nights and then twice a week in addition to my job in the advertising department. I then went to half-time in the ads department and started doing mornings at the day desk under the supervision of Joe Bloomberg, a patient and wise teacher. If there was anything I came to love it was watching Joe and the other editors laying out a page, choosing fonts and headers, the considerations that went into headlines, the ability to condense the essence of a story to a few choice words. Then the rushing off of proofs to the proofreaders and the subsequent interaction between editors faced with deadlines and proof-readers whose job it was to spend time checking the details. The whole place seemed like one big Swiss clock, every department independent yet working together to produce a product day after day, every day, but ever different. Joe was incredibly forgiving of my absolute inability to edit other people's copy, something I learned is an art in itself. I found myself rewriting other people's copy and getting deeper and deeper into a mess as I did. Even Joe's patience was wearing thin and it seemed as if I would be relegated back to the advertising department when Asher Wallfish, the paper's Knesset correspondent, saved me by taking me in as his assistant. He had noticed my first piece written for the weekend magazine and called "The Loneliness of a Long Distance Jumper" about a parachute jump I had done in the reserves and said he liked the way I wrote.

Asher was from Manchester, England, had been on kibbutz and then served with the Military Censor's office in Jerusalem. How he made the metamorphosis to journalism was never quite clear to me, but that did not get in the way of his being the best mentor I could have wished for. He taught me how to condense ten-hour debates into 300-word reports and how to listen to politicians "skeptically but politely." He introduced me to government ministers and took me along to all his interviews. Asher explained and made me read up on parliamentary procedures so I would understand how the country's democracy worked and how the political system functioned. He introduced me to people who would be important to my career in the future: Moshe Dayan, Golda Meir, Men-achem Begin, Yigal Allon and many others who all surprised me by the mutual respect they had for Asher, demonstrating that it was possible to be a hard-nosed, acerbic, critical journalist without making enemies of the people you write about.

Then during the parliamentary recess of 1971 I covered the highly publicized trial of an Israeli businessman suspected of fiddling the books at the Abu Rodeis oil fields. Israel had seized these from Egypt in 1967, kept them working and continued supplying Egypt's former clients, particularly from the Eastern Bloc. "What do you expect from someone selling stolen oil to countries we don't have relations with? Honesty?" asked the paper's deputy editor, Leah Ben Dor, when discussing the subject with me. She had previously served in the Mossad, and had a very practical view of things.

My work on the trial brought me to the notice of Ted Lurie, the paper's editor. One early evening we met in the corridor as he was leaving his office. He told me to follow him, which I did, all the way into the men's room, where he proceeded to take a leak. While doing so he asked me if I wanted to be the paper's military reporter. Zeev Schul, the incumbent, had suffered a heart attack while on a lecture tour in Australia and it looked as if it would be months before he came back. If he did and wanted his job back I could serve as Zeev's deputy, Lurie said. With that he shook off the last few drops, washed his hands and shook mine, wishing me well.

It did not take me long to understand why my predecessor had had a heart attack. Between June 1967 and January 1972 when I took over there had been a combined 5,720 military operations over all fronts. The job I inherited would include a full-scale war with Egypt on the Suez Canal, the War of Attrition that was ultimately going to cost Israel more casualties than the Six Day War, constant terrorism over the Lebanese border, ongoing battles with the Syrians and the fast-developing phenomenon of international terror culminating with the murder of eleven Israeli athletes in September 1972 at the Munich Olympic Games.

My plate was full.

PART THREE

FROM VICTORY TO WAR TO PEACE

7

THE DAY THE EYE PATCH
BLINKED

*The critically important Israeli intelligence post on the Golan Heights fell
to the Syrians in the opening day of the Yom Kippur War. It was retaken
by Israeli forces after an especially bloody battle. I am second from the
right. My friend Moyal from the 1967 war is to my right with the
bushy hair. We were not yet thirty and this was our third war.*

OCTOBER 6, 1973, was both a Saturday and Yom Kippur, two Jewish holy days in one. At around 11 A.M. young men started disappearing from the synagogues. Some were called by men who came in and whispered something in their ear. As the word spread, others got up, folded their prayer shawls, said good-bye to those they could and went off to their units. At 4:30 that morning hard intelligence had come through the head of the Mossad from a senior Egyptian source in Europe who produced irrefutable evidence that by evening Israel would be at war. Finally, the political echelons were allowing the military to do what it had wanted to do for three months: call up the reserves.

The intelligence that there was going to be a war had been building up from various sources for several months now. Even I, a fledgling military reporter, had heard of massive Egyptian troop movements and a redeployment of Syria's forces from defensive to offensive positions. It was common knowledge that the Soviets had pulled out their advisors and nonessential staff from Egypt. In an off-the-record briefing with a senior intelligence officer I had even been made privy to the Egyptian plan for crossing the Suez Canal using barges and high-powered hoses to destroy the Israeli defenses on the other side. The acquisition of this intelligence had been described by him as a major coup.

Though all the signs were there, no one wanted to believe them, putting their faith instead in the assessments of General Eli Zeira, head of Military Intelligence, who had managed to win over Moshe Dayan, the defense minister, and then Golda Meir and her closest advisors, leading them to believe that the Arabs were all huff and no puff; that their posturing and threatening were designed to win points in the diplomatic process, but that they would not go to war.

In the days preceding the war, briefings from senior military commanders became intense. They did not like the material some of us had been submitting to the military censor reporting on troop movements in Egypt. As defense correspondents we had all signed an agreement of understanding with the army that we would be given a high security clearance and provided with sensitive information, but would have to submit all our work to the military censor for clearance before publishing. The officers charged us with causing public hysteria. One briefing a few days before the war was with Eli Zeira himself in his office on the third floor of General Headquarters. We found him sitting at the head of a long, highly polished table, his bald crown sparkling in the sunlight entering from a window behind him, creating a halo around his head. He spoke softly but intently while, with a silver penknife, he peeled almonds plucked by delicate fingers from a small glass bowl filled with ice water. His arrogance was almost overwhelming. Unlike his predecessor, Aharon Yariv, who was a bundle of humor, brilliance, self-deprecation and self-confidence, Zeira was as icy as a Prussian, his cold blue eyes Aryan, his interaction with people like that of an automaton.

We did not understand that the Egyptians were posturing, he said. That what we were seeing was an annual exercise, one that had taken place every year for the past three years, one about which the Israelis knew every detail. True, there had been a massive movement of Soviet weapons to the region, including frontline aircraft, anti-aircraft missiles, Sagger anti-tank missiles, artillery, tanks and the like, but there would not be a war. What the Egyptians and Syrians, together with their Soviet allies, were trying to do, he said, was to keep Israel on edge. Keep the country calling up reserves, as it had done twice that year in the face of similar scenarios, costing the economy billions. We knew their game and were not going to play it. The press should rely on the military, which has "extraordinary" intelligence resources, as he said, and stop inciting panic.

Who was I to argue? Zeira and the others had extraordinary intelligence resources and all I had was Chico, a former copy boy at the *Jerusalem Post* who was now serving at the air force intelligence unit situated a few miles outside Jerusalem. Chico may have only been a sergeant but he happened to be responsible for coordinating the intelligence flow from field units to headquarters in Tel Aviv. Chico had been telling me for weeks about the Egyptian troop movements, about how the officers around him were frustrated that their opinions were not being listened to back at headquarters, how there were serious differences of opinion over how to interpret the deployment of the Syrians' spanking new anti-aircraft missile defenses.

Chico was a font of information, none of which I could use other than in the most obtuse way or by pegging it on "a foreign source." My reporting, as well as that of Zeev Schiff of *Ha'aretz,* Ya'acov Erez of *Ma'ariv,* and Eitan Haber of *Yediot,* all of whom had their independent sources of information, pointed to war. To this day Erez has in a frame behind his desk a typed page of text on Egyptian troop movements that was "killed" by the censor two days before the war.

Why Israel was taken by surprise has never been fully determined despite extensive research and the volumes of work written on the subject. To be sure there was arrogance and a genuine misreading of the situation. Israel believed that it had superiority and therefore deterrence. And in retrospect, President Anwar Sadat of Egypt, who had been dismissed as a buffoon and a clown by Golda Meir, and had been threatened with having his bones broken by Dayan, apparently decided to feed into what the Israelis wanted to believe, exactly as the Allies had done in the Normandy landing. Hitler had believed the landing would be at Pas de Calais, so that is the impression the allies reinforced while preparing for Normandy.

So while threatening war in public, Sadat used Israel's own intelligence sources to convey that he was actually shaking in his boots. A key figure in all of this was described to us at the time as a *"mekor tsameret,"* an impeccable source, one at the very top of the Egyptian government. It later came out that this was none other than former president Gamal Nasser's son-in-law Ashraf Marwan, the head of Sadat's President's Bureau, who held regular meetings with the Mossad in London, got paid millions of dollars for his services and, it now seems, was feeding us exactly what the Egyptians wanted Israel to hear.

It was Marwan's information, it is now claimed, that had led to two previous call-ups, the last in August, and it was his information that this time encouraged Israel to let down its guard. Since the last alarm in August, Marwan's message had been that the Arabs had lost their nerve, that Israel did have deterrence despite the new Soviet weapons, a message that gained credibility when, on September 13, Israeli Phantom and Mirage jets shot down thirteen Syrian top-line MiG-21's with only one Israeli loss. The conclusion was the Soviets may have given them weapons, but the Arabs don't have a clue how to use them. It was only on that Friday night that Marwan told Mossad head Tzvi Zamir in London that the Syrians and Egyptians would attack at 6 P.M. the next day. That too was a deception. The attack came with precision and determination on two fronts, the Egyptian and Syrian, four hours and five minutes earlier at 1:55 P.M.

While Marwan had been meeting with Zamir and as Egyptian and Syrian forces prepared themselves, I had been at an all-night poker game with friends in Jerusalem. It was the first time I had ever done such a thing on the eve of Yom Kippur and to this day I am convinced that in some way the war was my punishment from God. Chico phoned my home at about nine that morning to say war was on the way. I then noticed the movement of cars outside my window, only a few, but no one, absolutely no one, ever drove on Yom Kippur. At 11:00 the army spokesman's office called and said there would be a briefing with Zeira for the military correspondents at 1:30.

It took place in the same office we had met in a few days before, except this time there were no almonds. The meeting was called to tell us that there had been a change in the intelligence assessment and that hostilities were likely to break out in the evening. Zeira was explaining the background to the change with Pinhas Lahav, the army spokesman, at his side, when the head of Zeira's bureau came rushing through the door and whispered something in the general's ear. He looked as if he had been hit by a thunderbolt and rushed out of the room. A minute later he came back in, grabbed his red beret from the table and rushed out again. War had broken out, yet another surprise.

We correspondents were left to linger, as was the nation. Everyone knew that something was happening but no one knew what. At about four that afternoon a few of us who were hanging around the corridors of GHQ and the adjacent defense ministry managed to corner Pinny Lahav as he rushed between buildings. Usually a humorous man, he now seemed subdued and shocked as he quickly laid out the situation and told us to say nothing: Egyptian forces were streaming over the Canal virtually unhindered. Israeli defenses were paltry, the front line being held by the reserve Jerusalem Brigade made up of men in their late thirties equipped with bolt-action Czech rifles from the First World War and almost no armor. Because the Egyptian front had been considered a passive one since the cease-fire, Israel's frontline forces were mainly deployed in the north, where there was ongoing tension. The Syrians, Lahav said, had taken the Hermon listening post and had started to move on the Golan. The Israeli air force was encountering heavy anti-aircraft fire. The defense minister and chief of staff would hold a formal press briefing later giving us plenty of time to file our stories for the next morning's editions.

I had never been so scared. From what we were hearing from those around us, the situation was actually far worse than Lahav had described. There was serious concern as to what the Jordanians would do. Their well-trained and disciplined forces, the Royal Jordanian Legion, were but hours away from Jerusalem and there were no Israeli defenses at all between them and the Israeli capital.

That night after attending the briefings and news conferences, huddling in the halls with generals and their aides, exchanging a few private words with Dayan and Chief of Staff David Elazar and eavesdropping on what Golda was telling the Labor Party's *Davar* reporter, I ran to the *Post*'s Tel Aviv office to file. All the streetlights were off in anticipation of Egyptian air attacks. That afternoon an Israeli jet had managed to intercept two missiles fired from over the Mediterranean in the direction of Tel Aviv. The few cars on the roads were traveling slowly, their headlamps painted blue. There was an eerie silence in the air.

Having been convinced by the rosiest of scenarios, I opened my piece with "Israel forces yesterday contained invading Egyptian and Syrian units which crossed into Sinai and the Golan Heights under heavy artillery and air cover. The attack began shortly before 2 o'clock. Two positions, one on the northern tip of the Canal and the other on Mount Hermon, which were taken by Arab forces in the late afternoon, were recaptured yesterday evening. No casualty figures were available last night, but Syrian and Egyptian losses were reported to be 'heavy.'" The headline: "Egyptian-Syrian attacks held. Tanks battle as Syrians penetrate Golan Line, Egyptians cross Canal, Israel planes maintain air supremacy."

I got back to Jerusalem well after midnight and went to the *Post*'s offices in Romema, where the presses were still rumbling. I met Ted Lurie, his eyes glazed by whiskey, stumbling toward the men's room. Thankfully, this time, he did not ask me to join him. Leah Ben Dor, the deputy editor, looked shattered at her desk. The former head of legendary Mossad chief Isser Harel's bureau for many years, Ben Dor was caustic and had a sharp sense of humor. She despised Golda Meir, worshipped Moshe Dayan and, offering me a brandy, was quick to blame Meir and her cadre, as if Dayan was not one of them, for the war.

It was around 2 A.M. when I drove into the parking lot of our San Simon apartment, a new building project near a monastery of that name, in time to see Rafi, my friend and neighbor, an officer in the Armored Corps, rushing out to the road where friends from his unit were waiting. The stairwells of our five-entrance, four-story building were hives of activity. In the basement of each was the communal shelter where families would sleep if an emergency was declared, and every vessel, pots, pans, bottles, bathtubs, was filled with water, Jerusalemites remembering the 1948 siege when water was so scarce that one washed in it, then used it for doing the laundry and then for flushing. All windows were taped, lights blacked out and sandbags placed at all entrances.

Beulah was awake when I opened the door. She told me that Leo, another close friend and neighbor in the artillery, had been called up and that I had been given orders to be outside the Girl's School on Rachel Imeinu Street by 3 A.M., less than an hour away.

In the bedroom next to ours, Shai, two, and Maya, ten months, slept. I kissed them on their foreheads, not allowing myself to get emotional. I had done so much reserve duty in their short lives that going into the army for active duty was a matter of course. The chances of getting killed were always there.

Then I had a long, long shower knowing it would be my last for a while, found my uniform and brown boots and packed a few things into a bright yellow duffel bag, including a small gas camping stove, coffeepot, teaspoon, tin of strong coffee ground with "hell," Arabic for cardamom, and another tin with sugar. It was unthinkable to go into the army for even a few days without the paraphernalia for making the perfect cup of thick coffee, or *"botz,"* Hebrew for mud, this being more of a reserve duty ritual than anything else. One had to let the coffee boil up gently and then add exactly the right amount of sugar at just the right time.

The story I had filed that night would be the last for five months. From the Girl's School a truck took us to our base camp in the center of the country, near Petah Tikva, an old British airfield called Sirkin. There we stood in long lines in the cold early dawn, dew heavy on the ground, crickets chirping in the eucalyptus trees, receiving kits, signing out personal weapons and trying to crack jokes. The news reaching our commanders and trickling down to us was universally bad. Despondency descended through the ranks. There was none of the excitement of the Six Day War when surprise and tactical advantage were on Israel's side, when one felt like part of a winning team.

As dawn turned into early morning the news became more and more dire. The Egyptian advance was continuing at lightning pace. Shmuel Gorodish, the recently installed commander of the Southern Front, was overwhelmed and his headquarters in disarray. The Hermon had not been recaptured, as I had reported. Instead Syrian tanks were racing across the Golan toward the Galilee with virtually no Israeli forces in their way. With the late call-up of reserves God knows where the Syrians would be by the time they eventually reached the battlefield. With nothing between the Syrians and the Galilee, the Jordanians and Jerusalem, and the Egyptians and the Negev I thought that we were about to face a second Holocaust.

My company had earlier been assigned to a course in 120 mm mortars, which the Israeli Defense Forces command decided should be integrated into paratroop units to provide close ground support. We had jumped out of airplanes each lugging some part of these unwieldy monster weapons, and had carried them like mules through the sands of the Shifta training base, only to discover that the idea was impractical. The solution, which we now put into practice, was to pull the mortars by a command car, a jeeplike vehicle, which also carried an array of ammunition ranging from shrapnel bombs to phosphorous bombs, boxes of hand grenades, rifle and machine gun bullets, a crew of six, their equipment and mortar equipment like sights and rods, and for the four of us in the back of the command car, it was like sitting atop a volcano waiting to explode.

From Sirkin we went to battalion stores at Tsrifim, another massive former British military camp in the center of the country between Tel Aviv and Ramlah, where we carefully packed our new command car and mortar. Then, for what seemed like hours, we waited in the autumn sun, making coffee, while the brass decided what they should do with us.

I was 27 years old, had been in Israel for seven years, and this was the third full-scale war I was to participate in. At first we were deployed on the Jordan River as the only military units standing between Jerusalem and a possible attack from Jordan. The only other defenses were charges laid by sappers in the cliffs on both sides of the road going up to Jerusalem, known as the King's Highway, it having been completed by King Hussein just months before the 1967 war. All other forces had been rushed up to the Golan and down to the Suez Canal to contain the Syrian and Egyptian attacks.

A 120 mm mortar battalion and a few obsolete tanks near Beit Shean to the north were all that stood between the Jordan River and the Mediterranean Sea should the Jordanians have decided to go to war. We would have been outnumbered, outgunned and probably slaughtered. Its main population centers now emptied of young men and self-defense units off fighting the war on distant fronts, Israel would have been cut in half with Jerusalem back in Jordanian hands.

The six of us in our crew were Yeruham, a former merchant marine captain with twinkly eyes and an amazing knowledge of the stars; Golan, a Moroccan-born economist with a massive chip on his shoulder against the Mapai establishment, comprising Labor Party members, mostly of Eastern European origin, who worked at the defense ministry; Ketzele, a thin, bespectacled, intense man who worked at the nuclear facility in Dimona; Yossi, a cerebral economist who worked on secret projects he loved to talk about; Giora, a jumpy little fellow, a clerk with the Israel Lands Administration; and myself, the journalist.

That night, the second night of the war, we lay on our backs, sleepless, next to our command cars and their Soltam mortars, thinking about the dangers to our families, our country and ourselves. We heard Aharon Yariv come on the radio. Until a few months back, for eight years, he had been the head of military intelligence and a revered figure. Since 1971 and after the massacre of the Israeli athletes in Munich he had headed the fight against international terror and, as a defense reporter, I had met him many times in that capacity. Filling the role that Chaim Herzog had played so well in 1967 as the national explainer, Yariv made no bones about how dire the situation was.

But, he said, the attacks were far from Israel's heartland, reserves were being mobilized quickly and in many places the attacks were being contained. We believed him. It was very reassuring, as was a conversation between Ketzele and Yossi, who could not tell us what weapons Israel possessed but promised that we would never again, as we said, go like lambs to the slaughter. We may die here, this night, the six of us, on the Jordan border, but we will do so knowing our People will live on. Alternating every four hours, three of us stayed on guard and three slept.

By dawn Israel knew conclusively that Hussein had decided not to enter the war. We were ordered by the battalion commander to pack up and within half an hour were on our way to the Golan Heights. From a base in an apple orchard at Neve Ativ, in concert with other artillery forces deployed on the Golan, we pounded the slopes of the Hermon Mountain intelligence post with hundreds of shells, as our planes swooped in and dropped loads of fragmentation bombs and napalm in and around the captured Israeli intelligence base.

Night after night Golani infantry troops tried to make their way up the mountain to dislodge the Syrian defenders, but to no avail. The bombs of the aircraft and the shells from the guns of all that impressive artillery we had been writing about prior to the war were not able to shake the Syrians off despite their heavy casualties. We had built it too well and the natural rock face around the intelligence post made it almost impossible to penetrate.

We were then moved in even closer to the base of the mountain to where a cable car had operated before the war. From here we pounded the positions with thousands and thousands of shells, until finally on the night between October 21st and 22nd, on the last day of the war, the Hermon was taken. It had been a horrendous fight. What Israeli troops found when they recaptured the position was even worse.

The Syrians and their Soviet advisors knew exactly what they were doing when they took the Hermon intelligence facility in the opening move of the war. Inside the base, manned by fifty-four men, was Israel's most advanced intelligence gear used to monitor all movements in Syria, Lebanon and beyond. Some of it was American, the rest Israeli made. It included radars, electronic listening equipment, scramblers, codes, jamming equipment, all invaluable for both the Syrians and the Russians and constituting a devastating loss for Israel. Very quickly the Syrians and Russians took the men and machines they wanted. They destroyed the rest of the equipment. The bottle washers, cooks and maintenance personnel they had no need for, they lined up in front of a ditch with their hands tied behind their backs. According to the burial squad from the military rabbinate, the blood flow indicated their penises had been cut off and stuffed in their mouths while they were still alive.

For three long cold months we were stationed on the Hermon's snowy, misty slopes, carrying out patrols against terrorist incursions from Lebanon and living under constant mortar fire from the Syrians as we moved between the mountain's peaks. We then spent a few more months living in a chicken coop on a *moshav* on the Jordan River, from where we were sent off on all sorts of missions on the Golan Heights, but we mainly lay about doing nothing for days on end. As reserves our salaries were taken care of by Social Security, though many in our battalion were either self-employed or farmers, who watched their businesses decline into bankruptcy as the months passed by.

Golda Meir and her inner cabinet had brought the country to disaster. The number of soldiers killed totaled 2,688. Thousands more were injured. The economic costs were virtually incalculable and, at one stage when it looked like the Soviets were about to intervene for the Arab states, the American president had ordered U.S. forces on nuclear alert, bringing the world the closest it has ever been to potential nuclear confrontation since Hiroshima and Nagasaki.

The 1973 war was a result of what became known in Israel as "The Concept." This was based on the premise that the Arabs were so weak and Israel so strong that the Arabs would rattle their sabers but not go to war. Those who ascribed to "The Concept," which included the country's top political and military leadership, believed that Israel had attained absolute deterrence that allowed them to disregard the portents of war. It also led them to reject the peace overtures made by Anwar Sadat in the months before war broke out, the Egyptian president first sending an open message to Meir with Nachum Goldmann, then president of the World Jewish Congress, offering full peace in return for all of the Sinai, and again, this time secretly, through then U.S. secretary of state Henry Kissinger. Even a dramatic gesture by Jordan's King Hussein was rejected after he secretly flew to Tel Aviv on September 25 and, at the Mossad's headquarters at Pi Glilot near Herzlia, explicitly warned Meir that Sadat would go to war if peace was not reached. Hussein had been to Israel in June and August of that year with similar warnings and had thus lost some of his credibility among fellow Arabs. This time, however, he was more forceful than ever and, for the first time, said that the Egyptians and Syrians would be making a concerted effort. His warnings were flatly dismissed.

"The Concept" was a product of Meir's "Kitchen Cabinet," a tight inner circle of ministers who met around the prime minister's kitchen table at her official residence, an art deco mansion surrounded by a high fence on Ben Maimon Street in Rehavia. The group included Defense Minister Moshe Dayan, Deputy Prime Minister Yigal Allon, Minister without Portfolio Israel Galili and Justice Minister Ya'acov Shimshon Shapira. While there were differences of nuance among them, they fervently believed that Israel could not relinquish all of the territories taken in 1967 and that no matter what Arab leaders may say from time to time, they would never fully accept Israel's existence.

Dayan had long argued that Israel could not give up control of Sharm el Sheikh, which controlled access to the Red Sea and to Israel's southern port of Eilat, through which the country's oil imports from Iran flowed. "Rather Sharm el Sheikh without peace than peace without Sharm el Sheikh," he said in the Knesset in 1969. He repeated this phrase often. Likewise, the West Bank was needed to protect Israel from an attack by Iraq and Jordan and the Golan was essential to face off the Syrians. Israel, formal government statements repeatedly said, wanted peace but all the seized territory would not be the price.

On September 3, 1973, the government articulated the essence of

"The Concept" and had come out with a 16-point plan later known as the Galili Document, which outlined Israel's territorial demands, including the Golan, most of Sinai, the Jordan Valley and the West Bank ridge. The document was accepted by the Labor Party Central Committee as its platform for the October 1973 elections. It led Sadat directly to the conclusion that if he ever wanted the Sinai back he had no alternative but to go to war.

I was in the reserves from October 1973 to March the next year. Once back home and over the initial bitterness, shock and exhaustion, I began to think about my own role in feeding into "The Concept"; how I was a part of the deception machine that helped create the myth of invincibility. Going over my files of the months before the war, I was horrified by the pattern that emerged. I had been writing about the military as a Holy Cow, something one dared not question. Each reporter's signed agreement to submit his copy to the military censor was a deal designed by Faust.

I also had to deal with the anomaly of being a defense reporter for around ten months of the year, interviewing the chief of staff and other higher-ups, while for sixty and sometimes ninety days a year I was Corporal Goodman serving in the same army I was writing about. Many of the officers who had been my immediate commanders five years before were now ensconced in the military's senior hierarchy. It was all very buddy-buddy. Journalist or not I still wanted our side to win and if bending the truth a little to make it happen was the price we had to pay, so be it.

In January 1973, Chief of Staff David Elazar had met with the senior editorial staff of the *Post*. His message was simple and we swallowed it hook, line and sinker. The Israel Defense Forces had seen its greatest year of growth ever in 1972. The Egyptians may try and destabilize the situation to help them on the diplomatic front, he told us, "but they are incapable of even the slightest measure of success since we are in a position as never before to prevent this." The Syrians have suffered heavy losses and "they have realized that they cannot challenge us militarily."

All this I dutifully reported, verbatim, unquestioning, uncritically impressed by the army and those who served in it, prepared to write anything that would enhance its status. Anything included a new 1.1-kilogram revolutionary helmet designed, conceived and made in Israel, which "was lighter, more protective and smarter than any other helmet in the world." Or the new *Reshef,* Flash class missile boat that had three times the range and twice the firepower of any ship in its class, again the result of Israeli ingenuity and battle experience. The ship, I wrote, had incredibly smart electronics, new fire control systems unlike anything anywhere on this planet, and had been miraculously pieced together from 5,500 different sets of plans, with 38 kilometers of electronic cable and over 50,000 electronic connections in each boat. Wow.

February was the month of the tank. I wrote of how, at a secret base, I had been shown an upgrade program that catapulted Israel's aging fleet of British Centurions into some of the most modern and capable tanks in the world. They had been given redesigned engines, a 105 mm cannon with new stabilized gun sights and revolutionary night-vision equipment, state-of-the-art fire control systems and extra fuel capacity that increased the tank's range by 100 percent and speed by 25 percent. The over 2,000 modifications made the vehicle "better than anything the Arabs have and on a par with the American Patton M-60," according to a senior officer who, of course, could not be named.

March was underwater time in what seemed to be a lengthy submarine trip deep in the Mediterranean. Of course this submarine, the *Dolphin,* almost thirty years old, had been modified beyond imagination, making it "by far one of the best equipped conventional submarines in the world, jammed with sophisticated Israeli-developed equipment." I wrote about the enviable professionalism of 27-year-old Gad the captain and how magnificent it was to watch the crew, some from Jerusalem, others from development towns, all the children of immigrants, some immigrants themselves, work with clockwork harmony (a scene quite unlike anything above water where Israelis were notorious for pushing, shoving and rudeness).

Also in March, from the depths of the ocean to the previously impenetrable Armament Development Authority, or RAFAEL, where we were shown the Shafrir, the most brilliant air-to-air missile, 250 centimeters long with a 93-kilogram explosive head and solid fuel engine. This, we were told by the organization's head, Zeev Bonen, was "the secret of the success of Israel's wars in the air" and "the best in its class and capable of destroying any plane in service today."

In April came the world's "most revolutionary assault weapon," the Galil 5.56 submachine gun. And to prove that the Israeli Defense Forces was not just about high technology but devoted soldiers as well, I parachuted with and then wrote a puff piece about four brothers, the Rozenfelds, all paratroopers whose father had lost his entire first family to Nazis in Hungary during the war. The Jews will live on.

That month Israeli commandos made a daring raid into Beirut and killed three Black September leaders in their beds, including Muhammed Yusef Najjar, who had masterminded the terrorist attack on the Israeli contingent to the September 1972 Munich Olympic Games. Led by Ehud Barak dressed as a woman, the commandos from the top-secret Sayeret Matkal unit had landed on the city's outlying beaches, jumped into waiting taxis, assassinated the three, destroyed a seven-story building that served as headquarters for the Popular Front for the Liberation of Palestine, hit seven other targets in and around town, altogether killing over fifty terrorists, and left town by the same route two-and-a-half hours later.

National morale could not have been higher as Israel neared its 25th Independence Day celebrations. The May 22nd extravaganza on the streets of Jerusalem would have made the Kremlin proud: an unbroken 90-minute parade of 2,000 troops, 450 tanks, hundreds of artillery pieces, missiles and mortars, and a simultaneous 17-minute flyby led by Israel's new American Phantom jets. Israel's power would be evident not only to the 300,000 at the parade, but surely, we were told by our military briefer who was assigned to explain the huge outlay in such economically difficult times, to the enemy as well.

It is not difficult to see why we reporters were beguiled. In retrospect one can also understand why the government did not want to heed the warnings and ignored Sadat's overtures for peace. To have responded positively would have been an admission that the government's policies since 1967 had been misguided, that the massive investment in military muscle and settlements had been a waste, that the Arabs wanted peace and not the war that the government had been telling the people about as they bought more planes and tanks. As was oft told to me by even the most senior people, you just couldn't trust the Arabs. They would never come to terms with the Zionist presence in Palestine. It was all a sham.

Israel was prepared to compromise and give back some territory for peace, but not to the 1967 borders, making war inevitable. There was a genuine fear that Israel could not survive in the confines of the 1948 cease-fire lines. After the French embargo in 1967, which banned the sale of all weapons to Israel, the country's belief in the tenacity of alliances was tempered. There was a feeling that Israel could only rely on itself, and so could not give up most of the territories captured in 1967. When "territorial compromise" was mentioned, it was assumed in Jerusalem that it would be the Arabs doing the compromising.

Further, there was terrific arrogance. Eli Zeira, the intelligence chief, was arrogant. Unlike the tradition in the intelligence branch where young officers were asked to speak their minds, he would not listen to the opinions of those under him. He had a strong hold over Moshe Dayan, their relationship going back to 1954 when Zeira served as his aide-de-camp. Dayan was equally arrogant, even nasty. He thought he could do anything, from being an open philanderer to stealing national antiquities. He was rude to reporters and those who served under him, giving one the distinct impression that you were an idiot. He had won fame in the stunning military success of the 1956 Sinai Campaign, and being defense minister in 1967 added to his glory. But neither made him more of a *mensch*.

Remarkably, or perhaps not since Dayan dictated part of its composition, a Commission of Inquiry set up after the war found the political echelons to be clear of all blame. Zeira, of course, got chopped, as did Chief of Staff Elazar, who had begged Meir and Dayan to call up the reserves earlier, and who had then gone on to fight a brilliant and brutal war that ended with Israeli forces only 40 kilometers from Damascus, the Egyptian Third Army encircled in the Sinai and Israelis on the Egyptian side of the Suez Canal.

He deserved better.

One would have thought that the Yom Kippur War would have taught Israel and its leaders about the limits of brute strength and deterrence. It did neither. Instead, it set the stage for fundamental political change that, ironically, had as part of its core belief that the Arabs will never make true peace with the Jewish State and that Israel, at the end of the day, can rely only on strength and deterrence in order to survive.

8

WHAT GOES AROUND
COMES AROUND

In November 1974 Yasser Arafat addressed the United Nations.
Jews around the world were outraged and in St. Louis, where I was an
emissary from Israel at the time, youngsters at the Jewish Community
center organized a petition to send to the UN. On the poster is a cartoon
by the Jerusalem Post's *legendary cartoonist, Dry Bones, complaining*
that from hijacking airplanes Arafat and the PLO had graduated
to hijacking the world

By EARLY 1974, tensions between Israel and Syria were mounting steadily and it seemed I was back in the army, this time in civilian clothes as a military reporter.

During the war Israeli forces had fought a long battle to conquer the Syrian Hermon peak, the highest point on the range at 2,814 meters above sea level, several meters higher than the Israeli intelligence post that had been lost. Now the Syrians tried to retake it. Israeli intelligence believed this was an attempt by Syria's President Hafez Assad to encourage a war of attrition, a war he knew Israel did not want and could not afford. Less than six months after the Syrians were trounced, lost 600 square kilometers of territory, 1,200 tanks and 200 aircraft and thousands of men (exact casualty figures were never given), they were back at it. First they bombarded Israeli positions on the Golan, and then the bombardments became mutual.

By April Syrian and Israeli jets were attacking each other's positions across the cease-fire line. By the time a new cease-fire was reached in June, 68 Israelis had been killed, 180 wounded and three Israeli aircraft lost. Syria's losses were significantly higher.

That meant bouncing around in armored vehicles, sleeping out at nights, drinking coffee with old friends, the *hevra,* avoiding land mines and dodging Syrian mortars. I even made it up to Hermon Peak, where I found my former corporal in the paratroops, Nehemia Tamari, now the commander of Sayeret Matkal, in charge of the contested position. He looked terrible. Unshaven, dark, sunken eyes and crumpled clothes. No wonder. They had been there for weeks in the freezing cold under constant artillery and mortar fire.

The work was relentless. On April 11, 1974, eighteen civilians, including nine children, were killed in the northern town of Kiryat Shmona when three terrorists from Ahmed Jibril's Popular Front for the Liberation of Palestine went on a shooting spree in an apartment building on the edge of the city. I remember well the look on the face of Yitzhak Hofi, the acting chief of staff, as he surveyed the scene, children and women shot at close range in their homes.

Just one month later, on May 15, the Ma'alot school massacre took place, when eighty-six children on a school trip in the Galilee were taken hostage by three terrorists demanding the mass release of prisoners from Israeli jails. Negotiations and attempts to mediate by the Romanian and French ambassadors to Israel failed to end the impasse. Late that afternoon, when it was judged there was no alternative, orders were given to storm the school. Twenty-one children and five adults were executed by the terrorists or killed in the exchange of fire.

In response, Israeli jets started pulverizing targets in Lebanon. Dayan, still the defense minister, explained that if Israeli citizens in the north could not be safe, there would be no safety on the Lebanese side. By this time I was wary of Dayan's one-liners, tired of hearing generals explain why they could not effectively seal Israel's border. I was disillusioned with the army I had so proudly written about in the months preceding the 1973 war. The transition from being in the reserves to being back in the army as a reporter had been too quick. I felt I needed time to breathe, to lead a normal life, to have a weekend, to be able to go out for dinner and actually get to finish it.

So I applied for a job as a Jewish Agency emissary abroad. The kids were still young and I was curious to see the world. I was offered the opportunity to go to St. Louis, Missouri, for two years, where I was to work out of the Jewish Community Center as the community *shaliach* from Israel. First I had to complete a three-month course at the Hebrew University campus on Mount Scopus, where we were taught Israeli and Jewish history, Arab perfidy, the great Zionist thinkers, the structure of the American Jewish community, good manners, youth activities and what programs the Jewish Agency, our employer, was offering to overseas youth.

Little of what we learned remained with me for long, the courses being long-winded, uninspiring and somewhat flat after the experience of the Yom Kippur War. These folks were still in the *"hora*-in-the-fields" stage and I had become cynical about Zionist heroes and what an egalitarian, democratic state we were—"the only democratic state in the entire Middle East," as was pounded into us time and again. I do, however, remember the last night when in a moment of levity one of the class, Moshe Fass, sat himself down on a bar stool under a light, threw his head back, crossed his long legs and began to read *Fanny Hill, or Memoirs of a*

Woman of Pleasure in Yiddish, without doubt the funniest thing I had ever heard: *"Er het der groise ding arois genemen und arupt gestupt. . . ."*

Things did not start well in St. Louis. The director of the Center, Bill Kahn, was a giant of a man, physically huge, with huge hands and a huge voice. I felt like a dwarf when ushered into his huge office with its huge desk. This was America and everything was overwhelming. On the first day in America I had been sent to buy some milk for the kids and was astounded to find about twenty types on the supermarket's shelves. I fled in panic.

Bill Kahn had also built a huge Center, a model emulated by Jewish communities all over America. It had ultra-modern health and sports facilities, a rich cultural program, an especially good home for senior citizens, a kindergarten with a national reputation and camp facilities tucked in deep woods surrounding the Center. It was a fantastic community facility in every way. But there was a problem. Teenagers were just not coming in. Only nerds went to the JCC's youth programs.

This was my first real meeting with Kahn and his youth staff, with whom I was supposed to work closely toward the goal of injecting Jewish and Israeli content into their programming. I listened to the debate on how to get youth involved and when each of the department heads had had their say, I asked whether it would not be a good idea for us to find an old house in a nearby suburb that we could rent, have the kids fix it up and turn into their *bayit,* going back to my experience in Habonim in South Africa, where having our own "home" was such an integral part of the social experience. Kids don't come to the Center, so the Center, I said, should reach out to them, by taking a dilapidated house and transforming it into an ongoing youth project.

Silence. Absolute, total, silence. The six or so staff members sat still, their eyes fixed on the floor. It was, I could tell, the calm before the storm. Kahn turned redder and redder behind his desk. He seemed to puff up at the neck, thick veins protruding from his temples.

"You fucking Israelis," he screamed, "always know better. I've built a multimillion dollar Center so that you can move into some dilapidated fucking house." And then, in one quick movement, standing up and turning toward the wall behind him he lifted a framed plaque from the wall and read out the inscription giving him the highest award for community service of any Jewish professional in the United States and Canada.

"The highest award and you come here and tell me what the fuck to do," he screamed, his eyes bulging. With another swift movement he hurled the plaque at my head, missing me by inches. I stood up, walked the three blocks home to the apartment we had moved into earlier that day and told Beulah to pack. We were leaving.

It was six or so in the evening and since we had no pots and pans we went out to a nearby Dunkin' Donuts for dinner. I felt I had made a huge mistake and we both felt so dejected, so far from home and family and so very alone.

That evening when we returned to the apartment, two staffers, Hank and Terry, were waiting for me on the stairs to call me back to the office. When we arrived at his office Kahn was extremely apologetic and gave me an absolutely overpowering hug and handshake. I and the family went on to spend a fabulous two years working at the Center, living in a great community situated in a fascinating part of America and traveling through the states.

In the end, we brought kids, lots of them, into the Center and on programs to Israel. We brought Israeli culture to the Center and the community at large, ran a vibrant Hebrew program and developed Zionist youth programs where none had been before. It was lots and lots of fun.

But it was also an important lesson for me. I got to know and appreciate organizational Jewish life in America and was exposed for the first time to non-Orthodox Jewry, the Reform and Conservative movements. For the first time I had to wrestle with a notion that until then I had considered axiomatic: that every Jew should live in Israel. Here I met Jews who were proud Americans, proud supporters of Israel and conscious of their power.

Very early in my work I realized that I should not encourage *aliya,* emigration to Israel, but focus on strengthening the Jewish component of the existing curriculum. Bring Israel, Hebrew, and Jewish history and culture into the schools, youth groups, temples, publications, universities, camps; try to inculcate a love for and identity with the Jewish people wherever they may choose to live, even outside Israel. This involved weekend sleepovers with Israeli songs around a campfire late into the night, Israeli folk dancing, Israeli movies, falafel and pita instead of pizza. At summer camp we created games with *Palmach* defenders and Arab insurgents and again lots of campfires, just like those we had at the Habonim camps in South Africa so many years ago.

We regularly took ten-day canoe trips down the beautiful and protected Bufflo River in deepest Arkansas. Every time we went down there, deep into "redneck" country where everyone walked around with a rifle and looked like they could be members of the Klan, the counselors would beg me and the kids not to let out that we were from Camp Sabra, the Jewish camp. If anyone asks just say you are from Camp Mohawk in the Ozarks, we were told.

But that changed dramatically on a trip we took in July 1976 when we stopped our bus on a bridge somewhere between Ponca and Pruitt, Arkansas, to watch a group of mean-looking young men catching snakes with forked sticks. It seems four rattlers had moments before escaped from a snake hunter's bag and were putting up a hell of a fight about being put back in again. The job eventually done, our thirty or so kids clapped while the snake hunters and their entourage of hillbilly-looking women cracked open beers that they slugged down with alarming speed.

"Where ya'll from?" one of the men asked.

"Camp Sabra, we're all Jewish," the kids shouted. "Israel is also our country and we're going to visit."

"Oh, you guys are great man," said the snake hunter, his drawl so pronounced that his words were hard to understand. "Just faaaaaantastic man. Long live Israel."

The reason for the change in the kids' willingness to be identified was Israel's brilliant raid on Entebbe, Uganda, on July 3rd, 1976, when Israeli commandos operating 2,200 miles from base managed to rescue ninety-eight hostages who had been hijacked there by Palestinian and German terrorists. The terrorists had first forced the Air France flight from Paris to Tel Aviv to Benghazi, Libya. There they refueled, separated the Israeli and other Jewish passengers from the rest, put them back on the plane and flew on to Entebbe, where they were welcomed by Idi Amin's army. Amin had once been a big Israeli ally and had even come to the jump school at the Tel Nof base for parachute training. He had been at Tel Nof one course before ours and story had it that he and the chief army chaplain, Shlomo Goren, who was on the course with Amin, had to be pushed out of the "Eichmann," the smaller of the two towers from which one is taught to simulate an exit from an airplane (the taller was called "Hitler"). Now a sworn enemy of Israel, Amin continued to wear his silver Israeli parachute wings above the many rows of medals on his chest.

In October 1975 there had been the humiliating adoption of the "Zionism is Racism" vote at the United Nations, and less than a year before that Arafat's appearance at the UN wearing a gun in his holster and vowing to the delegates that "now Zionism will get out of this world." What the Six Day War had done for the Jewish community nine years before, Israel's daring raid was doing again, making it desirable to be identified as a Jew and associated with Israel's success.

As my stay in the Midwest came to an end, the *Jerusalem Post* agreed that when I came back to Israel I would return to my job as military reporter. I had been replaced temporarily by two of my colleagues, who agreed they would be more than happy to have me come back and take over.

In August 1974, just as I had arrived in St. Louis, a group of Israeli Air Force officers and defense ministry personnel made a trip to the city to visit the headquarters of McDonnell Douglas, where they made a decision to purchase twenty-five F-15 advanced aircraft for a total outlay of $624 million, or roughly the equivalent of five months' salary for every Israeli family.

The first of these planes was due to be delivered to Israel in December 1976, so in March, several months before leaving St. Louis, I telephoned McDonnell's representative in Israel, George Lavin, and attempted to convince him that since I was already there it would make sense if I could do the "inside story" on the plane and its capabilities and that I would not jeopardize the security of its systems.

It took time and bureaucratic dexterity, but finally the McDonnell Douglas people opened up after clearing it with Israeli Air Force field security. I spent days at the plant watching these magnificent flying machines coming together, miles and miles of thin strands of wire, new technologies that dazzled the mind and capabilities that had seemed unattainable in previous generations of aircraft. I was also impressed by the respect the American engineers had for the Israeli Air Force personnel working opposite them, including Eitan Ben Eliyahu, who I had met years before as a gung ho member of the Air Force aerobatic team and who was destined to become the commander of Israel's first F-15 squadron, and later commander of the Air Force.

In building this advanced fighter, the Americans brought new technologies and the Israelis brought recent battle experience. But an equally important element was a feel for the human dimension of the aircraft. Human engineering was one of the main reasons that Western weapons, other than artillery, were so superior to those in the East. The Soviets produced weapons that had good statistics, could go far and shoot far, but they cared nothing for the environment in which the men operating them had to work, thus greatly reducing their efficiency.

The Israeli version of the F-15 was significantly re-engineered, keeping in mind both the human factor and that other F-15s would soon be available to the Saudis and other pro-Western Arab regimes, meaning that Israel's F-15 had to be unique if the country was to maintain its qualitative military advantage to offset its quantitative disadvantage. The hundreds of changes made by the Israelis ranged from systems that helped pilots deal with the problem of information overload—sometimes so intense that they landed with their wheels up—to the angle of recline of the pilot's seat. The aircraft's American-designated role as an interceptor made it difficult for Israeli pilots, who used the jet in a multirole capacity, so changes had to be made to accommodate that difference. The Israeli changes basically put the David into the Goliath to ensure that ever important critical edge over the capabilities of the enemy.

I received permission to go to Washington at the paper's expense since my editor, Ari Rath, thought it would be useful for me to understand Israel's strategic relationship with the United States as the two became more closely allied. Washington was like no other place I had been, a modern-day Rome, ancient Athens reincarnated, a place where power and urgency oozed out of every pore of every official. I was taken around the capital by Wolf Blitzer, now of CNN fame, then the *Post*'s newly installed Washington correspondent. Wolf, recently married and living in an apartment in Bethesda, Maryland, knew the city and corridors of power as well as any young man, having spent several years working under the watchful eye of Morrie Amitai, the director of the American Israel Public Affairs Committee (AIPAC), the pro-Israel lobby in D.C.

We went from the plush offices of deputy assistant secretaries in the State Department to the more austere quarters in the Pentagon, meeting the officials who made the giant wheels of policy turn. And then to the Congress to begin to understand how they dealt with the executive branch and with their voters back home. In a week or so Wolf opened many doors onto a whole new world; it was an experience that would forever change how I covered defense issues.

With each new F-15 eventually costing around $30 million and Washington being as complicated as it was, defense, I concluded, was not a beat on the paper, but a profession. To avoid my earlier mistakes of naiveté and shallowness, of uncritical reporting of what we were told, I had to understand the geostrategic environment, political trends in the Middle East, modern technologies, the inner workings of Washington, U.S. interests and their interaction with those of Israel, global economics and what was really going on in the Soviet Union.

Meanwhile, as sometimes happens with weapons, the first target shot down by Israel's three maiden F-15's was a friendly one—the government of Yitzhak Rabin, the nation's first native-born prime minister and chief of staff in the Six Day War. The aircraft, after an 11-hour nonstop flight from St. Louis with one aerial refueling, touched down at Tel Nof airbase twenty minutes later than scheduled and only seventeen minutes before the Sabbath. Because the aircraft's arrival would be so close to the Sabbath, a ceremony originally planned for 3,000 guests was canceled and 290 were invited instead.

This failed to placate Rabin's religious coalition partners, ten Knesset members from the National Religious Party and two from the religiously more extreme Agudat Yisrael faction, who left the government in protest, claiming that because the ceremony had been planned so close to the Sabbath the government had forced some of those present to desecrate the holy day. Thus losing his solid majority, Rabin resigned in April 1977, ostensibly over an illegal bank account his wife was reported to have had in Washington. This initiated a leadership battle with Shimon Peres for control of the Labor Party that was to last almost until the day Rabin was murdered in 1995.

By the time we left the United States, Beulah, myself and the children had traveled through forty-eight of the fifty states; I had given dozens of lectures, half of them to non-Jewish groups in the Bible Belt, who chastised me for Israel's being too soft on the Palestinians, and cursed those who had built the "abomination" on Temple Mount, referring to the Al Aksa Mosque. These people, it soon became apparent to me, were prepared to fight the Muslims to the last drop of Jewish blood. I also had the dubious experience of demonstrating with the Ku Klux Klan in demanding that the "Kikes" leave America for Israel.

The occasion was a lecture we had organized at Washington University in St. Louis for Serge Klarsfeld, the famed Nazi hunter. The Klan had come to demonstrate, as they did at many Jewish events, and when I saw a placard calling on the "Kikes" to leave I joined in, in the cause of *aliya,* as did dozens of the Jewish students who had come to hear Klarsfeld and were now having a whale of a time making fools of the idiots in white hoods.

My first Yom Kippur in America was a more profound Jewish experience. Hank, the youth worker who had persuaded me to return to Bill Kahn's Jewish Community Center, took me to his temple for *Kol Nidrei,* the holiest of all prayers on the holiest of all nights. We parked far from the temple, having been directed there by a line of attendants in red waistcoats, and managed to get seats for the second session at 9 P.M. On a normal Sabbath the rabbi would have been happy to fill a quarter of the synagogue, let alone hold a second session.

Exactly at nine with all of us in our seats, having been directed to them by an army of ushers, the lights dimmed. Then a single spotlight went on and Rabbi Rubin appeared, rising through the floor on an elevator, his hands spread like the wings of an eagle, his *talit* draped over him, and to the music of a lone cello he began intoning a blessing about the good Lord looking over us. Then, from a balcony, a huge Black woman who, like the cellist and two violinists, had been rented for the night from the St. Louis Symphony began to sing the prayer in perfect Hebrew in a spine-chilling soprano.

At first I was appalled that Judaism had been diluted to this degree. But then, I thought, when was the last time I had been in a synagogue, any synagogue? No matter how shallow, superficial or theatric the Kol Nidrei service may have been to me, it brought tears to Hank's eyes, and the eyes of so many others. One of the great things about America is its belief in personal freedom, in the principle of each to his own as long as it is not at the expense of others. Tolerance, especially religious toler-ance, like so much else, is something Israelis have yet to learn.

St. Louis was an interlude and an education. It was a time to rest and heal, and by teaching others about what we loved, to begin loving again. It was also time to leave. Shai, after two years in an Orthodox Jewish school, the Epstein Hebrew Academy, came home on the afternoon be-fore we were leaving and told us that he had learned God's real name.

"And what's that?" we asked.

"Jesus Christ," he replied.

"Where did you learn that from?" we asked.

"From Sean upstairs," he said.

We arrived back in Israel in the summer of 1976 via Amsterdam and Copenhagen. Rochie, my older sister, Monty, her husband, and their four kids were there to meet us. They had emigrated to Israel from South Africa in May 1973, also graduates of the Zionist youth movement in that time. We climbed into their white Peugeot station wagon, the roof rack loaded high with our new American possessions, and headed for Jerusalem. I thought back to the moment just before landing when I had seen the Israeli coast from the plane's window and the mixed feelings I had about being home. I had enjoyed America, was still dazzled by the sheer happiness of Tivoli Gardens and the uncomplicated freedoms of Holland, and now the airport staff had been rude and unhelpful, the cus-toms people were atrocious and leering, and the other passengers pushed and shoved, mindless of our two relatively small children.

And when we finally arrived at our apartment that Rochie, Monty and the kids had valiantly tried to spruce up for our arrival, including leaving freshly baked cakes, flowers, food in the fridge and everything spotless and clean, our hearts sank. We had rented it out to a seemingly nice Dutch couple. Our oak rocking chair had been painted purple, the walls of our bedroom deep red. Pieces of cupboards and shelves were missing, as were some of our books and records. The place felt so grungy and gray, stifling and small. I hated it.

As for the country, something had changed in the two years we had been away. It only took a visit to the bank or grocery store or a chat with the neighbors, none of whom could believe that we had actually come back. There was an air of dissatisfaction and resentment, and loss of belief in the country's leaders. The government's arrogance had disappeared, but so had the spirit of unity and common purpose.

Shai's new school was a disaster, with underpaid, exasperated teachers trying to educate over thirty children in a class, some like Shai, who knew very little Hebrew. Many of the children came from poor families from the Katamon area with ten children or more who could not go home and do their homework or get any real help from their parents, a problem the school was not equipped to address. There were no sports facilities other than a paved playground with two netless hoops at either end. The playground and the language were rough. On his third day there Shai came home and informed us that everyone in the school hated his mother. "Why?" we asked. "Because everyone calls me a *ben zona*," he said. Son of a whore.

This was obviously no Epstein Hebrew Academy. A good Jewish education, it seemed, was reserved for those in the Diaspora.

Political tensions, always high in Israel, were now shriller, debate was less tolerant, more extreme, more acrimonious and threatening, than in the past. The National Religious Party, which had always been in alliance with Labor and had limited itself to guarding the status quo on issues of religion and state, was transformed into a militant, messianic, loud and pugnacious nationalistic movement that now cared about one thing: building settlements in Judea, Samaria and Gaza to ensure that *Eretz Yisrael,* the Land of Israel, never be relinquished.

Young men and women, all graduates of the Bnei Akiva Zionist religious youth movement, were now grabbing hilltops and abandoned Jordanian army camps on the West Bank and trying to turn them into permanent settlements, coming into direct confrontation with soldiers ordered to remove them. I had never seen a Jew attack an Israeli soldier before.

At the same time Menachem Begin had forged the Likud Party out of a group of right-wing secular parties, including those vehemently opposed to Labor's socialism. Begin, a Polish Jew, the consummate hand-kissing gentleman, also became the hero of the mainly Sephardic underclass. Their support for Begin derived from their hatred of Labor, who they blamed for the degradation of being placed in tent and shack transit camps and de-loused with DDT when arriving in Israel in the early 1950s. The country had also eventually decided to punish Labor for the Yom Kippur War. The chant of "Begin, Begin King of Israel" reverberated round the land as opposition against the white, Ashkenazi, socialist rule of Labor reached a crescendo. The whole mood was ugly. I felt like a stranger in my own country. I remember wondering why we bothered unpacking our suitcases at all.

Things did not get off to a good start at work either. My first big piece was for the weekend magazine and titled "Wasted Dollars." It ruined my relationship with the organized American Jewish community for years to come. I reported that an estimated $69 million a year was wasted because the three hundred organizations representing American Jews refused to give up turf and would not cooperate or innovate despite some of them being anachronistic and having served causes long gone. I criticized the high salaries and lifestyles of some Jewish executives and was especially hard on the United Jewish Appeal, which, I claimed, had armies of emissaries and bureaucrats who were so inept that a fund-raising campaign on the campus of Washington University in St. Louis in 1975 raised a total of $600 from 5,000 Jewish students.

That Saturday night I was called into the office by Ari Rath, the managing editor, who told me that the wrath of the Jewish world was upon me, that some of the major non-Israeli shareholders of the paper, themselves big deals in the UJA and other organizations I had criticized, wanted my head. Particularly irate was Irwin J. Bernstein, the all-powerful head of the UJA, who was so furious with me, Rath related, that he had almost choked on the phone. My idiocy, Bernstein had yelled, was going to cost the Jewish people millions. My article, he went on, would be thrown in their faces while trying to collect money for Israel, adding that I was a liar, saboteur and menace and should be fired and fed to the dogs.

To escape the fire I took myself down to Dahab, a Bedouin encampment on the Red Sea coast equidistant between Eilat to the north and Sharm el Sheikh to the south. The Israelis had also built a small cooperative settlement there called Di-Zahav, where I had friends and diving partners, and where rudimentary diving services were available. Red Sea diving was my solace and love. It was quiet down there, no news, no phones and, strangely, no pressure.

My love affair with the Sinai started in 1966, a decade before, when I was posted on reserve duty in Eilat, on the Jordanian border, before the Six Day War. My friend Yoel, who would later be killed in the Yom Kippur War, and I spent hours snorkeling in the Red Sea's pristine azure waters. We were stationed across from the Jordanian port city of Aqaba in a tiny intelligence station on the beach, where we guarded a shack opened twice a day by a secretive diminutive Iraqi Jew who never said hello or good-bye once he had finished twiddling his knobs on the radio sets inside. Six of us, now all close buddies having survived basic and advanced training together, lived in a tent. We had a small outside kitchen where we competed in knocking up imaginative meals from the very basic rations the army provided, my specialty being making eggplant taste like chopped liver.

And then, after the 1967 war, I discovered the rest of Sinai, an unbelievable treasure of largely untouched miracles despite the conflicts that had taken place on its soil. Its interior, at the center of which was Mount Sinai, from where one can watch the most spectacular and spiritually uplifting sunrise on earth, is a combination of starkness, bareness and beauty, yet sensual at sunset when the hues become pastel and daunting mountains soften.

It was always to the Sinai that we escaped from the heavy atmosphere in Israel, several families camping together at secluded *wadis* and bays along the coast. There was no feeling of this being occupied territory, but rather "head space" where the kids ran along virgin beaches, their bottoms getting brown in the sun, and one's only worry being whether the children were drinking enough water.

Unlike the West Bank, there was no ideological conflict here. This was not part of Greater Israel or the Biblical Promised Land; it was a place the Jews spent forty years trying to leave after escaping bondage in Egypt by following Moses to the Promised Land. There were no conquered people here; the area's 10,000 indigenous Bedouin were only too happy that the Egyptians, who had treated them deplorably, were gone. Very quickly they adapted to catering to the needs of the thousands of Israelis who had begun to discover the desert peninsula. For just a few shekels one could take a trip in a Bedouin taxi, an ancient Peugeot held together with string and rubber bands, to the interior, bouncing down *wadis* and recklessly overtaking camel trains on tracks where only camels should tread.

The Bedouin even became integral to the operation of the Israeli army. They built most of the bases and ran many ancillary services, including providing the troops with as much hashish as one could smoke. In the mid-seventies I spent a fabulous thirty days on reserve duty at Jabl Hammam Mussa on the coast of the Gulf of Suez. There, from our vantage point above the Gulf, it was our duty to record all incoming shipping and to present these reports to the intelligence officer at the A-Tur base a few miles to the south. It was also our job to patrol the coast twice a day with a Bedouin tracker to see whether anyone had infiltrated from the sea, there always being a fear of Egyptian intelligence missions landing behind the lines.

The base at A-Tur was a story in itself, one that I wrote but that was blocked by the military censor on the grounds that reporters could not report on what they saw while on reserve duty. I was no whistle-blower, but three times during that period we could not carry out our daily patrols because the command car had a puncture and the Bedouin who changes tires had not come in that day. Dishes went unwashed for a week because the Bedouin dishwasher had been off at his mother's funeral. Even considering having a shower in the base was suicidal, the

Bedouin who kept the WC clean being off because it was date harvest season. The front gate to the base was locked because the Bedouin with the key had lost it, so a hole had been cut in the fence wide enough for a vehicle to pass through with relative ease. Not once could we find the intelligence officer to whom we were supposed to hand our diligently written records. He was either on leave or at meetings in Sharm or places so secret we could not be informed. Our records were so "secret" that according to our instructions we could not entrust them to anyone but the intelligence officer himself.

After the censor "killed" my piece I asked for a meeting with Chief of Staff Rafael Eitan, who had been my brigade commander in the Six Day War. I explained that I had written the article to try to bring about change in what I saw as a potentially disastrous situation. He promised me that within a month he would deal with all the problems listed in my unpublished article. He did that by firing everyone from the commander all the way down the line. He then flew me to Sharm, where a jeep was waiting to deliver me to one Colonel Jackie Even, who was balancing on his head eating a quarter of an orange when I walked into his office. Colonel Even then took me off to A-Tur to show me that everything had been set right, which it seemed it had.

While in the states I had completed a diving course and bought some expensive diving equipment, the first time I remember spending so much on myself. It was one of the best investments I have ever made. The beauty of the Red Sea is indescribable, as were the friendships made and the unforgettable evenings under the ever-so-bright stars.

One such unforgettable night was Thursday, April 7, 1977. We had come up from a night dive off the reef at the Sharm field school run by the National Society for the Protection of Nature. I had seen the moon from 50 meters under water and my head was spinning from the experience. There were three of us; myself, Rafi, my neighbor in Jerusalem; and Ilya, a friend who lived at the field school where he taught and guided nature tours. We shed our heavy gear and drove back to where our families were camped out in a beautifully secluded spot on the beach between Na'ama Bay and Ras Nasrani.

Two tents were up and the children were already asleep when we arrived. The day's sun had exhausted them. Five or six friends were seated around a campfire, a bottle of wine was open and a coffeepot was slowly boiling on a bed of embers. Dinner had been fresh fish and pita purchased from the Bedouin. I did not eat the fish. I could not dive and eat fish, and it pained me to see the remnants on the plates, everyone being too mellow to bother cleaning up.

Suddenly, in the distance, a pair of headlights came bouncing down the *wadi*. Howard Rosenstein, the owner of the dive shop at Na'ama Bay and a pioneer in bringing the Red Sea to the attention of the world while militantly safeguarding its ecology, arrived breathless with the news that Rabin had resigned and, more importantly, Maccabi Tel Aviv had beaten Mobilgirgi of Varese, Italy, by one point in the European Cup basketball finals.

"Who gives a shit" was the unanimous reaction, as we passed Howard the bottle of wine and a paper cup and told him about seeing the moon from 50 meters under water.

I had first met Rabin when, as a soldier stationed in El Arish following the Six Day War, I was selected to be part of the detachment chosen to protect the chief of staff's convoy as he and his generals surveyed firsthand the carnage of the battlefield. I had been immensely impressed by this blue-eyed, calm, self-confident *Sabra,* his deep, soft, yet evocative voice asking questions with precision and listening with genuine respect and interest as junior officers made their reports. As a politician, however, I found him lackluster and disappointing, notwithstanding those instincts that had first brought him the leadership of the Labor Party and then the prime minister's office. Just a few weeks before his resignation, Ari Rath, the paper's co-editor and former diplomatic correspondent, and I interviewed him in his Jerusalem office. He chain-smoked throughout the conversation, which was diffuse and pointless, most of the time spent complaining about Shimon Peres and his subterfuge. The interview was so thin on content that Ari and I worked hard to find a lead.

Elections were held on May 17, 1977, and Menachem Begin indeed became King of Israel. The Likud trounced Labor, 43 seats to 32 in the 120-member Knesset. Begin forged a coalition with the National Religious

Party, which was at the forefront of Israel's settlement movement in the West Bank and that Begin fervently supported, and with the ultra-Orthodox party Agudat Yisrael, which cared little about the politics of modern Israel but saw their participation in government as a way of ensuring funding for the *yeshiva* system and their constituents. Together they controlled only 61 seats in the Knesset, a majority of one, but this later grew to a solid 76 in October 1977 when a new party, the Democratic Party for Change, headed by world-renowned archaeologist Yigael Yadin, joined the coalition. Yadin had gone into the election promising clean government and social change and had won an astounding 15 seats, mainly from voters who were disappointed with Labor. Begin now had a comfortable majority. Almost three decades of Mapai socialism had ended and the stage was now set for a historic shift in the political, social, economic and psychological makeup of the nation.

The underdog had come to power. The politician that David Ben-Gurion in June 1948, just a month after Israel was created, accused of "attempting to crush the Israeli army and murder the Jewish State," and only referred to in the Knesset as "that man seated next to Knesset member Bader," was now prime minister. Labor's settlement policy, governed by strategic considerations, was replaced by one governed by ideology and religion. The monopolies owned by the unions were to be privatized, the kibbutz movement's massive subsidies were to be cut, and resources were to be reallocated to the benefit of the ultra-Orthodox and the development towns and the encouragement of private industry. In a single election the face of Israel was changed irrevocably.

On May 19, two days after the election and before he had formally taken office, together with his agriculture-minister-to-be Ariel Sharon, under a *chupa* made of a prayer shawl held up by four poles, Begin carried a Torah scroll into the temporary West Bank settlement of Eilon Moreh, grudgingly established by the Labor government after a massive settler sit-in at the abandoned Sebastia army camp threatened to turn into a violent confrontation.

Standing under the *chupa*, Torah in hand, Begin, his voice quivering with emotion, his eyes magnified behind the lenses of his thick glasses, declared that "there will, in a few weeks or months, be many more Eilon

Morehs. These are not occupied territories but liberated ones in which Jews have every right to settle." Sharon beamed in the background.

Later, speaking to a small cluster of foreign correspondents, he said: "You annex foreign territory, not your own country, not Judea and Samaria." He went on to offer the Palestinians Israeli citizenship, something he was to repeat many times and mean sincerely. He believed in democracy but was disdainful of demography, pointing out that when Israel was created the Jews were but a speck in an Arab ocean. One must have faith.

He, and others in the Likud, genuinely believed that if one could raise the local standard of living and allow minority rights in terms of local governance, the Palestinians of the West Bank and Gaza would be only too happy to be Israelis, or at least live quietly under Israeli rule.

In August, Begin announced that "action" had begun on equal rights in the territories. A labor policy was to be instituted in Rafiah that would prevent the exploitation of Palestinian workers and guarantee them an honorable wage. There was to be a health scheme for the West Bank and Gaza and credit was to be offered to Palestinian bus companies to upgrade their fleets. It was stressed that these services would not be financed by the Israeli taxpayer, but from the more efficient collection of taxes from the Palestinians, or "the Arabs of *Eretz Yisrael*" as Begin meticulously called them.

My own work was far from politics. In September I made an amazing voyage on an Israeli missile boat down to Djibouti at the entrance to the Red Sea between Yemen and Eritrea, where a civil war potentially threatened to block Israeli shipping through the strait. The farther south we went the more spectacular the sea became, dolphins following us for miles and miles, the blueness of the water reminding me of the little cubes of dark blue dye my mom used to dissolve and wash into her hair.

On the third night, off the coast of Sudan, the ship came to a standstill. The crew was ordered not to speak. All radios were turned off and only one light burned low above a map table on the deck. An officer measured off distances with calipers and once his calculations were done that light too was extinguished. Then the captain asked me down to his cabin, where the porthole had been latched down. He apologized and locked me inside, saying he would be back in about an hour. It took four.

A boat being a small place, and seeing a gray rubber dinghy being washed down by men in rubber dive suits, it did not take me long to ascertain that several Mossad agents had been dropped off on the Sudanese shore from where they were to make their way inland to the temporary camps that had been set up for the flood of Falasha Jews fleeing Mengistu's cruel regime in Ethiopia. These agents would guide the refugees, on foot, back into Sudan and the relative safety of the camps there, until the final voyage to Israel. It was truly amazing what Jews were prepared to do to save other Jews. The problems started once they arrived in Israel and had to live together.

Later that month fighting in the north became fierce and in October the army agreed to take a few of us to see what until then had been a semicovert operation, the training and arming of the South Lebanon Army. We met at Bialik Belsky's hotel in Metullah. From there we proceeded in a minibus to a gate in the border, our guide being the former Israel Radio correspondent in the north, Yoram Ha'Mizrachi. He was now a liaison on behalf of the Defense Ministry to the South Lebanon Army, an Israeli surrogate force made up of Lebanese Christians, Druze and Shia Muslims who wanted to keep the Palestinians out of southern Lebanon and end the painful succession of Israeli retaliatory raids against terrorist bases on their lands. To do so they had allied themselves with Israel, seized a several-kilometer-wide corridor along the Lebanon border, thus theoretically taking Israel out of the range of terrorist Katyusha rockets, and created an Israeli-armed and trained fighting force that was quite effective. This way they protected their own interests by protecting Israel's, a win-win situation as the military saw it. Israel could now open up its border with southern Lebanon at the "Good Fence" southeast of Metullah, where hundreds of workers, mainly young women, could enter Israel for daily jobs, mostly in the textile industry. Israel also provided water, electricity and almost all food supplies. Yoram Ha'Mizrachi acted and was received as if he were the High Commissioner.

On the Israeli side of the border four Mercedes-Benz limousines, a bit the worse for wear and with Lebanese license plates, waited for us, each driven by an SLA militiaman wearing the old Israeli Defense Forces canvas leopard-spot training fatigues. Having been found unsuitable for use in the Israeli climate, these had been withdrawn from stock and recycled as the official uniforms of the SLA.

We drove a short way to the village of Marj Ayoun, where Major Saad Haddad was waiting for us in his modest home. Diminutive next to the giant and portly Ha'Mizrachi, he described the rationale for his alliance with Israel: Since King Hussein of Jordan had expelled the Palestinians in September 1970, the lives of the people of southern Lebanon had become intolerable, caught between the hammer of Palestinian terrorism and the anvil of Israeli counterstrikes.

Haddad's charming, well-dressed wife and two children, none of whom were introduced, laid out small cups of sweet tea and Osem biscuits from Israel, and one by one we were introduced to the senior commanders. I then went off with one of them, also named Saad. Together with three armed bodyguards we got into a red Dodge jeep commandeered from three journalists from Beirut who the SLA claimed were Palestinian spies. The three were being kept at the Tel Nahas prison, a place I was later to visit and never forget, the conditions there being appalling.

Leaving Marj Ayoun and setting off into the southern Lebanese hills, one can see how vulnerable the towns and villages along Israel's northern border are. Metullah, Israel's most northern town, made an easy target for even an inept sniper. So it was all along the border.

We traveled at a 100 kilometers an hour along the narrow, undulating roads to villages that for me, until now, had been targets on a map—Klea, Dir Mimas, el-Meri, Kila, a-Deisa and the beautiful gorges of the Litani River. Everywhere, but everywhere, children of ten or so were toting guns and pistols and saluting us as we drove past, ending up at a position overlooking Tel Shreifa and the village of Khayam, where the SLA and Palestinians had fought a pitched battle a few weeks before.

In the position stood a lone French-made 155 mm cannon, being lovingly cleaned by its young crew of militiamen. It had fired over 5,000 shells at Tel Shreifa, one proudly told me, adding that this was the same cannon Israel had used in the battle of Kalkilya in 1954, twenty-three years before. What goes around comes around.

9

MY LAND IS HOLY

*In Alexandria, Egypt, at the very start of the peace process, 1978.
My three companions were Egyptian secret service agents who never
let me out of their sight. A fourth took this picture.*

IT WAS ABOUT 7:15 on Saturday night, November 19, 1977. I was standing with Eitan Haber, then *Yediot Aharonot*'s military correspondent and later Yitzhak Rabin's closest aide, in a crowd of about two thousand journalists from the world over who had come to cover Egyptian president Anwar Sadat's visit to Israel, the first ever by an Arab head of state. We were at the Jerusalem Theatre, where, with miraculous efficiency, Zeev Chafets, head of the Government Press Office, had in less than two days organized the installation of 250 phones, 60 teleprinters and 20 television sets. The theatre itself was ideal for press conferences and briefings, while the foyer served as an impressive press center where government bureaucrats roamed around looking to be interviewed and journalists interviewed each other.

Sadat was due to land in about 45 minutes. Shouting over the noise Eitan said this was not something he wanted to watch with two thousand others, and I suggested we head over to my apartment, about ten minutes away. Other than the thousands of police deployed along the route Sadat would take while in Jerusalem, the streets were deserted. The entire nation was glued to their TV sets waiting for the unbelievable: the leader of the most powerful Arab country on a peace mission to Jerusalem, the capital of the Jewish state.

We parked with a few minutes to spare and bounded up the three stories to the apartment, which was empty. Beulah had taken the kids to a friend's house, not wanting to be alone and convinced, correctly, that I would be at work for most of the night. I switched on the television as the camera panned the hundreds of journalists pushing and shoving for space on the makeshift elevated stands. It looked as if a riot was about to break out.

Despite being November, it was not cold. I opened the floor-to-ceiling window overlooking the Jerusalem University Botanical Garden while Eitan made himself comfortable on the blue tweed couch. On a Saturday night eighteen years later, November 4, 1995, Eitan would hold up a blood-stained sheet of paper with the words to the "Song of Peace" on it, taken from the breast pocket of Prime Minister Yitzhak Rabin's shirt after he had been shot three times in the back by an assassin, and tell the world that Rabin was dead.

Sitting there that night, though, blood and death seemed far away. We watched mesmerized as the Egypt Air Boeing 707, with Arabic writing on its body and the Egyptian flag on its tail, appeared over Tel Aviv's skies accompanied by four Israeli-made Kfir jets. Then it slowly banked to the right and came in to land from the east—a short 90-minute journey from Cairo that had brought the Egyptian leader an incredibly long way.

It had taken four wars in less than thirty years for Sadat to make the decision that war was no longer a viable strategic option for his country. His armed forces, even with the element of surprise and a coalition of other Arab states, had not been able to defeat Israel.

At home, Egypt was faced with a population explosion, mounting poverty, collapsing health services and sliding literacy rates, burgeoning Islamic fundamentalism and a bankrupt socialist system. He had cut his ties with the Soviets and needed to build a relationship with the West, primarily the United States. The only way to do so was by pursuing peace.

This visit, born out of necessity and not goodwill, was still a masterstroke of diplomacy. By announcing that he would come to the Knesset to offer his hand in peace in return for the territories conquered in 1967, Sadat placed the Israeli government on the defensive. If Israel refused, it would exacerbate Jerusalem's already tense relations with the United States, deepen the political divide in the country and force Israel to spend heavily on preparations for a possible war. As Sadat had demonstrated in 1973, he did not need to conquer Israel to make a point, but only cross the Canal.

This dramatic gesture not only placed Egypt in a win-win situation, but also proved again that Sadat was capable of surprise, and that despite his reputation as a lackluster leader, he was one of the great statesmen of the century. In the end he would manage to win back every inch of conquered Egyptian territory without firing a shot, and to create a bond with the United States that revolutionized Egypt.

It was the night before Sadat landed, at a party at the Diplomat Hotel with about twenty or so Egyptian journalists, that I came to understand that peace with Israel was considered by them to be not a prize but a punishment. They had never anticipated having to come to terms with Israel's existence. Now Egypt had no alternative. They resented the re-action in the Arab world, where Sadat was being called a traitor and worse. And they were still under the spell of their own rhetoric that was viciously anti-Israeli and, in many cases, anti-Semitic.

The party was held in the luxurious penthouse suite of Haim Schiff, the hotel's owner. The Egyptians were guests at the hotel and Schiff had been nice enough to invite about twenty Israeli journalists for a social event. He laid on the booze, which the Egyptians pounced on, covering the Black Label in their glasses skillfully with a napkin, as well as good food and music. The atmosphere, however, could not have been more somber. When the wife of one well-known Israeli broadcaster started singing *"Heveinu Shalom Aleichem"* ("We Bring Peace Unto You"), she was greeted by stony silence from everyone except for Mr. Schiff, who gave up after a second or two.

Unperturbed, the broadcaster's wife then tried *"Hava Nagila"* ("Let Us Be Merry"), presumably on the assumption that the lack of participa-tion was a result of the Egyptians not knowing the first song, whereas everyone knew *"Hava Nagila."* This caused a mass exodus to the bal-cony with its night view of the Judean desert. It was cold on the balcony and from my conversations with Egyptian colleagues it seemed clear that the best we could hope for was a cold peace. As a cameraman with Egyptian State Television explained, this was better than no peace at all. Just because we had decided to stop fighting, he said, did not mean that we had to love each other or even stop hating each other, a mind-set I had not considered.

The next night, Saturday, at 8 o'clock to the second, the shining white aircraft pulled up at Ben-Gurion Airport, its front door aligned with a red carpet along which the Israeli prime minister, members of the cabi-net, main opposition leaders, religious heads, judges, diplomats and oth-ers had been patiently waiting. Begin looked stiff, unsmiling and anxious, as if the burden of history rested entirely on his shoulders, his head shining under the bright lights, the thick lenses of his glasses mag-nifying his eyes in a grotesque manner. Stairs were quickly driven up to the aircraft's front and rear doors and the chief of protocol at the Foreign

Ministry bounded up the front stairs knowing the world's television cameras were hot on his back.

The door opened and for a few moments nothing happened. Then, with a great sense of drama, wearing a silver suit, a gray tie and immaculate white shirt, his black hair sleek, a prayer mark clearly visible on his forehead, Sadat appeared, his hand slowly waving in greeting. As he descended the steps the Israeli Defense Forces Orchestra, under the baton of Lieutenant-Colonel Yitzhak Graziani, began to play the type of martial music we used to march to in basic training. Both Eitan and myself were quietly sobbing. Cold peace was better than no peace, and watching Sadat put his foot on Israeli soil for the first time was, for me, an experience no less grand than Neil Armstrong's first step on the moon.

Sadat walked stiffly down the receiving line, stopping to shake hands and exchange a few words with each of the dignitaries until he reached Ariel Sharon, now the agriculture minister. More than anyone else, Sharon was responsible for having routed the Egyptian army in 1973 and was now seen as the government minister most associated with Israel's settlement drive. There was an awkward moment, then Sadat clasped Sharon's hand, smiled and said something we could not hear but that sparked applause from those close by.

There was more applause when he greeted Golda Meir and Moshe Dayan, each with a brief, warm exchange. Sadat came across as a giant of a man, dignified, erect, proud and determined. He seemed to grow even taller as, together with President Ephraim Katzir, he reviewed a guard of honor of Israeli men and women representing all branches of the armed forces, looking almost too neat and polished to be Israeli. After that, as all stood to rigid attention, soldiers presenting their arms and officers saluting, the band played first *"Biladi Biladi,"* "My Land," the Egyptian anthem, and then *"Hatikva,"* "The Hope," the anthem of Israel. Though we were alone in the apartment, Eitan and I stood as well. It would have been indecent not to have done so.

And then, quick as a flash, it was over as Sadat entered a limousine with Katzir and sped up to Jerusalem. Eitan and I went back to the press center at the Jerusalem Theatre and from there I walked over to the King David Hotel where Sadat was staying. I was stopped two blocks away by a policeman who was not at all impressed with my press card. Luckily, I saw Ephraim Poran, then Begin's military secretary and a former army spokesman, whom I knew well and who managed to get me through about five rings of security into the hotel's lobby.

There I was herded into a roped-off pen for authorized pool reporters, where we waited for hours for absolutely no purpose. Sadat and his entourage were on the sixth floor and the meeting rooms, while on the ground floor, were barricaded from the press and others. I was very frustrated the next morning when I saw that I had little input in the historic front-page lead piece. My total contribution to the report of Sadat's visit so far was an account of Friday night's interaction with the Egyptian journalists who had arrived early, including my encounter with the cameraman who spoke to me about cold peace.

I arrived at the *Post* office early that morning and waited in front of Ari Rath's door like a puppy dog, eager to be handed a scrap of that day's coverage. As defense reporter including me in the Sadat roster was not a logical choice, but I was determined to be part of this story. I was awed by its importance and knew that it was one of those rare events that actually was history in the making, no matter what the end result. Ari, a newsman to his core who could not help acting like a reporter even when editor, understood and assigned me to cover the Begin-Sadat press conference at the Jerusalem Theatre at three that afternoon.

There was a feeling of high expectation in the main concert hall of the Jerusalem Theatre. Only a hundred and fifty journalists had been allowed into the Knesset to witness the speeches there. Now there must have been three hundred or so inside the hall, with hundreds more arguing with Government Press Office staff outside the doors. They were willing to sit in the aisles if need be. American-born Zeev Chafets, the newly appointed head of the GPO, who had never organized anything larger than a tea party, was behaving like a seasoned professional. Polite but firm, cajoling and pleading, he directed the angry mob locked outside to the television screens in the adjacent auditorium where the event would be broadcast. At least, I thought, we had someone with perfect English dealing with the press and not some Israeli *bok* who could hardly speak the language.

At three the lights went on and Sadat and Begin appeared. Both looked as if they had just walked out of the shower, immaculately dressed, hair neatly combed. They sat down and one could tell immediately by their body language that these two men were not comfortable together. From what I had gleaned, the two meetings between the leaders had consisted of long silences punctuated by frosty, very formal exchanges. So it was here at the Jerusalem Theatre. There could have been a wall of ice between the two, though both had started to perspire under the bright stage lighting.

That morning Sadat had given a hard-nosed speech in the Knesset, saying that he had not come to Jerusalem to make a separate peace with Israel but with the goal of ending the occupation of all Arab lands. He called for the creation of a Palestinian state and spoke not of the spirit of peace but simply of ending belligerency, expressing the hope that the "past wars were the last of wars and the end of sorrow." It was said that Begin was deeply disappointed, almost offended, feeling that the speech did not conform to the understandings reached in the series of secret meetings between Dayan and Sadat's deputy field marshal, Mahmud Hassan Tahamy, in Morocco that had taken place in preparation for the visit.

Begin's response in the Knesset was dull and unfocused. Had Begin and his ministers directed the proper staff work rather than running the prime minister's office as if it were a secretive underground organization petrified of leaks, they would not have been surprised. Shlomo Gazit, the head of Military Intelligence, had predicted exactly what Sadat's speech would contain in an assessment he presented to Defense Minister Ezer Weizman a few days before the visit.

Gazit had warned with amazing accuracy that Sadat, mindful of the reaction to his visit in the Arab world, which was vociferous and violent, would announce that he had not come on a bilateral mission and that a Palestinian state was a minimal demand. Begin had kept the defense minister and the general staff completely out of the loop on the Dayan-Tahamy talks. While paying lip service to the intelligence assessments, he thought he knew better. What he did not take into account was that what Sadat told Tahamy to tell Dayan to tell Begin in secret talks was one thing, and standing before the Knesset and the world was another.

Now at the Jerusalem Theatre the air was heavy with tension. Short statements were made and the floor was opened to questions. It was all rather predictable and banal until the issue of territory was raised. Begin put on his schoolteacher pose, his finger darting into the air as he made his points, his glasses making his eyes look huge, perspiration forming on his brow.

He spoke about strategic needs and biblical rights, evoking Israel's narrow waistline and the threat from a still hostile Arab world, ending his monologue with the dictate that for the Jews, land is holy. This led Sadat to turn to him and say laconically, in his deep baritone, that for Egypt, land was holy too. I thought the peace process was dead then and there.

That may well have been the case if it were not for Ezer Weizman, former head of the Israeli air force and architect of the 1967 air war that had reduced the combined Arab armies to rubble before the war even started. Weizman was not at the airport to greet Sadat because he was in a hospital bed at Tel Hashomer, having been involved in a car crash two days before while driving up to Jerusalem in a rage about Chief of Staff Mordechai Gur. Gur had given an interview to *Yediot Aharonot,* the country's largest newspaper, claiming that the Sadat visit was a deception and that the Egyptian leader was actually planning to go to war in 1978.

Gur left on a family vacation abroad without telling the defense minister what he had done. Ordinarily the chief of staff needs the minister's permission to give an interview, and he had not even informed him about it after the fact. Weizman, always tempestuous, was flaming mad. He ordered Gur back to Israel. Gur arrived midweek, a few days before the Sadat visit, and went straight to the defense ministry. There, as one top aide to Weizman later put it, Ezer wiped the floor with him. He demanded that Gur, who was due to end his term in June the next year, should leave in December. Gur, also in a rage, said he'd resign on the spot. Weizman said fine, and was on his way to get Begin's approval when his car turned over several times while trying to avoid someone crossing the highway. The accident left Weizman badly injured.

So it was from his hospital bed, drugged with painkillers and attached to tubes, that Weizman watched Sadat arrive and, to his great annoyance, shake hands warmly with Gur, who was fitted out in full military regalia and looking as proud as a peacock. Weizman later admitted that he would gladly have strangled Gur had he been able to do so.

On the second day of the Sadat visit Weizman could no longer contain himself. Despite medical advice and with three doctors in attendance, he insisted on being driven up to Jerusalem on a heavy dose of painkillers. He endeared himself to the Egyptian president forever when, upon meeting Sadat for the first time in Begin's office in the Knesset, he jumped out of his wheelchair, raised a crutch as if it were a rifle and crossed his right hand over it in military salute.

Sadat cracked up and said, "I like that Ezra"—which was how he referred to Weizman from that day on. Weizman's humor was to save the night on Sunday at the formal dinner Begin hosted for Sadat and his retinue at the King David. His witticisms, some of them horribly out of place, were the only rays of light in what was described to me by one participant as an evening where the atmosphere was positively funereal. It was as if Begin in particular thought he had made a huge mistake. The Sadat speech in the Knesset and the unpleasant news conference had left their mark.

Begin had good reasons for having picked up the glove thrown down by Sadat when he offered to visit the Knesset. At the time the Carter administration and the Russians were planning to hold an international Middle East peace conference in Geneva that would have brought the PLO in as a full negotiating partner with, for the first time, the Russians. Both prospects were anathema for Begin. The conference would also put on the agenda the return of all territory taken in 1967, unlike the early understandings Begin thought he had reached with Sadat, which related only to the future of the Sinai.

As for Sadat, he seemed to be extremely satisfied with himself as he calmly puffed at his pipe. Yes, relations between he and Begin may be frosty, and yes, they may be burning his effigy in the streets of Beirut and

Damascus, but his act had brought only benefit to Egypt, even if their effort were to collapse. Sadat's armed forces had not recovered from the Yom Kippur War, leaving him without a war option, and he had burned his bridges with the Soviets when he expelled their advisors in 1973, leaving him without a viable strategic ally. Sadat recognized that he needed to forge a relationship with the West if Egypt were to turn itself around and not become a basket case nation. He was wary of the Geneva meeting because he knew Egypt's needs could not wait the eternity it might take for Israel to give the Palestinians a state and return the Golan Heights to the Syrians. If the bilateral track worked, he would have brought Egypt into a new era; if it failed, he would be the darling of the West for having tried and Israeli stubbornness would be blamed for the failure.

That morning he had prayed at the Al Aksa Mosque on the Haram al-Sharif, Islam's third holiest site, and visited the Church of the Holy Sepulcher. He had been greeted by tens of thousands of enthusiastic Israelis wherever he had driven, visited the Yad Va'Shem memorial to the Six Million, addressed the Knesset, met with old adversaries like Golda Meir and Moshe Dayan and had his small victory over Begin at the press conference when he told him that Egyptian land was holy as well. All in all Sadat, it seemed, could not have been happier with the way things were going.

I was not on the first flight to Cairo on December 13, three weeks after the Sadat visit, when Cabinet Secretary Eliyahu Ben Elissar and a small delegation of Israeli negotiators and newsmen left for the Mena House talks, where the sides sat down to frame a formal agreement. The *Post* sent Rath, the diplomatic correspondent David Landau and the Arab affairs editor Anan Safadi. Anan, an Israeli Arab whose father had once been the *mukhtar* of Beit Shean, was shocked by the hostility with which the Egyptians greeted him. One television interviewer accused him of being a Zionist quisling.

Of course I was devastated about being left behind, very anxious to have been with the first delegation of Israelis to return to Egypt since the Exodus, but I found salvation a week later when, on the 22nd, I was assigned with Yehuda Litani, the Arab affairs correspondent, to cover an overland bus trip to Egypt by a delegation of 164 West Bankers. The day started badly. I met Yehuda outside his apartment about a block away from mine at dawn and together we took a cab to Zion Square, from where we would take another cab to El Arish, where we were to meet the West Bank delegation.

Unfortunately, at Zion Square I got out of the backseat of the cab first and as Yehuda reached for the door frame, I slammed the door shut on his hand and the tip of his index finger fell to the ground. I thought I was going to faint.

I quickly pushed some money onto the driver and told him to rush Yehuda to Hadassah hospital. I phoned Yehuda's wife from a call box telling her what had happened and then, to the everlasting ire of Yehuda, hopped into the cab that was waiting to take me to El Arish, on my way to meet the West Bankers and to become the first Israeli journalist to make the trip to Cairo overland.

The trip was not to be, however. The West Bankers, led by Hussein Shiyoukhy of Ramallah and Borhan Ja'abari of Hebron, with their $160,000 mother-of-pearl table inlaid with the Dome of the Rock in tow as a present to Sadat, were turned back three times from the Hirbe border crossing for reasons unknown. My passport was taken away for hours, supposedly for close examination, and came back with an Egyptian visa that had been granted, then annulled, then regranted on appeal and finally canceled with two thick X's. I was left in the middle of nowhere with no story. Managing to hitch a ride to El Arish and another to Jerusalem, I wrote up a feeble article and phoned Litani to tell him how lucky he was not to have come along. He was not amused.

I finally made it to Egypt on Christmas day of 1977. On December 20, Weizman had made a secret trip to see Sadat at an air force base 25 kilometers north of Alexandria. There Sadat promised full normalization with Israel in return for all of the territory and a solution to the Palestinian conundrum. He was totally unaccommodating on Israeli security issues and demanded mutual demilitarization on both sides of the border. Despite their unpromising meeting it was decided that Sadat and Begin would hold a summit at Ismailia five days later, on the 25th.

We landed at Egypt's Abu Sweir airport about an hour before Begin's El Al Boeing 707 was due. Over a hundred journalists were there, including a large Egyptian contingent, some of whom I recognized from the November trip to Jerusalem. Greetings between us were much more collegial now. Standing to the side of the pack was Mohammed Abdul Moneim, the military correspondent of the venerable *Al Ahram* daily and later President Hosni Mubarak's spokesman and trusted aide. Mohammed and I were destined to have some great times together, including smuggling him through Israeli lines at El Arish fairly late in the disengagement process to be the only Egyptian journalist to see and photograph the Israeli Sinai town of Yamit before it was destroyed. The town had been built inside Sinai a few kilometers south of Gaza and Israel's pre-1967 border with Egypt and was intended as a wedge between a then hostile Egypt and Palestinian Gaza. When Israel returned the Sinai to Egypt after peace between them, the Begin government decided to raze the town rather than risk that it might become a large Egyptian population center close to the Israeli border and Gaza.

Also there was David Rubinger, the wonderful press photographer who, among other memorable pictures, had shot the indelible snap of the three Israeli paratroopers at the Wailing Wall moments after it had been captured in 1967. Rubinger was perched atop the aluminum four-step folding ladder he always carried with him. Rubinger's real secret, however, the one that gained him access to places from which others were barred, was his practice of always making copies of pictures for the security guards he photographed with their famous wards.

The atmosphere at the airfield was heavy, with no sense of celebration. There were no flags, Egyptian or otherwise, in evidence, nor any banners of welcome. Sadat's portrait was everywhere. Begin's plane landed at 11:02 and pulled up at a very short red carpet. Two highly polished Egyptian lancers placed themselves at the foot of the stairs that were brought up to the front door of the plane; they stood at rigid attention, their eyes unblinking. Sadat's deputy, Mubarak, and the war minister, Abdul Ghani Gamassy, were on hand to greet the Israeli delegation, which included foreign minister Dayan and defense minister Weizman, who was now walking with a cane. When Begin reached the bottom of the steps, a ten-year-old girl came forward and shyly handed him a small bouquet of flowers. That was the extent of the ceremony.

While the delegation and a few senior editors went off to Sadat's holiday residence atop a hill overlooking the city and the Suez Canal, the rest of us were herded onto buses and driven to the Port Authority building where we were to wait for a joint press conference not scheduled for any specific time. The option of leaving the compound was not encouraged by our very nervous Egyptian hosts from the press office, and anyway there was not much point in walking around the city's muddy streets with nothing to offer other than more portraits of Sadat and one small sign in Hebrew at the entrance to the Port Authority: "May Peace be Upon the Land."

Finally in the late afternoon the press conference took place and I even got to ask a question. What, I do not remember. I only recall that Ya'acov Erez, the defense reporter for *Ma'ariv, Yediot*'s rival, told me later that it was "stupid." Whatever, both leaders seemed to give me an elaborate and lengthy reply, while the whole affair was being broadcast live in Israel and Egypt. In the mayhem following the conference, with reporters rushing off in a hundred directions either to file their stories or to try and interview some of the principals, I nonchalantly strolled onto one of the minibuses returning delegates and editors to the holiday palace.

Within a few minutes I found myself in a large hall-like waiting room where Sadat and Begin were standing, handkerchiefs to their brows, greeting guests as tea and sweet cakes were being passed around. I managed to shake Sadat's hand and Begin gave me a limp paw, a flash of recognition in his eyes. I had only met him once or twice in the Knesset. I was struck by how he seemed to have become smaller, more fragile than I remembered. He had had two heart attacks and obviously they, together with his tremendous responsibilities, had taken their toll. I then helped myself to a small glass of sweet tea and bumped into Ari Rath, who looked more than surprised to see me. I gave him a wink and he gave me a scowl.

My head was buzzing with excitement when in the early evening about a dozen of us who had received permission from the Egyptians to stay over for a few days started out for Cairo. We were all defense reporters and the extension had been arranged by Weizman, who wanted to build up as many levels of contact with the Egyptians as possible. Having Israeli journalists in Cairo was one way of keeping the process alive.

We bounced along for what seemed to be hours and hours, avoiding donkey carts, bicycles and careening trucks. Every moment brought a new experience, another glimpse of Egypt: trains with dozens of people hanging out of the windows and clinging to the roofs of the carriages, oxen patiently swishing around water wells in fields to the side of the highway, the sheer masses of humanity everywhere.

We drove past the airport and the soccer stadium on the outskirts of Cairo and began to traverse the city with its crazy drivers. We passed roadside stalls with bright lights selling fresh juices and *foul* from huge copper pots. People were everywhere, thousands of them despite the late hour, rushing about, clambering onto buses belching out black smoke, passengers clinging to every available handhold, most wearing *galabiyas* and seemingly happy with their lot. Also hundreds, if not thousands, of khaki-clad soldiers were deployed along the roads, on bridges and in front of buildings, all looking disheveled and unsmiling. I wondered what Sadat would do with them all if there was peace and, apparently, so did he.

Seeing the Nile and later, as we pulled into the Mena House Hotel, the Pyramids and the Sphinx was like nothing I had ever experienced. I remember being overcome with awe, disbelief, gratitude and a very strong desire to share the moment with others. Mena House itself, with its wooden lattice screens, copper tables and oriental atmosphere, made one feel as if one were in a dream. Later that night a few of us took a taxi downtown to the Nile Hilton, played a few rounds at the casino, walked over to the central railway station to buy the early morning Arabic newspapers to see how the Begin visit had been reported in the Egyptian press and made our way back to Mena House, astounded at how naturally we had walked around the city, unafraid and at ease.

When asked by merchants, who never seemed to close their stores, where we were from, we answered Israel and they immediately offered us a "peace price" on goods ranging from perfume essence to leather jackets. That we were yesterday's enemy seemed irrelevant. Even the taxi drivers seemed to be welcoming, though in one case the driver had been a POW in the Six Day War, thankfully not in Rafiah, while another had lost a brother at Mitla Pass, where he served in an anti-aircraft unit. Enough war, we all said.

The most striking thing about being in Egypt in those early days was just how genuinely warm the people were. Peace with the Egyptians seemed a real possibility. These were people with humor, and a gentleness that expressed itself in the way they treated children, the constant willingness to help, the lack of crime and their inefficiencies softened by the charm with which they carried off their inefficiency. The local post office at Mena House, for example, was selling first edition commemorative stamps of Sadat's visit to Jerusalem, a hot item with the visiting Israelis. It took about an hour to get served, but the clerk was more than happy to adjust his rubber stamp to any date we requested. Obviously we all wanted the date of Sadat's visit, November 19th. "No problem, no problem," he said as the queue got longer and longer.

My next visit to Cairo was in January for the start of the military talks. We checked into the Sheperd Hotel on the Nile, near the center of town. Weizman and his delegation were out at the Tahara Palace, where the talks were taking place, and we had arranged for a bus to take us back and forth.

The Sheperd used to belong to the same chain that owned the King David in pre-state Palestine, but by now it was fairly run down and neglected. The room I shared with Erez was definitely depressing, the plumbing from another century. Not wanting to spend one unnecessary moment in the room, we headed for the starlight bar on the roof. As we walked through the door the pianist immediately stopped whatever tune he was playing and started to play the theme song from *Exodus*. How he knew who we were at first glance I never found out, but he did tell me later that he was a Copt and had lived in an area that once had a lot of Jewish people. The talks between the sides were to go on for months through March 26, 1979, when the peace treaty was finally signed in a five-minute ceremony on the White House lawn. The sides spent over two hundred days negotiating a few hundred meters of coastline at Taba on the Red Sea just south of Eilat. There was a dispute over which border markers, the British or the Turkish, were authentic. After all, every inch of land was holy.

At one point in January, when the political talks taking place in Jerusalem broke down, the few military reporters and a skeleton defense ministry delegation were asked to stay on in Cairo for however long it took to get things back on track. It was an ugly period with vitriolic Egyptian press. Mustafa Amin, the senior columnist for *Akbar el-Yom,* a state-controlled paper like most of the others, was calling Begin a Shylock again, and the caricatures of Jews with hooked noses and blood dripping from their jaws were horrendous. The Egyptian security personnel recommended we stay in the hotel and a guard was posted on every floor "for our protection."

After two days of confinement I slipped through the front door, hailed a taxi and headed for the Muhammed Ali Mosque in the heart of the old city. There I went to the Egyptian War Museum, paid five piasters for a ticket and walked down a path lined with captured Israeli tanks and cannons and parts of destroyed Israeli aircraft. I wandered through the halls looking at models of Israeli encampments on the other side of the Canal, the signs on the miniature buildings all in perfect Hebrew. There was a *Sefer Torah* in a glass cabinet and a huge picture of an Israeli POW saluting an Egyptian officer. I then attached myself to a group of schoolchildren being taken through the display and watched the pride on their faces as they were told how 80,000 brave troops in a thousand rubber boats, aided by two thousand cannons and two hundred aircraft, heroically crossed the Canal and defeated the Zionist enemy.

The stories were endless; every hour of every day the copy virtually wrote itself. On my first Friday night there five of us—myself, Eitan Haber, Ya'acov Erez, Zeev Schiff, the military correspondent of *Ha'aretz,* and Ronny Daniel, the *Kol Yisrael* reporter—set off for the one still operating synagogue in Cairo. We were received with suspicion and a quiet fear by the few worshipers, their eyes darting to the security men at the entrance and in the gallery above. There were forty-two Jewish families left in Cairo; there had not been a wedding or a *Brit Mila* in a decade. No one invited us home for Friday night dinner.

By contrast, in Alexandria the following Friday we were warmly welcomed by the wonderful Clement Setton, chairman of the 150-member-strong community, who played golf daily at age 76, spoke four languages fluently and was proud to announce that the previous month the community had celebrated its first wedding in seven years when Mr. Palasiano, 43, finally decided to take a wife.

When we entered the synagogue with Mr. Setton in the lead, Leon Samuel, the 66-year-old voluntary cantor, broke out in an operatic *"Baruch Haba Be'Shem Adonai"* ("Blessed Are Thee in the Name of God") that sent shivers down my spine and brought tears to my eyes. When I asked Mr. Setton to explain the difference in our welcome between Cairo and Alexandria, he explained that Alexandria was not really Egypt, but a Mediterranean implant on Egyptian territory.

Looking back now, peace between Israel and Egypt has, as the cameraman predicted on the balcony of the Schiff penthouse at the Diplomat Hotel all those years ago, been cold, even hostile at times. But it has held up. Sadat was assassinated in 1981 and Mubarak took over. He has not been a great statesman but a competent leader, steering a course between the West and the Arab world, faced with essentially the same problems as Sadat, though all to a lesser degree: overpopulation, fundamentalism, poverty, illiteracy.

Begin made peace to protect Israel's hold on the West Bank, Gaza and the Golan. Sadat got the Sinai back and the West on his side. Sacrificed on the altar of the bilateral peace was the Palestinian issue, which was "fig leafed" with a preposterous plan for some form of autonomy, but that set the stage for a massive settlement effort by the Begin government with Ariel Sharon at its helm. Sharon had erected dummy settlements in the Sinai at a critical stage of the talks in order to undermine them. I remember Weizman literally hitting the roof of the Dakota transport plane en route to Cairo when he saw them from the air.

On the West Bank and Gaza, however, Sharon was not erecting dummy settlements. With a nod and a wink from Begin and the blessings of a right-wing government and its National Religious Party partners, the bulldozers started to roll. Sadat had retrieved his "Holy Land"; now it was Begin's turn to settle his.

PART FOUR
BAD TO WORSE

10

MARCH TO FOLLY

In January 1982 Ariel Sharon, as Israel's defense minister, made an overland trip from Tel Aviv to Cairo and back. Here, on the southern bank of the Suez Canal he met some Egyptian officers. One claimed his brother had been killed fighting forces commanded by Sharon in the 1973 war. I was listening attentively at right, quite taken in by Sharon's charm. Five months later Israel was at war in Lebanon.

As for myself, I was spending more time covering war on the Lebanese border and in southern Lebanon than writing about peace with Egypt. As predicted by military intelligence, the Sadat visit gave impetus to the Palestinian effort to derail any process of reconciliation between Israel and its principal enemy, Egypt, and terror across the Lebanese border became endemic. The Lebanese army was impotent and unable to control the Palestinians, who had created an area called "Fatahland" along Lebanon's pre-1967 border with Syria, from where they staged their operations.

Because he did not want to jeopardize the talks with the Egyptians, Weizman had so far reined in the army and offered muted retaliations, but on March 11, 1978, while he was in the United States negotiating with the Egyptians, the terrorists crossed the line.

It was late on a spring Saturday afternoon and we had spent a wonderful day on the Herzliya beach with friends. While parked at the traffic light at the Glilot Junction patiently waiting to take a left turn toward Jerusalem, the radio news came on. Terrorists had landed south of Haifa in a rubber dinghy, and had killed a young American, Gail Rubin, who had been photographing birds near the spot where they disembarked. It was not clear where the terrorists were now or where they were heading.

Instead of taking the turnoff to Jerusalem, I sped to my sister Rochie's flat in Ramat Hasharon a few kilometers away. My first thought was to get the family off the road and into a safe place as quickly as possible; the second was to get to a phone. I also knew that this meant I would be heading to the Lebanese border instead of home, because Israeli retaliation would follow as sure as night follows day.

It was impossible to get through to the army spokesman's office, all three lines being busy. The radio now reported that the terrorists had hijacked a bus and were heading toward Tel Aviv along the coastal highway.

I got back into my car and returned to the Glilot junction, through which the bus would have to come if it was on its way to Tel Aviv. As I neared the junction I heard the sound of gunfire and sirens as ambulances and security vehicles converged from every direction. I pulled up and parked on the side of the road near the entrance to Mossad's headquarters and ran like a madman the six hundred or so yards to where the fighting was taking place. The bus stood on the far lane of the highway, its tires punctured. Its windows had been blown out and a fire was flickering inside. Soldiers were running west through the fields and toward the sea in pursuit of the terrorists, who had apparently fled in that direction.

Around the bus was a scene of sheer horror. Bodies were everywhere, women, children, men, old and young, all of whom had been on their way home from a family picnic organized by the bus company they worked for, Egged. Others lay dead or bleeding inside the bus, with that horrible look of shock that comes when one looks death in the eye. Thirty-seven Israelis were killed that day.

I drove into Tel Aviv and went to the army spokesman's office, where the duty officer filled me in on the details, and then to Ichilov Hospital nearby, where some of the injured had been taken. I needed an eyewitness account. I filed from the Tel Aviv office by midnight, punching my story out on an old Royal typewriter and then having it transferred to a tape for telex transmittal to Jerusalem. I was starving. The telex operator, a colleague who was also working late, and I went to a nearby all-night grill for something to eat before I headed up to Kiryat Shmona in the north, from where any military operation against the Palestinians would be launched. I did not get to eat. The minute I walked into the restaurant and smelled the burning meat on the grill, the stench of burning flesh came to me. I ran to the restroom, vomited and became a vegetarian for the next nine years.

I met my colleague Ya'acov—Yankele—Erez from *Ma'ariv* in Kiryat Shmona and together we drove up to Metullah, Israel's northernmost town, where we checked in with Yoram Ha'Mizrachi, Israel's liaison with the Christians in southern Lebanon. Yoram, a former newsman, knew everything. The army was going to punch roughly 10 kilometers into Lebanon up to the Litani River and then systematically clear out the terrorist infrastructure there—training camps, munition dumps, everything.

We slept over at Pension Belsky in Metullah, which, as always, had been turned into an advance command post by the army and the usual cadre of military reporters while the army awaited their orders to proceed. Finally, after three days camped in the mud, the attack began at 10 P.M. on the night of March 16.

Erez went off on his own, using his extensive contacts in the Northern Command to get the best vantage point possible, which he was not inclined to share with me. I drove to an assembly point down by the border where I met Yoram and we both squeezed into a personnel carrier of the 13th Golani Battalion.

Yoram was well over six feet tall and weighed, at a conservative estimate, two hundred pounds. He was like a bear, covered in hair everywhere except his head, which was bald and shiny like that of a monk. He put on a helmet, barked instructions to the driver and pushed up into the turret next to me, smoking and wheezing at the same time, as we drove into battle at the head of a force of khaki-armored vehicles, bumping along barely discernable tracks to some terrorist camp in the region of El Kiyam, a PLO stronghold that threatened the Lebanese Christian villages of Klea and Marj Ayoun.

It took us seven hours to traverse 3 kilometers. At 7:15 A.M., just as I was listening to a newscaster on the radio reporting how well the invasion was going, we hit the first mine and then the second. Yoram bashed his head on the steel rim of the turret and started to bleed. The driver was either unconscious or dead. The four soldiers with us started to shout and scream as the vehicle rocked and reverberated, like an injured bull moments before death in the ring. We clambered through the back door and onto the path. Two of the soldiers carried the driver, shouting for a medic over the radio, while I half-carried, half-pushed Yoram out of the APC, which could have exploded any second. Once out it became apparent that Yoram had been blinded by the blow. He could not see a thing, not even a shadow. I was terrified.

The closest vehicle was about one hundred meters behind us. Usually mines out in the open like this are laid as part of a wider ambush; we knew we could not be outside the protection of an armored vehicle for long. With strength I did not know I possessed I hefted Yoram onto my shoulders and trotted toward the nearest vehicle, fully suspecting that at any moment I would step on an anti-personnel mine. They too were usually planted around larger anti-tank mines to target the crews evacuating the vehicles.

We made it. We removed Yoram's helmet and gave him some water.

Slowly his vision returned, though he had no memory at all of what had happened. Then we hit another mine. The APC lost a track, which put it out of action. I left Yoram and the nice bunch of good-humored youngsters in the stricken vehicle and hitched a ride in another passing APC.

We arrived at El Kiyam at around noon and the troops began to systematically go through the streets looking for terrorists. Not a building in this once picturesque village in the foothills was unscarred, not the church nor the mosque. Damage and devastation were everywhere, first from PLO shells when they captured the town from the predominantly Christian Israeli-backed South Lebanese Army and then from SLA artillery as they tried to get it back.

By four in the afternoon I knew I had better start heading back to Metullah to file my story. I also needed to get some background for color, which would take time. Every vehicle in sight, however, seemed to be traveling in the other direction, away from Israel and toward the Litani River. I was miles inside "Fatahland" with no prospects of making it back before nightfall when an ambulance came hurtling toward me with three soldiers sitting in the front cabin. I waved them down and begged for a lift. "Your choice, hop in the back," said the driver. I watched mesmerized as a corpse covered with a rough blanket, boots poking out from under it, swayed in rhythm as we headed to the border.

I rushed up to the central command post where Doron Rubin, the silver-haired commander of the Golani Battalion, was conducting battle. I understood the picture fairly quickly and rushed off to Belsky's to quickly write my story and get in line for one of the few available phones. I was finished by nine, but the line at the phones was interminable. A German correspondent was shouting into one phone, red in the face and getting redder by the moment, at an operator somewhere in Tel Aviv who would not let him make a collect call to Frankfurt. Screaming, he slammed the phone back in its cradle and walked away. I rushed to pick it up and was dialing when the German returned and demanded the phone back. I told him to get fucked. He told me Hitler had not done a good enough job. A young soldier standing next to me hit him in the face with his elbow. The German screamed with pain and I continued dialing Jerusalem.

The phone at the other end rang and rang and rang. No one answered. Ahuva, the operator, had gone for a pee and left her post unattended. Sheepishly I handed the phone over to some young stringer for *Ha'aretz* who proceeded to whisper his file into the mouthpiece. By 11:20 I finally managed to get through to the *Post*. Ahuva, after much screeching and shouting from her booth down the corridor to the newsroom, eventually managed to get someone on the desk to take my call.

It was Abe Rabinovich, a talented reporter who had been saddled with desk duty due to someone being ill and was not at all happy about it. "You have three graphs," he said. "Anything longer won't make it into print. It's late you know."

I had been up and running for thirty-six hours. It was almost midnight. I had been jarred by three mines, carried a two-hundred-pound-plus bear through a minefield and ridden home with a corpse. I had seen a German correspondent's face split in half and had to spend over an hour waiting in line for the phone a second time because Ahuva went off to the toilet and three paragraphs were what I got that night, squeezed in as if by favor on the bottom of the left-hand column of the front page. Anybody reading the story probably thought what an idiot Goodman was with a war going on and three graphs of basic copy being all he could manage.

Israel withdrew three months later, in June, leaving Saad Haddad's South Lebanese Army in place and confident that the terrorist problem had been capped if not solved. An international force that Israel did not want, UNIFIL (the United Nations Interim Force in Lebanon), was deployed to police southern Lebanon, bringing in a mixed bag of foreigners who could not tell an Arab from a Jew. It ultimately cost Israel a heavy price in its relations with some participating countries like Holland and Ireland, whose forces would often clash with nervous Israeli troops in the region. The only UNIFIL people who were happy with the job were the Fijians, their participation being a significant foreign income earner for their country and their brilliant rugby team having found some worthy opponents in Israel.

But my work was not all blood and guts, like the time in May 1979 when I was selected as pool reporter on the first passage of an Israeli naval vessel, or any Israeli ship for that matter, to sail through the Suez Canal. There was always something magical about Ophira, as Israel had renamed Sharm el Sheikh, but on this Sunday morning, May 28, it was bewitched. I had flown in the night before and after a few hours with my friend Howard Rosenstein, who owned Red Sea Divers in Sharm and was about to lose his home and business as a result of the peace treaty, I checked into the naval base, where I was given a bunk bed for the night. The naval port was situated in a beautiful protected cove where the sea was azure and still and reflected the barren and stark landscape of Saudi Arabia to the east, just where the Red Sea meets the Gulf of Suez and Africa.

I was awake at dawn and sipped a cup of oversweet tea as I watched the crews skillfully loading 24 Leyland trucks into the cavernous bellies of the three vessels that were to make the 71-hour, 400-kilometer trip. The *Achziv, Haifa* and *Ashdod* were all landing craft that had been built by the Israel Shipyards in 1966 and had been based in Sharm since 1974.

After a hearty breakfast and much hugging and kissing between the lucky 125 sailors selected to make the journey and those being left behind at base, all hands were called onto the parade ground to hear a special prayer that had been composed by the base chaplain in honor of the historic occasion. Then Commodore Yitzhak Davidi, the commander of the Red Sea Region, who was to captain the *Achziv* and lead the small flotilla, said a few words and handed over the parade to a petty officer who gave orders for final preparations. About noon, with a great blowing of whistles and horns, the three clumsy, gray, elephantine craft slowly churned their way out of port into the Red Sea, past the string of islands around Ras Muhammad, perhaps the best diving spot in the world, and west into the Gulf of Suez. It would take two days to reach Port Tawfik at the mouth of the Canal. There we would pay a $15,000 passage fee and join a convoy of forty-one ships heading for the Mediterranean. Israel, for the first time, was making the journey together with the family of nations.

It was dawn off Port Tawfik when Master Pilot Abdul Halmy, a rotund man, arrived on board via a little motorboat. He saluted us for at least a minute, looking splendid in his white uniform awash with golden braid and white peaked cap, his shoulders laden with rank. He climbed up the ladder to the deck and presented one of the three women sailors aboard with twelve pink roses freshly picked from his garden.

The 160-kilometer, 14-hour passage through the Suez Canal was like sailing through a desert. Images of war were still evident on the sand banks on either side. By midafternoon the slow journey, including a five-and-a-half hour wait in the Great Bitter Lake to allow the southbound convoy to the Gulf to pass, was becoming monotonous when a signal was received that electrified the atmosphere: President Sadat, we were told, would be waiting on the balcony of his home in Ismailia to greet the flotilla as it sailed past in less than three hours' time.

An order was given to the crew to change into the formal white uniforms they had been keeping in pristine condition for the arrival ceremony in Ashdod the next day, and to practice lining up on the deck to return Sadat's greeting with a salute from the ships' officers while the men stood at rigid attention.

At 6:15 in the evening Ismailia came into sight and to the left, on a balcony high above but clearly visible, was Egyptian president Anwar Sadat. Immaculate in a white naval uniform, his right hand fixed to his temple in a salute, he stood erect as a lamppost until the last of the three Israeli vessels had steamed past. On the decks of the three ships, 122 men and 3 women of the Israeli navy saluted back as a lone bosun whistle pierced the late afternoon silence, like a clarion call of thanks from these young soldiers who were seeing the first manifestations of peace in their lifetime.

But in the background, looming larger all the time, was the continuing instability over the Lebanese border. The PLO had established a solid presence in the south and along the coast. With Syrian, Iraqi and Libyan connivance and help the Palestinians were becoming expert at attacking targets in Israel with Katyusha rockets over the northern border, and from the sea along Israel's coast, hitting deep into its cities and settlements. They also used hang gliders and hot air balloons to deliver bombs. All of this was fueling growing public outrage.

Ezer Weizman, as defense minister, was focused on peacemaking with the Egyptians, fighting battles inside the government where he felt there was foot-dragging on the negotiations. His policies on Lebanon, however, were indecisive and wavering. He punched back at terrorist bases with the air force, navy and ground forces, and occasionally allowed an incursion into PLO territory to "clear out the vipers' nest," but they were blows into thin air. As fast as the air force could bomb terrorist camps they would sprout up again like mushrooms. The Katyushas were fired from simple metal stands that were hard to find and easily replaced.

At first Weizman's policies were retaliatory, then preemptive and finally punitive, using military force against civilian populations in southern Lebanon to get them to purge the terrorists from their midst. "Israel will stop shelling the PLO when the Palestinians stop shelling the Christians," he told the Knesset in August while trying to explain to opposition parties why in the previous four months Israeli shelling in southern Lebanon had killed a hundred people, injured 280 more and destroyed 270 buildings.

Weizman resigned in May 1980. He had threatened to do so seven times before, but this time he followed through. He was furious with Begin, his cabinet colleagues, everything. The defense budget had been cut against his objections, Begin was not consulting with him on policy issues, Sharon had gone mad with settlements—thirty-eight new ones were to be built in 1980—there was foot-dragging with the Egyptians and Lebanon had become a lose-lose situation. Being defense minister had become a burden.

Begin took over the job for the next sixteen months, a disastrous decision for a man with an ailing heart and already overburdened as prime minister. But he had little choice. Had Begin not taken the job himself, he would probably have had to appoint Sharon, something he did not want. Begin is famously reported to have remarked that were he to do so, the first thing Sharon would do is order tanks to encircle the Knesset and declare a putsch.

Begin came into the defense ministry on Thursdays for meetings with the general staff and top defense officials, but day-to-day defense policy fell to Rafael Eitan, who had replaced Motta Gur as chief of staff. Begin suggested changing his title to Field Marshal.

Eitan was a tough paratroop officer and a man of few words. His speech on becoming chief of staff lasted fourteen seconds. Universally referred to as Raful, he was a soldier's soldier who tried to bring some discipline and decorum into the army and was known to get out of his car at bus stops near military bases to admonish troops who were not properly dressed.

His views on Lebanon were very different from those of Weizman and Gur. He had been commander of the Northern Command and knew the situation in Lebanon intimately. He believed that Israel should forge an alliance with the Christian forces to the north under the leadership of the Gemayel family to face off their common enemies, the Syrians and the Palestinians. Israel's relationship with Gemayel's Phalange militia had gone back to 1976 when the navy picked up a messenger off the coast of Lebanon near the Christian-controlled port of Junieh and brought him to Tel Aviv, where he told Prime Minister Yitzhak Rabin that unless Israel was prepared to extend help to the Christians, within a very short period of time the community would be wiped out. The Syrians, who had originally come into Lebanon to save them, had now turned against them and key Christian cities like Zahle that controlled access to the Beka'a Valley were in danger of falling. Rabin was sympathetic but said that Israel could do no more than help the Christians help themselves. Israel would supply the weapons, but would not fight their wars for them, a policy Weizman had carefully adhered to, but one that Raful was now anxious to change. He also believed that Israeli forces should establish a deep and continuous presence inside Lebanon to ensure that the PLO's rockets and artillery remained outside the range of Israel's northern border. Relying on Sa'ad Haddad's militias in the south would never, in his view, be enough to control the problem.

In the meantime Israeli reprisals and preemptive raids against the Palestinians in the south continued relentlessly, which for me meant steady work. But I was frustrated because I always seemed to be reporting what others were telling me, whether they were intelligence sources, pilots coming back from sorties or soldiers returning from behind enemy lines. Several of us had tried hard to be allowed to go on behind-the-line missions but the army spokesman had consistently refused, claiming that we lacked the training and physical ability to keep up with the troops and that our presence would endanger them. We argued that there were serving officers and former paratroopers among us. In the end it was agreed that two of us, Amiram Nir of Israel Television and myself, would be allowed to go as a test case.

So in December 1980, after being kitted out with a uniform and Uzi, I was taken by an army representative to Raful's office at General Staff Headquarters in Tel Aviv. There I was to wait for the chief of staff himself, who was going to give me a lift in his plane to an airfield up north, where I would join the Golani force I would be going into Lebanon with that night.

I was ushered into a small waiting room at the entrance to Raful's office when his wife, Miriam, a stodgy woman you would not liked to have wrestled with, came in with a brown bag of sandwiches and thermos of coffee. Her ability for small talk equaled that of her husband, so we sat in silence alternately looking at each other and the walls.

At about three in the afternoon Raful emerged, greeted his wife with a short birdlike nod and took his thermos and brown paper bag. He greeted me with a slap on the back and together with a small retinue of staff officers and aides we headed for Sde Dov airfield, where four of us boarded a military twin-engine propeller aircraft. With Raful at the controls we flew up north, landing at Machanayim, where I was attached to a unit of young soldiers who immediately called me "grandpa." I was then the ripe age of 34.

Toward evening steaming pots were brought out of a command car and placed on trestle tables. A cook called for the men to come and have their "last supper," yet another in the long line of macabre jokes the men seemed to delight in telling. It was their way of dealing with fear, I suppose.

After dinner, with hot cups of tea cuddled in our hands as shields against the bitter cold, we sat down on the edge of the runway for a final briefing by a matter-of-fact intelligence officer using aerial photos to point out targets and potential problems. Then came a short sequence of orders and instructions from the force commander and the commander of the Northern Command and, finally, a few words from Raful, who told the men to be careful, that dead soldiers were of no use and that they had been privileged to have been chosen for the task of bringing security to the citizens of northern Israel. Pointing to the lights of the communities on the hills above and around us, he said: "They sleep well tonight knowing you are out here. They are depending on you."

The plan was to hit seven targets simultaneously in and around Mahmoudiya, a PLO stronghold with a strategic height advantage over territory held by the South Lebanese Army and a source of endless attacks on the Christians. We reached the border by around seven. It was pitch dark though a full moon was beginning to rise, its silver beams reflecting on the snowy slopes of the Hermon. Very quietly, without speaking, the men took off jackets and sweaters despite the bitter cold, put on 25-kilo packs and quickly organized into strike forces. I was placed in the charge of a sweet, chubby redhead kid from Beersheba who was to make sure "grandpa" kept up with the pack.

It took two-and-a-half hours to reach the Litani River, the slope down and then up the other side soggy after two weeks of solid rain. All I could hear in the cold silence of the night was the heavy breathing of the men lugging their loads of ammunition, explosives, communications gear and medical equipment. Not a word was said. Once up the slippery slope of the river we had another three hours of a half run through pine forests with the danger of booby traps and snipers always a possibility. It had taken almost six hours to traverse 18 kilometers inside enemy territory on foot. We had reached Mahmoudiya.

The plan had been to attack the targets simultaneously but one of the forces was detected early and all hell broke loose. The fighting continued for about two hours, with one of our men being killed and three others wounded. It was amazing to me how the unit's doctor and a medic attended to them calmly and efficiently as if they were in a pristine hospital environment, not in the middle of a battlefield with bullets, grenades and mortars exploding.

By 3 A.M. it was all over. We carried the dead and wounded a few more kilometers to an open field whose perimeters were pounded by Israeli artillery to protect the nine helicopters that landed to fly us back to base. At six, Raful arrived to congratulate the men on a job well done and to offer them the thanks of the Jewish people. I personally thought that I had just witnessed a folly. This was the twentieth such raid this year against the PLO in southern Lebanon and the terror had continued unabated. It was a high-risk operation exposing troops to multiple dangers deep inside enemy territory where the Palestinians knew the battlefield far better than we did. They also had a topographical advantage, Israeli forces always having to come up to the plateau from the Litani Valley. We had suffered one dead and we counted twelve dead terrorists. If anything more had gone wrong, the results could have been very different and, I asked myself, for what long-term advantage?

In January 1981 Begin called an early election for July. The polls did not look encouraging and with good reason. The economy was out of control, inflation so high that my daughter Maya used to wake me up at midnight to change her babysitting money into dollars because by morning her shekels would be near worthless. The security situation was precarious and relations with the United States were at an all-time low over the settlements, Israel's policies in Lebanon and its continued resistance to American arms sales to "friendly" Arab regimes like Saudi Arabia and Egypt. Lebanon was taking up a lot of our attention. But in the background the air force, on Begin's instructions, was training for a project so secret that not even the pilots involved fully knew what the target was until the night before they were to take off.

Why Begin ordered the raid on Osirak, the Iraqi nuclear reactor, has long been an open question. Shimon Peres, the head of the Labor Party who was running against Begin, claimed it was an election stunt. Begin said he did it to save the Jewish people from another Holocaust. What is beyond question is that Iraq was on the verge of acquiring both nuclear weapons and the means to deliver them over long distances, including to Israel. The head of the Mossad at the time, Yitzhak Hofi, and the head of Military Intelligence had made frequent trips to Washington to ring warning bells, but they fell on the deaf ears of an American administration fully in support of Iraq in its war against Islamic fundamentalist Iran.

Israel had also tried to stop the program by other means. In a 1979 Mossad operation, a well-placed explosive device in a container at the port of Seyne-Sur-Mer south of Toulon, France, left a good section of the Osirak-bound reactor destroyed, setting the program back some-what. Then, in June 1980, one of its chief architects, Egyptian-born nu-clear scientist Yahia al-Meshal, was assassinated in Paris. But the program went on, and by the end of that year the unequivocal assess-ment of the Israeli intelligence community was that the French-made re-actor at the Tamuz One complex at Tuwaitha, 17 kilometers south of Baghdad, was only months from being operational. If the attack was postponed beyond the first week of June 1981, the reactor's full load of 70 megawatts would have been in place, making it impossible to destroy without massive doses of radioactive materials being released into the at-mosphere and posing the danger of heavy civilian casualties.

Begin ordered the attack in the first week of June, the month before the election. Had he not done so, he later told a press conference in Jerusalem, Iraq would have had three to five 20-kiloton nuclear weapons within four years, each of which could have killed 200,000 Israelis. If he had to do so again, he said, he would without hesitation.

A bitter Peres had called a small group of us into his office at Labor Party headquarters on Hayarkon Street in Tel Aviv for a background chat the Friday morning after the attack. As usual he was impeccably dressed in suit and tie, his full head of hair combed backward. He rose from his desk on which, as always, there was a pile of books in English, French and Hebrew waiting to be read. He gave us each a weak hand-shake and motioned us to a couch and a few easy chairs. He claimed the attack was a cynical use of the air force for political goals. The Iraqis, he claimed, were nowhere near having weapons-grade material. The French had sold them yellow cake, and any fissile materials produced by the Iraqis were returned in tightly controlled and measured quantities.

He reminded us that he was one of the architects of Israel's nuclear program, and that he was in a position to have excellent intelligence. I had never trusted or liked Peres particularly, considering him a politi-cian with no shame, with a penchant for backbiting and subterfuge. I liked him even less now. What was the point of casting doubt over Be-gin's decision after the fact? Especially as I also knew Peres was lying. I could see it in his eyes.

The attack may not have been an election stunt but it did win Begin the election by one seat. The Likud went up by 5 seats to 48, the largest number it had ever held, while Labor went up 14 to 47, gaining back the seats lost to the Democratic Movement for Change, which voluntarily disbanded in April 1981. Instead of opting for a government of national unity, Begin went for the most right-wing, nationalistic and religious coalition in the country's history by joining forces with the National Religious Party, now at the height of its messianic fervor, the ultra-Orthodox parties and the small but vocal extreme right-wing Techiya, Redemption Party. To fortify his hard-nosed, uncompromising message, Begin named as foreign minister Yitzhak Shamir, a hawk who had abstained on peace with Egypt, a former Irgun terrorist and later head of Mossad operations in Europe.

Ariel Sharon, the man Begin had earlier said would encircle the Knesset with tanks, was appointed defense minister. Sharon was a controversial man who Ben-Gurion had said was talented but not to be trusted. By appointing Shamir, Begin was telling the Americans that he had no intention of moving on any peace process beyond that already agreed upon with Egypt, or of offering the Palestinians anything more than functional autonomy, and that the Syrians shouldn't even think about getting the Golan Heights back. By appointing Sharon he was saying that if he had to, he would use muscle to enforce his policies.

Watching Sharon enter office in August 1981 I was reminded of a conversation I had had with Raful about a year before. I was interviewing him and, being a man of few words, the interview was over before either of us had finished our coffee. I got up to leave but with his right hand he motioned me to sit down. He asked me how the skydiving club was doing. A short while before he had given us some help in getting permission to use an airfield.

Then, out of the blue, he said that Sharon was never to be trusted and that it would be a disaster if he were ever to become defense minister. "He is a man quick to send others to their deaths," he said, relating how Sharon had sent a paratroop battalion under Raful's command to jump into the heavily defended Mitla Pass in the 1956 Campaign "for no reason other than his own personal aggrandizement."

He accused Sharon of "chronically exceeding his orders" and related that he and his other senior commanders—Mordechai Gur, whom Raful succeeded as chief of staff; Yitzhak Hofi, later head of the Mossad; and Aharon Davidi, who went on to become a legendary commander in the paratroops before retiring to farm cattle in the north—had threatened in 1956 to resign in protest over an operation "of no military advantage and heavy in the subsequent senseless loss of life." He could have been speaking about the Lebanese war to come.

I hardly knew Sharon at all, his military career having ended when my career in journalism began. But the changes felt as he entered the ministry were dramatic, making it seem more like a putsch than a ministerial takeover. He quickly brought in his own inner group of lackeys, including Uri Dan, a controversial journalist, as his spokesman. Sharon created a quasi-military strategic planning unit that was intended to circumvent the chief of staff and the general staff, not all of whom he trusted, to carry out his goals.

Within a very short period of time the brown-gray austere defense ministry building in central Tel Aviv began to take on the nature of the Kremlin at the peak of the Cold War. The press was shunned and made unwelcome, other than a few court journalists who could be "trusted" to serve as reliable couriers of Sharon's message. Professional civil servants who had worked for generations of ministers now looked worried and harassed and would speak only in whispers, fearful for their jobs. Others had been cut out of the loop and spent long days at their desks looking into space as Sharon's cadre took over all key functions within the ministry.

I had first met Sharon in 1973 when he commanded the southern region. He had earned a fearsome reputation for the ruthless way in which he dealt with terror in Gaza, literally setting up hit squads that tracked down suspected terrorists. Unless the person was needed for interrogation by the security services they took no captives.

As a military commander he had been affable when guiding the press around the borders and he was always a gracious host. Food, a big thing in Sharon's life, was everywhere at all times. He was unorthodox and arrogant. He had little respect for orders from above, for hierarchy or authority, and he seemed incapable of holding a conversation unless he was pointing to a map. Above all he was bitter and paranoid, convinced that his advance to the top of the military pyramid had been hampered by his enemies because of his anti-establishment politics, rather than his own limitations.

Just weeks before the outbreak of the Yom Kippur War Sharon had slammed the door on the army when he was not made chief of staff. Against all regulations and without the permission of either the chief of staff or the army spokesman, as required, he called a press conference at his Southern Command headquarters to announce his decision to go into politics. We were shocked. At the time there was a strict delineation between elected government and the army that carried out the government's orders. Having a general still in uniform announcing that he was going to join the Likud, the opposition to the government he was supposed to be serving, was unprecedented. But that was Sharon.

As agriculture minister, which put him in charge of settlement, Sharon had managed to double the number of settlements in the West Bank and to quadruple the Jewish population there, making him extremely popular with both the right wing of the Likud and the religious parties. He had become so popular that Uri Dan now said in a famous and prophetic quote that "those who did not want Sharon as chief of staff now had him as defense minister and those who do not want him as defense minister would still get him as prime minister."

Begin and Sharon could not have been more different in every way, but they had a confluence of interests on the issue of territory. It was Sharon whom Begin took with him to the settlement of Elon Moreh on the morning after his election victory in 1977. But whereas Begin's motives for keeping Judea, Samaria and Gaza were historical, biblical, emotional and ideological, for Sharon the issue was one of security.

He saw the potential threat from the east—Iraq, Jordan and Syria—as an existential danger to Israel in its pre-1967 borders. Iraq's army was huge, Jordan's well trained and the Syrians were bent on reaching strategic parity with Israel, which they were approaching with some success.

Unlike the Labor strategists before them who were prepared in principle to give up at least some territory for peace, Begin and Sharon settled the territories not only to give Israel strategic advantage in any future war, but also as a way of ensuring that the territory would never be given up by any future government, no matter what its ideological base. Labor had for the most part restricted settlement to areas in which there were no concentrated Palestinian populations; the Likud did exactly the opposite. They wanted to create facts on the ground that clearly said this is ours forever, and this Sharon had done with alacrity.

My first extended close-up experience with Sharon came in January 1982 when, as defense minister, he visited Egypt for the first time with the goal of wrapping up some unfinished details as the date for the final withdrawal from the Sinai, on April 15, drew close. His mission was also to solidify relations with Egypt's relatively new president, Hosni Mubarak, elected following Sadat's assassination the previous October.

Unlike any other minister before him, however, despite the logistical and security nightmare involved, Sharon decided to make the journey over land. We all met at the Sinai settlement of Neot Sinai at dawn on a Sunday morning. Sharon and his entourage, including his wife Lily and 15-year-old son Gilad, arrived ensconced in three silver limousines followed by an army of security personnel. The twenty or so journalists who had been invited along were piled in a bus. Formally the military correspondents were boycotting Sharon because he had cut them out of the loop, canceled all briefings, refused to meet with them and had spokesman Dan inform them that he considered them the enemy. But despite his genuine hatred of the press, Sharon always had a good nose for publicity. He knew he could use this trip to establish his image as a statesman by having his meetings with Mubarak and other top Egyptians reported back home, and that by going overland, stopping off at past battlefields and posing for the cameras, he could reestablish himself as a military authority.

From Neot Sinai this convoy of military proportions drove to El Arish and from there to Refidim and Tassa, where we stopped for a short break. Though Sharon and the press were not formally speaking, we were invited over by his military aide, Gadi Dror, to some tables that had been set out in the desert and covered with stiff white linen tablecloths. From the boot of one of the limousines trays of little sandwiches, obviously made with great care and at no small expense, were produced, together with petit fours, hot coffee and tea. Sharon, as we were to learn, liked his little luxuries.

His manipulation of the press was masterful. At the Chinese Farm, the scene of a bitter battle in 1973 that the public associated Sharon with, as well as heroism, victory and leadership, reporters jostled in line to interview him and photographers yelled at him to move this way and that so they could get the perfect shot.

We got to the town of Suez by driving through the Ahmed Hamdi Tunnel, recently constructed under the Suez Canal, and on to an enormous lunch at the Port Tawfik Maritime Club before heading for Cairo and the Hilton Ramses Hotel, a notch down from the Nile Hilton, where we had become accustomed to staying, but still in the heart of Cairo.

I learned to respect some aspects of Sharon on that trip. He worked incessantly, meeting with Mubarak, Abdul Halim Abu Ghazala, his Egyptian counterpart, and Foreign Minister Kamal Hassan Ali. And then, into the small hours of the morning, he gave interviews to the press that the day before was boycotting him; we were now pounding on his door. The big issue with the Egyptians was the fate of the town of Rafiah in Gaza, which would be cut in half if Israel went back to the 1967 line. Fifteen years of occupation had obfuscated the border between the former Egyptian and Gazan sections of the city.

"You take Rafiah," Sharon said to Ali, arguing that it made no sense for people to be cut off from their families as the price for peace.

"No, no, please you take Rafiah," Ali urged back, Egypt having enough of a population crisis on its hands. In the end the city was officially divided but remained united with a network of subterranean tunnels that Israel could never fully shut down and that would, twenty years later, serve as vital conduits supplying arms to the Palestinians in their war against Israel.

The trip to Egypt had eased some of the distrust between Sharon and the press, but the relationship reverted to enmity back in Israel. The smiles and congeniality disappeared as he and his cadre disappeared back into the Kremlin, doors shut to all but a few, and secret plans were put into place. Summer was fast approaching and so was Israel's sixth war.

11

THE BIG LIE

Covering the Lebanese war often meant witnessing scenes of intense destruction, like this home in West Beirut once owned by Lebanese Christians. I'm holding the gun, for protection, and to the right, fellow journalists Zeev Schiff of Ha'aretz *and Ya'acov Erez and Shmuel Rachmani, both of* Ma'ariv.

It was a Saturday afternoon in June 1982 and about a hundred of us were in the Jerusalem Forest just below the memorial to John Kennedy, a cement structure of fifty ribs—one representing each state—that come together like a tree trunk cut off sharply to denote the president's death before his prime. It was a friend's son's Bar Mitzvah and the family had the novel idea of organizing a mass picnic in the woods rather than a traditional reception in some hall.

The crowd was typical secular Jerusalem, journalists, academics, midlevel government bureaucrats, all friends of varying degrees, and there was more politics than religion in the air. The Bar Mitzvah part of the event was totally incidental. The main topic of conversation was the press conference held by six senior reserve officers at Beit Agron in Jerusalem to decry Sharon's "Iron Fist" policies in the territories. These officers, including Yuval Neriah, had won the highest citation for heroism in the Yom Kippur War.

They said they had gone to the press because no one in government or the military command had responded to what they had to say, and what they had to say was shocking. They spoke about brutality, violence, atrocities, collective punishment and repressive measures being carried out systematically by the Israeli army against the Palestinians. They said they could no longer remain silent and could no longer serve in the territories with good conscience, and they demanded that the public respond, which it did a month later with a demonstration of 100,000 people organized by the Peace Now movement in Tel Aviv's city hall square. The government responded by organizing a counter-demonstration attended by 200,000 in which Begin and Sharon delivered fiery rhetoric about being stabbed in the back, and Sharon launched his war on the media as the seed of all evil in the country.

The sentiments of our crowd, of course, were uniformly with the 100,000, but my own thoughts were far away. I had just been up north for a briefing with the chief intelligence officer and was told that there was a buildup in progress of Israeli forces on the Lebanese and Syrian borders. The goal, he said, was deterrence. Begin, who had slipped in the shower and was in a hospital bed with a broken hip, had decided to annex the Golan Heights a few weeks before. This, I was told, was a precautionary move, something I only half bought and he half sold. We both knew that there were detailed plans for an invasion of southern Lebanon, an incursion just waiting to happen given the escalation of border violence and the growing number of clashes with the Syrians, including dogfights as Syrian aircraft tried to intercept Israeli planes on missions against the Palestinians.

On June 3, the Thursday night before the picnic, Israel's ambassador to Great Britain, Shlomo Argov, had been shot by a Palestinian gunman as he was leaving the Dorchester Hotel in London's Park Lane. He had been badly injured and doctors were fighting for his life. The next day Begin had called a security cabinet meeting at his home in Rehavia, where he was recovering from his fall. I knew that Sharon was not there, being in Romania on a state mission. I had spoken to one of the ministers by phone after the meeting; without divulging content he let me know that no major decisions would be taken without Sharon and that I could relax over the weekend.

At about two in the afternoon I became edgy, excused myself from the picnic and drove to the *Jerusalem Post* office where I could read the Reuters and AP wires while making phone calls, something I hated doing on the Sabbath. At 3:15 Israeli planes attacked targets in West Beirut and at 5:20 Katyusha rockets started falling on the Galilee. By eight that evening over five hundred of them had fallen on thirty towns and rural communities, just as Israeli military intelligence had predicted they would. This was clearly the prelude to war and it was in that atmosphere that the cabinet met again at Begin's home in Jerusalem, this time with Sharon, who had just returned from Bucharest.

The assembled ministers were briefed on the situation by the chief of staff and decided that the time had come to take drastic action against the Palestinian terror infrastructure in southern Lebanon. They voted to put into action Operation Small Pines, a broad thrust into Lebanon that officers in the Northern Command had been working on for weeks. This plan had the Israeli Defense Forces attacking along three lines from south to north and consolidating on a front from Sidon on the Mediterranean in the west to Lake Karoun in the east, roughly 40 kilometers up the Zaharani River, thereby removing all Palestinian rockets and artillery from within range of Israel.

Sharon was asked by one of the ministers, Mordechai Zippori, a former deputy defense minister and commander of an armored division, how long the operation would last. Sharon replied, "twenty-four to forty-eight hours." He stressed that there was no intention of reaching Beirut and that the army "would advance no further than 40 kilometers."

When the vote was taken, two ministers, Yitzhak Berman and Simcha Ehrlich, both from the Liberal Party, voted against the operation. The rest, including the prime minister, raised their hands for what they were convinced was a serious but limited strike against the Palestinian terror infrastructure in southern Lebanon. Neither Yitzhak Hofi, the head of the Mossad, nor Yehoshua Saguy, the head of Military Intelligence, both of whom were at the meeting, were asked for their opinions.

An attempt by the prime minister's outgoing Advisor on Terror, Gideon Machanaimi, to inform the ministers who was behind the attempted assassination of Argov was silenced by Begin before he could speak. It was not Yasser Arafat's PLO or any of the factions based in Lebanon but rather Abu Nidal's group, the Revolutionary Council in Iraq and a blood enemy of Arafat and the PLO. The attempt on Argov was retaliation for the Israeli attack on Iraq's nuclear reactor the year before and had nothing to do with Israel's northern border. The gunman had been positively identified as Hassan Said, using a Polish-made WL-63 submachine gun traced back to Iraq and known to have been given to him by the Iraqi embassy in London.

That afternoon's strikes against PLO headquarters in Beirut was hitting back at the wrong enemy for the wrong reason. Those in turn unleashed the PLO's massive barrage that lit the fuse for Israel's war in Lebanon, the first war in the country's history that would be fought without public consensus, by an army kept in the dark as to its true goals by the defense minister; a war that would embroil Israel in Lebanon for eighteen years to come, yet leave the problem of Palestinian terror unresolved. From the outset Sharon had carefully planned every move for the implementation of his Grand Strategy that saw Israeli forces penetrating deep into Lebanon, linking with the Phalange, installing Bashir Gemayel as president and, most importantly, getting rid of the Syrian and armed Palestinian presence in Lebanon once and for all.

Early Sunday morning I drove up to Safed, where Northern Command had its headquarters. It was from there that any war would be directed, deep down in the underground facility known as "Noah's Ark," designed to survive attack by any known weapon, including a nuclear one.

I met my friend Ya'acov Erez of *Ma'ariv* at a nearby pension where we took rooms for two nights, expecting a forty-eight-hour operation. We had both brought our reserve uniforms along, hoping to be attached to one of the forces by the army spokesman, forgetting that this was Sharon's war and that he would not want the backstabbing press involved. We put on our uniforms anyway, and posing as reservists who had been called up, walked through the gate of the heavily guarded camp as if we owned the place. Since no journalists had been invited or were expected there were no facilities available and no formal briefings. All we could do that first Sunday was glean bits of information from the officers running around.

A formal communiqué was issued stating only that a Skyhawk fighter and a helicopter had been lost in Lebanon and that an operation had been launched, whose goal was "to push back terrorist artillery and rockets from Israel's frontier." I managed to reach an official who I quoted as saying that "the IDF and government make it clear that there is no intention of engaging the Syrians, that Israel has no territorial ambitions in Lebanon and no intention of intervening in internal Lebanese politics."

While no official details were coming from the Israeli side, a UNIFIL spokesman told me that by evening of the first day Israeli forces were in Tyre, a city of 17,000, mainly Palestinians, on the Mediterranean, in Nabatiya in the central hills and in Auroub in Fatahland to the north. We even had to learn from the foreign press that the operation had started at 11 that morning.

The next day, bowing to immense pressure, the army spokesman finally agreed to give a few of us a briefing so that we could report that thirty-one hours into the operation, the IDF was in control of a 750-square-kilometer area that stretched from the mouth of the Awali River on the Mediterranean to Hatzbaya in the north. The air force had flown fifty-seven sorties, including bombing PLO headquarters in Beirut, and had shot down a Syrian MiG-23, and Israeli forces were mopping up in Sidon, a city of 150,000 people 55 kilometers from the Israeli border, 15 kilometers farther than had been approved by the cabinet. We were told that the operation, now officially renamed Operation Peace for Galilee, was all but over. The headline on my piece the next morning, spread over the entire front page in bold type, read: "Tyre, Beaufort Fall as IDF Operation Nears Completion." It would take another four years before that headline would reflect anything near the truth.

By Tuesday, June 8, battles were raging in Tyre and Sidon. Both were major PLO strongholds and the Palestinians had been bracing themselves for the attack. In the central sector Israeli forces were 6 kilometers from the Beirut-Damascus highway, which meant that the Syrians would not be able to get reinforcements or supplies through to the Lebanese capital. By now Israel was in control of 11,000 square kilometers of Lebanese territory and almost half a million Lebanese and Palestinian civilians. The IDF was at Damour, 14 kilometers south of Beirut, a former Christian city pulverized by the Palestinians, who turned it into a terror base. Further pulverized by the Israelis, it was now a ghost town.

Meanwhile the messages coming out of the defense establishment were controlled to create a fog of war, hide Sharon's true intentions and keep the public and the cabinet in the dark. All attempts to get accurate casualty figures failed. Sharon himself lied about these to the Foreign Affairs and Security Committee in the command and control center of the Northern Command when he told them on Monday that there had been no Israeli casualties in the battle for the PLO-held Beaufort Castle the day before. In reality six soldiers had been killed and eighteen injured, facts known in the command and control center.

Government spokesmen went out of their way to play down the clashes with Syrian forces that had taken place during the second day. Six Syrian MiGs had been shot down and there had been brief tank skirmishes around the city of Jezzine, where the Syrians had three armored battalions just to the north. Again they reiterated that Israel had no intention of engaging the Syrians and that the goal was to push the Palestinians out of range of the Israeli border and get out of Lebanon as quickly as possible.

Then on Wednesday, as event followed event, the Israeli air force destroyed seventeen Syrian anti-aircraft missile batteries in Lebanon and shot down twenty-nine Syrian MiG-21's and -23's that tried to interfere, with no Israeli loss. The next day twenty-five more were shot down. These spectacular successes were achieved by Israel jamming Syrian air-to-ground communications with its newly acquired Hawkeye aircraft, rendering the Syrian planes, which still had no over-the-horizon radar capabilities, nearly defenseless.

By that afternoon tank battles were reported at Lake Karoun to the north and Israeli forces reached Khalde, just 3 kilometers from Beirut International Airport. Ariel Sharon decided that it was time to meet the press, which he did in a hastily prepared lecture hall on the base. There were, of course, sandwiches, cakes, fruit and other niceties, and the inevitable maps with arrows in different colors all darting north of the Israeli border.

Sharon announced that the decision had been made to attack the missiles when it was learned that the Syrians were sending more in. It had never been Israel's intention to engage the Syrians, he said, but Lake Karoun was still within terrorist range of Israel and it was "inconceivable that the IDF would leave terrorist guns threatening the Galilee." He reported that in the east the IDF was in pursuit of the Syrians, pushing them from Karoun to the Hermon foothills, and said that "the collapse has started. Within a very short time the last areas of the Galilee will be removed from enemy artillery and rocket range." How long, we asked, was a "very short time"?

No reply. Instead, as if unhearing, Sharon went on with his systematic delivery, all the time pointing to the arrows on the maps as we scribbled furiously. "We have taken the terrorist infested city of Damour," he said, "and have offered the Christian community aid in rebuilding it." Then he casually threw in that "an IDF vanguard unit has moved to take up positions on the outskirts of Beirut from where the IDF can control the crucial Beirut-Damascus highway, the focal point for Syrian reinforcements into Lebanon." Evading more questions, he summed up by saying that "no amount of pressure will prevent us from guarding Jewish lives. We have decided to live and will take all steps necessary to ensure this." With that, he turned on his heels and left.

Israel was at war with the Syrians, Israeli forces were on the outskirts of Beirut, on the verge of entering an Arab capital for the first time in the country's history, and were twice as deep into Lebanon as the 40 kilometers approved by the cabinet. Israel was almost five days into a war that was supposed to have been over, in Sharon's own words, in a day or two, yet he felt he needed to offer no explanations. His arrogance was monumental, his brazenness beyond belief. One very senior military officer who was at the briefing, having left the underground command post for the first time in four days, took me aside and said that Sharon was leading us to disaster. "Even the army doesn't know what his plans are," he said. Then he melted away quickly as we both saw Uri Dan watching us with a look of white anger distorting his face.

I first made it over the border on Thursday, June 10, when I managed to hitch a ride to Sidon on a helicopter taking Minister Without Portfolio Yitzhak Modai; the prime minister's newly designated Advisor on Terror, Rafi Eitan; and the head of the General Security Services in the North, Yossi Ginosar, to the city where Israeli forces were battling terrorists determined to fight to the last man.

Eitan, a former senior member of the Mossad who had been on the team that brought Adolf Eichmann to trial in Jerusalem, was universally known by his nickname "Smelly Rafi"—Rafi Ha'masriach—and this clammy June afternoon one could understand where he got it from as he boarded the helicopter looking disheveled and sweating profusely, his short-sleeved white shirt dripping wet.

The flight to Sidon was supposed to be relatively straightforward. Both pilots were reservists, one from Jerusalem, the youngest son of a well-known family that owned a large bakery in the city. We took off and first headed up north to Metullah and then west toward the Mediterranean using the contours of the Litani and Awali Valleys to fly low and evade Syrian and PLO missiles. I had managed to get myself the seat nearest the cockpit facing outward. Looking down at the Litani I remembered the hard slog I had endured with those young Golani troops, fighting the same enemy we were fighting now. I then craned my neck to the left to see what was going on in the cockpit, the sun descending over the ocean to the west blinding me for a split second as I screamed "wires, electric wires. . . . "

The pilots dropped the helicopter like a stone, narrowly missing the electric cables that were spanning the valley. They had both been consulting a map for just a moment when I turned and spotted the thick cables maybe a hundred meters ahead. We had had a miraculous escape.

We finally landed in Sidon and were met by an armored personnel carrier that drove us to the center of the city. There we ascended four flights of steps in a partially completed building. From here young paratroop commander Yitzhak Mordechai was conducting the battle against several hundred terrorists who had holed up in the local hospital with an undisclosed number of hostages in the middle of a large residential area. By dropping leaflets and using loudspeakers his forces had managed to get about 40,000 civilians out of the area the day before. These civilians were now camping down by the mouth of the Awali River with a promise that they would be able to return to their homes, what would be left of them, the minute the fighting was over.

A young major appeared and invited us to join him for a tour of the area. We first stopped over at what used to be the headquarters of the local Communist Party and were shown a narrow opening behind a metal filing cabinet. Inside was a large arms cache containing everything from rockets to anti-tank grenades, explosives and tens upon tens of thousands of rounds of ammunition.

Sidon, built on three hills overlooking the Mediterranean, must have been a beautiful city once. Except for the massive destruction it was similar to Haifa in every way. We drove through what used to be the commercial center. Only one shop was open, a grocery, and a long line of people waited patiently as the owner served them through a small window in the front of the store. Had he opened the doors there would have been a rush for food and probably mayhem.

We took off in the late afternoon as the sun was setting behind us. It had been shocking to visit Sidon, a once thriving port city far north of the Israeli border and now a battlefield with the stench of death at every corner. "What were we doing all the way up there?" I asked Modai, shouting to make myself heard above the helicopter's engine.

"We have to wipe them out here. If we don't they'll only move back south when we withdraw," he said.

"So why state 40 kilometers in the first place?" I asked.

"War is not an exact science," he replied.

Casualties, however, are. On that day, the fourth of the war, fifty Israeli soldiers had been killed, and seven more were missing.

By now I was in Lebanon on an almost permanent basis, often leaving home at three in the morning, picking up Erez in Netanya at about four-thirty and making it to Rosh Hanikra, the crossing point from Israel into Lebanon, by dawn, and from there along the coastal highway to Tyre, Sidon and Beirut. Once over the border, usually wearing an army uniform and blending in with the traffic as supplies rolled in and the wounded were brought out, I would rub mud over the Israeli plates on my car and proceed to drive at 120–130 kilometers an hour on narrow and sometimes windy roads so as to avoid being shot at. This was not an unusual occurrence given that Israelis, Syrians, Palestinians, Christians, Druze and Shiites were all shooting at each other in a relatively small area.

By the end of the first week I had managed to get to Jezzine, a town set in the most startling scenery of mountains and valleys covered with majestic cedars of Lebanon, on to Lake Karoun and the Beka'a Valley, then back to the coastal road by Saturday, where heavy fighting had broken out on the heights above the highway into Beirut at Kfar Sil.

The Syrians had inflicted heavy Israeli casualties and destroyed several tanks, and the stunned Palestinians, who at first could not believe that the Israelis would actually enter Beirut, now began to fight fiercely, realizing that Sharon had no intention of stopping at the Awali or even the Beirut-Damascus highway. He was coming for them in West Beirut and there would be no mercy. This was a war to the end.

I first got to Damour, about 20 kilometers south of Beirut, that Saturday afternoon. I have never seen such complete, utter destruction. Not even the church remained intact. I stepped out of the car carefully. Yeku-tiel Adam, a former deputy chief of staff who'd been designated to be the next head of the Mossad, had been killed by a Palestinian sniper while relieving himself where I was now parked. I approached some officers from Amos Yaron's division and asked what was going on. One young officer removed a neatly folded plastic-covered map from his pocket and pointed to two axes of advance, both of them clearly leading to the outer suburbs of Beirut.

The one to the west along the coastal highway was now stalled at Kfar Sil just south of Beirut, but it would eventually place Israeli forces in control of Beirut International Airport. The other axis was to the north-east in the direction of Ba'abda, a Beirut suburb where the presidential palace was situated, then on to Ein Anoub to the north, and from there to Bassaba, a Maronite village under Phalange control. Once reached, it would forge a physical link between the IDF and Bashir Gemayel's Lebanese forces for the first time, all without the knowledge or approval of the Israeli government.

I slept the night in a borrowed sleeping bag at a battalion headquar-ters in Sidon. Battles were still raging around a mosque where 250 Pales-tinians were holed up with an unknown number of hostages, and at the Ein Hilwe refugee camp, where the Palestinians had taken an oath, or so our intelligence said, to fight to the death. I woke at dawn and went for a drive around the city, carefully picking my way around debris, cars crushed by tanks and fallen buildings. There was a constant sound of gunfire. I drove down to the mouth of the Awali, where civilians were still camped out with no water or electricity. "What have these people done to deserve this?" I wrote in my dispatch that night, adding that "Sidon has fallen. Now it remains to be conquered."

From Sidon I drove up to Ba'abda, where I knew I would find Yoram Yair, or Yaya, as he was known to all. He had been my company com-mander in the paratroops when he was a second lieutenant and I a pri-vate fresh out of basic training. Now he was a colonel, the commander of the Paratroop Brigade and set up in a temporary headquarters right across the road from the Lebanese presidential palace as he commanded

Israel's thrust to the northeast, now turned more westward to avoid a major clash with the Syrians encamped in the town of Aley.

I had little idea where exactly I was driving, winding my way through mountains of incredible beauty and opulent houses. I finally arrived in Ba'abda by late morning. A sign pointing north said it was 8 kilometers to Beirut. Yaya looked somewhat surprised to see me and, though exhausted, seemed to be in high spirits. He and his men had landed on a beach north of Sidon on the first day of the war, made their way on foot directly into the mountains overlooking the coastal highway and then marched more than 40 kilometers with full pack and encountering heavy Palestinian and Syrian resistance.

It seemed that most of the senior command of the brigade was there at the time, Rafael Eitan being expected for a final briefing before they moved forward from their current positions to forge a link with the Christians and complete the encirclement of West Beirut, an area of 400,000 Lebanese civilians under Palestinian control. Intelligence estimates put the number of armed Palestinians at 8,000, with fifty artillery pieces and thirty tanks.

Raful arrived, gave his briefing and then deliberately came up to me and offered a short interview, saying that the Syrians would be allowed to leave Beirut unharmed, with their personal weapons, if they chose to do so. He was emphatic that the IDF would guarantee the safe passage of any Syrian forces should they decide to leave the city, something he urged all noncombatants to do as well. I then asked him off the record whether the intention was for the IDF to enter Beirut. "Where do you think you're standing right now?" he asked, then turned and walked to a waiting car.

I was sitting on a pile of sandbags writing my notes when a young officer I knew quite well, a battalion commander, came up and said hi. We started to talk about the war and for the first time I began to hear misgivings at the senior command level. "Sharon's gone crazy," he said. "They're going to send us into West Beirut and we expect so many casualties that orders have been given to prepare the highway near Damour as a landing strip to evacuate the wounded." With that he went off in his jeep to join his men for the next push northward, farther and farther from the 40-kilometer line and deeper into all-out war.

By the start of the third week the war that had begun so quickly ground to an uneasy halt as uncertainty about the future set in. Beirut had now been encircled. A link with the Phalange had been established. The military high command had established itself in the grounds of a Catholic boy's school overlooking the city. The Phalange, however, were making it increasingly clear that they had no intention of fighting Israel's war against the Palestinians, and other than a token raid on the National Museum in Beirut on June 16th, they were refusing to field any men at all, leaving the Israelis, particularly Sharon, in a quandary.

This was being discussed at a meeting somewhere inside the school as Zeev Schiff, Eitan Haber, Erez and I sat on a fence in the yard outside overlooking Beirut. We had been promised a briefing at the end of the meeting, and were biding our time. It was dusk. Beirut airport could be clearly seen down to the left. To the right East Beirut was alive with lights and moving cars and, in the center, a large black patch of nothing was illuminated only by the incessant flow of incoming shells as they exploded in West Beirut. After a while Deputy Chief of Staff Moshe Levi, or Moshe-and-a-half as he was called for being so tall, came outside for a cigarette and some fresh air.

Thirsty for any tidbit of news we could get, we immediately surrounded Levi, who at first refused to say anything. Then he turned and uttered tersely, looking directly at Schiff, who was the most senior among us and by far the best connected: "He wants us to go into West Beirut. It's madness. We all think so." With that he ground out his cigarette with the stub of his paratrooper boot, picked up the remains and walked back into the meeting, indicating both nerves and discipline.

Standing just behind us during the exchange was a young, thin man in a uniform one size too large, Albert, who was doing his reserve duty with the army spokesman's unit. In ordinary life he was an aide to David Levi, a senior minister and member of the inner security cabinet. He noted that Begin was en route to the United States and that Sharon had probably taken advantage of the vacuum to order the army in. "Excuse me, I have to make a call," he said, and quickly disappeared and made a call to his boss. Others were also telephoned, including Finance Minister Simcha Ehrlich, Deputy Defense Minister Mordechai Zippori and Energy Minister Yitzhak Berman, none of whom had the faintest idea that Sharon intended to enter Beirut. On the contrary, he had told them exactly the opposite. They contacted Begin abroad, who rescinded the order. Denied entry into the city, Sharon ordered up a full siege, including cutting off electricity and water to the city and an ongoing artillery barrage to bring the PLO and Syrians to their knees.

On June 23, I met up with the Phalange for the first time at their headquarters in the Quarantina Quarter down by the port. The impression was not positive. The men were walking around toting their weapons like gangsters in a movie, most wearing sunglasses, none very keen to fight. A nice enough chap by the name of Eddy escorted me along the 7-kilometer Green Line that separated East and West Beirut, pointing out the landmarks and telling me that 7,000 Christians had been killed here by the Palestinians over the past eight years.

Back in the Quarantina headquarters, sitting in an eclectic collection of lounge chairs, the air thick with cigarette smoke, two bottles of whiskey on a small table in the center, it became clear to me that there was no chance these men were going to fight the Palestinians on Israel's behalf. It also became clear that while they hated what the Palestinians had done to their country, underneath it all they hated the Israelis even more for having created the Palestinian problem in the first place.

This point seemed to have been missed by both Begin and Sharon, who had relied on the Phalange to enter West Beirut and mop up the suspected terrorists. They would, however, fight their enemies, not ours. Judging from my conversations that evening and later over dinner at a restaurant in the fashionable Burmana Quarter, where I paid for the meal with Israeli shekels, which the proprietor accepted without blinking an eye, it appeared that all the Phalange wanted from their relationship with Israel was to get their man into the presidency with the help of Israeli-supplied submachine guns.

About a week later I was in Bhamdoun on the Beirut-Damascus highway, high up in the mountains, sitting with a few Israeli officers from a tank platoon guarding the junction. The inevitable little pot of coffee was bubbling away and to my astonishment I realized that the men were listening to an English-language Lebanese radio station. When I asked why, the young captain, a redhead from Netanya, said that's how they get their news on the war. You can't believe a thing on Israel radio, they said. As we talked, it came out that these young officers were becoming increasingly frustrated; they did not know where the war was going, or what its purpose was. On returning to Jerusalem I wrote a long magazine piece called "Doubts at the Front," which appeared the following Friday and caused a stir among the *Post*'s more conservative readers, of whom there were many, who did not appreciate my growing criticism of Sharon during a time of war. Their reaction was nothing, however, compared to that of Uri Dan, who phoned me at three in the morning.

"Look at your watch," he said. "We work around the clock and we will get you, you bastard." He hissed out the last two words with such venom that my blood turned cold. I told him he was mad and that, worse, his boss was even madder, that they had blood on their hands and that he should get some sleep. "Friend of our enemies," he screamed, "you defeatist, traitor. . . ." I put down the phone, deeply concerned that the country was in the hands of madmen.

During July the noose around Beirut tightened. The bombardment of PLO targets in the city was relentless. A series of Gabriel sea-to-sea missiles were launched against an underground garage the PLO command was thought to have moved into. As if playing a video game, a missile operator aboard the ship guided the missile with a joystick while closely examining a map, directing the missile around corners and down streets until it reached its target, whereupon it entered the underground garage and exploded.

The air force was used for both surgical strikes and to break the sound barrier low over the city to terrorize the population into leaving. Nevertheless, 150,000 civilians insisted on staying, unintentionally providing a human shield for the 7,000 Palestinian fighters and 2,300 Syrian troops still there. The siege was in its fourth week with a total blockade on power, water and food. A military spokesman, Paul Kedar, had the gall to tell the press that "Despite this the people of West Beirut are neither starving nor thirsty yet." A government spokesman in Tel

Aviv announced that Operation Peace for Galilee had thus far cost a billion U.S. dollars and that the army was expecting to spend the entire winter in Lebanon, an announcement that shocked the country.

On July 26 a colonel in the armored forces, Eli Geva, son of a general and at 32 the youngest brigade commander in the Israeli army, resigned his commission because he refused to lead his troops into Beirut. He would join his force as a regular soldier, he said, but not lead his men to their deaths in a campaign he thought was futile. Meetings with Begin, Sharon and Raful had failed to change his mind. The military censor at first tried to suppress the story but it came out in the foreign press. Geva, ironically, became the most remembered hero of the Lebanese war.

By the end of August, after sustaining some of the heaviest attacks on any city since the Second World War, the PLO finally agreed to leave Beirut in an American-brokered agreement negotiated by veteran American diplomat Phil Habib that would have the Palestinian fighters and their weapons ferried to Tunis, where Yasser Arafat would set up headquarters, with other splinter groups going elsewhere. Sharon, Raful and the army senior command watched the evacuation from the top of an eight-story building that had served as Amos Yaron's forward headquarters. The story that a sniper had Arafat in his sights and could take him out was true. But even thick-skinned Sharon knew what the consequences would be for U.S.-Israel relations, and told the sniper to lower his weapon.

I too watched Arafat's departure with some senior officers from the top of a nearby hill. They said nothing. There was no sense of victory in the air. The war was still far from over and they knew it.

Thousands of Palestinian fighters had surreptitiously stayed in Beirut and the camps around the city, armed with tons of ammunition left behind in secret caches by the departing PLO. Getting to them was going to be a problem. The evacuation agreement specifically guaranteed the safety of Palestinian noncombatants, which precluded Israel from using artillery or the air force to do the job.

The only people who could were the Phalange and the Lebanese forces loyal to president-elect Bashir Gemayel. If Gemayel's forces went in it would be perceived abroad as the Lebanese reclaiming Beirut, as opposed to Israel entering a foreign capital in pursuit of Palestinian terrorists, which would have caused international condemnation and possibly a break in Israel-U.S. relations. Bashir had now become critical to Sharon. Without a military success led by Bashir, how would the defense minister ever be able to explain having dragged the IDF to Beirut, getting Israel involved in a bloody war with the Syrians, sustaining 320 soldiers killed and hundreds more wounded and with Arafat's men still in control of West Beirut?

The two met on Sunday night, September 12. Unlike their previous meetings, where Sharon and even Begin could not get the Phalange leader to act, this time he was hot to trot. The numbers were massively in his favor and even if he could not get direct Israeli military support, the Israelis would contribute intelligence to make his job easier.

Unlike the earlier fight for Beirut when Gemayel had refused to go in and liberate the city for the Israelis, he was now fighting to establish his legitimacy as a Lebanese leader, retaking the country's capital on behalf of his people. It was a whole different opera and the two men, after eating a hearty dinner, departed on excellent terms. The Phalange were going to "clean out the last pockets of terrorist infrastructure while mindful of the Habib accords," and Sharon was to have his terrorist-free Lebanon. The future could not have seemed rosier to Sharon.

At four o clock on Tuesday afternoon, just two days after their meeting, Bashir, as he always did at four on Tuesday afternoons, went to the Ashrafiya branch of the Phalange Party to give a lecture to a group of women activists. It was just several days away from his scheduled inauguration and there was a heightened sense of expectation in the air. In the apartment above, Habib Tanious Shartouni made the final touches to a bomb he had placed directly above the lectern where Gemayel would be speaking. The bomb had been smuggled into the apartment, which belonged to his sister, in a fridge that morning.

Shartouni raised no suspicion at all, his family long having been highly respected members of the Phalange. What no one knew was that in recent months he had broken away from the Phalange and joined the Syrian National Party, a tiny clandestine group dedicated to incorporating Lebanon into Greater Syria. Once satisfied that everything was in place, Shartouni crossed the road to the roof of an adjacent building and activated the bomb. It exploded with such force that it reduced the entire apartment building to rubble. The devastation was so great that only after nine that night was Bashir's body positively identified in the morgue of the nearby Hotel Dieu de France Hospital, stretched out on a slab, as cold and dead as Sharon's dreams for Lebanon.

The next day Israeli forces moved even deeper into West Beirut and sealed off the major refugee camps, including Sabra, Shatilla and Burj el-Barajneh south of the city and in the vicinity of the airport. The Americans were furious, but Begin explained that Israel was doing this to protect the Palestinians from the wrath of the Christians. With that he and the rest of Israel prepared themselves for the weekend and the Jewish New Year.

And then it started, as if a plague had been sent down from the heavens to devour household after household. Commencing after sunset on Thursday night and continuing to Sunday, Phalange gunmen set about with the systematic slaughter of Palestinians in the Sabra and Shatilla refugee camps, killing anywhere between 460 men, women and children, as counted by a Lebanese government report, and 2,000, as the Red Crescent later claimed. Israeli intelligence put the number of dead at 700–800, which would be the figure used by the Kahan Commission of Inquiry subsequently set up to apportion blame.

Like all things born out of a lie, this war too was ending badly. The Phalange had done the killing, but Israel had been in charge of those camps, its forces encircling them and its spotlights and flares illuminating them. The Phalange had gone into the camps with Israeli permission over the warnings of the head of Military Intelligence, who pointed out that revenge would be an inevitable result. Israeli soldiers may not have perpetrated the actual massacre, but the mark was on Israel's forehead. Israel was responsible.

The exposure of the massacre was largely accomplished by the Israeli press. Ron Ben Ishai, Israel Television's intrepid reporter, was on a helicopter back to Israel when he heard a rumor of what was going on in the camps and returned to report on it. And Zeev Schiff, once informed about what was going on, used his connections in the government to try and stop the slaughter.

My own contribution was modest. On the morning after the killings a senior officer in the intelligence community gave me a call. He served in the counterintelligence section and knew the situation in Lebanon well. We met in his office and he handed me a cable to read. It was a report from an intelligence officer in the north that had reached Israeli military intelligence on Thursday night at 11 P.M., the night the killings started, saying three hundred people, including civilians, had already been executed. The memo had been circulated to about twenty people in the military and defense hierarchies, and it proved that Israel knew about the killings almost two days before Sharon and Raful claimed.

"This you must publish," he said, handing me a copy. An account appeared in the *Jerusalem Post* the next day and was added to the mounds of evidence weighed by the Kahan Commission, reluctantly established by Begin after an unprecedented public outcry for justice, including a now-legendary demonstration of an estimated 400,000 people, ten percent of the population, in the square outside Tel Aviv City Hall.

Begin said he first heard about the massacres on the BBC on Sunday evening at the end of Rosh Ha'shana and was saved by the Commission from any embarrassing retribution. Sharon, however, was declared unfit to be defense minister, was fired and was immediately rehired as a minister without portfolio, taking up another seat at the same table with the government he had so cynically misled. His spokesman Uri Dan was now walking around quoting himself, saying, "Those who don't want Arik as defense minister will get him back as prime minister." Again, he would be proven right.

Among the major players the highest personal price was paid by intelligence head Yehoshua Saguy, of all people, who had been opposed to Israel's involvement with the Phalange from the outset but, according to the Kahan Commission, had not been forceful enough in making his case. He was the only one to pay with his career. Other officers, like Amos Yaron, were internally disciplined. Raful, who was due to end his term in the coming month, was chastised but left in place.

In the meantime the situation on the ground continued to get more complicated. In the Shouf Mountains the IDF was caught in a new war between the Christians and 800,000 Lebanese Druze, half of whom lived along the Beirut-Damascus Highway between Zahle and Hatzbaya. The Druze supported Walid Jumblat as their leader and under no circumstances would consider bowing to Christian authority.

A bloodbath was clearly in the making with Israel caught in the middle, both protagonists being its allies. To the south in Tyre and Sidon clashes continued, as they did in and around Beirut. And in another dangerous development, Israeli forces and U.S. Marines who had been sent in to monitor the Beirut agreement were reporting growing friction and tensions were mounting. Captain Charles B. Johnson of Neenah, Wisconsin, became instantly famous when photographers and television cameras caught him stopping three advancing Israeli tanks on the Beirut-Damascus highway, shouting "Over my dead body" at them.

It was now winter. On January 13, I met my friend and colleague from the *Sunday Times* of London, David Blundy, at the gaudy villa of a former Saudi sheikh that now served as a field office for Military Intelligence and the Mossad. Blundy could not believe where he was, inside the heart of the black empire, the mythical Mossad, and he scribbled away furiously in a small notebook with a spiral coil at the top.

At about eight in the evening he said, "Want to come to West Beirut?"

"You mad?" I asked.

"We'll just go to the Commodore, no big deal. All our mates are there," he said, referring to the sizable foreign press contingent that lived in the PLO-owned hotel. The Commodore had been where the PLO held all their press conferences before Yasser Arafat's departure.

I phoned a taxi driver I had been dealing with, who picked us up at a shoe store several blocks away. We drove downtown and then through a barricade into West Beirut, which seemed remarkably intact given the months of bombardment it had sustained. Some store windows were still lit and displaying Louis XV furniture, crystal chandeliers and fashionable clothes and shoes. Some had Christmas decorations in them.

We got to the Commodore and went to the check-in counter, where I was immediately picked out by two burly security men standing to the side, who carefully watched my every move. "Be calm," Blundy said, "be calm." He then turned to one of the women behind the counter—he had a way with women—and asked whether Colin Smith was in. He wasn't and neither were any of the other names Blundy rattled off.

"O.K. Two rooms. One for me and one for my friend here. *Sunday Times* credit card O.K.?"

We were asked for our ID's. All I had was an Israeli press card. "I've left mine in the cab it seems," I said, my heart pumping.

"No problem," she answered, raising an eyebrow in the direction of the security men.

In room 405 I got under the covers of my bed and prayed for morning, which seemed years away. After midnight I went down to the lobby trying to find a familiar face. Blundy was at the bar and I told him I had to get out of there. Bad things were going to happen. I was going to be taken hostage, my family would never see me again. He told me to have a drink.

Eventually I crept out of the lobby, found a taxi, and prayed he would take me to an East Beirut address, which he did, for a whopping fee of course. That weekend I wrote a magazine piece called "Journey into Fear" illustrated by my room key with a big plastic tag labeled "Hotel Commodore/Beirut Lebanon/405," which for reasons of prudence I had not returned to the front desk.

Blundy, who I adored, was killed in El Salvador in 1989 covering a story on the rape of several nuns. Everyone else on the organized press tour had gone back to the minibus. Blundy, of course, had to go back for just one last look at the crime scene. He was shot by a rebel marksman and died instantly.

On the evening of February 10, I was in the office finishing up a piece about visiting troops in the Shouf Mountains of Lebanon when my phone rang and I was told by the news editor that there had been a terrorist attack outside the prime minister's office about a ten-minute drive away. I was there in less. It was not a terrorist attack but an attack by a right-wing extremist, Yona Avrushmi, who had thrown a grenade at a crowd of Peace Now demonstrators marching against the war in Lebanon. The explosion killed Emil Grunzweig, 33, a paratrooper reservist who had served in Lebanon. It was an event that shocked and divided the nation even further. I could not remember a time of such a lack of national cohesion.

The piece I had been writing was about how I had found soldiers deployed in the Shouf Mountains in early February angry, confused and restless. The commander and his men could not have been blunter in telling me that they felt they were sitting ducks, under orders not to fire at either the Christians or the Druze, but coming under constant fire from both. I noticed that one soldier had pasted a picture of Eli Geva on the wall of the tent beside his cot. "He's our hero," he said when he saw me looking at it. "Mine too," I answered.

In February 1983, when Moshe Arens took over as defense minister, 466 soldiers had been killed in Lebanon and 2,567 wounded. Arens, an American-born engineer who was ideologically a member of the right-wing Herut Party, very close to Begin and very similar in his gentlemanly ways, inherited an impossible situation that he was determined to sort out. In August the IDF began pulling its heavy equipment out of the Shouf and in the first week of September, like thieves in the night, pulled all forces back to a 115-kilometer line along the Awali River, leaving the Druze, Phalange, pro-Syrian Maronites, Shiites and the other factions north of it to fight it out.

I was with the Israeli forces that early September as they withdrew from the Shouf, one of the more ignoble moments in IDF history. I was with Reuven Merhav, the Mossad representative who was trying to negotiate with the Druze and Phalange to hold their fire until the last Israeli had left the area, which they did.

While waiting for the pullback I sat with a Phalange commander named Oscar at a villa in the hamlet of Ras el Jabl, a kilometer south of Alay. Oscar had about thirty men with him. They would soon constitute an island of Christians surrounded by 2,000 armed Druze. These men calmly smoked on a bubbling *narghile,* the smell of hashish heavy in the air, not giving a damn about anything anymore.

"Say farewell to Oscar," he said to me. "You are abandoning us to our deaths. You have turned our former friends, the Druze, into our enemies, and you have created new enemies, the Shiites. There are now 1,200 Syrian tanks here instead of 400 and with 40,000 Syrian troops."

I stared at the ground, letting his accusation sink in.

"The devil," he said, "could not have done what you people have done here."

Half an hour later we were gone and it was not long before the sound of gunfire disturbed the distant silence. Who knew what would happen to Oscar.

12

YOM YAVO—
THE DAY WILL COME

Just days before his assassination Yitzhak Rabin granted
The Jerusalem Report *an extensive and philosophical interview*
in which he outlined his conditions for peace with Syria. We scheduled a
session to complete the interview for Sunday, November 5, 1995.
He was murdered the night before.
(Copyright Cathy Rath, for The Jerusalem Report*)*

IN MAY 1983 I had been invited to Sweden to give a talk at the Royal Swedish Defense College in Stockholm and to lead a seminar on the impact of the Lebanese War on the Middle East for researchers at the Stockholm Institute for Peace Research. The payoff was that I got to interview Olof Palme, the socialist prime minister of Sweden and respected international diplomat, and to fly over Lapland in a Swedish air force jet, which was by far the more impressive of the two experiences.

Palme was a mouselike man with twitchy features, who spat rather than spoke his comments. He had recently likened Israel to Nazi Germany and, the week before, on May Day, had invited Yasser Arafat to attend the Socialist International being held in Stockholm. Shimon Peres, the leader of the Israeli Labor Party and one of Israel's main advocates for peace, was told not to come.

Palme was furious when I suggested he was biased against Israel. "How dare you," he hissed, his eyes red. "Because I am critical of Israel's policies does not mean I'm an anti-Semite. I was emotional when I made the slip about Nazi Germany but your policies in Lebanon and against the Palestinians in the territories are atrocious."

Then he added: "And, for your information some of my best friends are Jews. We even had a Jewish maid in Latvia. That doesn't mean I have to like what Begin and Sharon are doing.

"I told, begged Arafat when he was here last week to recognize Israel, to give up on all of Palestine, to accept a two-state solution before it is too late. And I am telling you and you can tell your readers," he said loudly, enunciating each word with a dramatic pause between them, "it will be too late. You have to stop the occupation now, speak to the PLO now, otherwise much blood will flow."

The next day, my formal escort from the Swedish Foreign Ministry phoned the hotel and asked me to join him for lunch. He took me out to the island of Waxholm in the Archipelago to a grand hotel that boasted twenty-three different types of herring, each of which I had to taste and each of which, my host insisted, had to be washed down with a tiny glass of vodka. He had taken me out, he said, because he was incredibly embarrassed by Palme's behavior and wanted to make it up to me. By the fourth type of herring and corresponding glass of vodka, we could not have been agreeing with each other more.

Palme's delivery was pig-headed, but his message was right. I did not need a Swedish prime minister to tell me Israel's occupation of the West Bank and Gaza was eating away at the nation. "Israel's occupation has been benign," I wrote in a piece several months later, "but it has been occupation" with punitive actions like "administrative arrest, banishment, demolitions, forced evacuation, curfews, roadblocks, censorship." And worse, I wrote in another piece, these actions did not help: "You stop the stones in Jalazoun only to be faced with rocks in Kalandia. When you use water cannon to subdue Kalandia you face riots in Dahariya. You get things under control in Dahariya and tires are burned outside Deheisha."

The piece was called the "The Curfew Cycle" and by then it could have been an allegory for how I was feeling about my job. Between rushing to meet demoralized troops in the Shouf Mountains in Lebanon, demoralized troops serving on the West Bank, demoralized staff officers increasingly at odds with the defense establishment and government policy makers, I was ready for a change.

Fortuitously for me around that time I was invited to have breakfast at the King David Hotel in Jerusalem with two researchers from AIPAC, the pro-Israel lobby in Washington, D.C., Steve Rosen and Martin Indyk.

They had shared with me several of their monographs on the Middle East's balance of power and wanted to know what I thought of them. I said I thought they were terrific but that no one would take them seriously since they were being published by a lobby, which by definition meant the work was being written to make a case. There was so much stuff coming out of think tanks on every aspect of the Middle East that I doubted whether they would ever make it to the top of anyone's reading pile.

I don't know whether our talk that morning contributed to Martin's thinking, but in a short while he broke away from AIPAC and established the Washington Institute for Near East Policy, and invited me to be a visiting fellow for a few weeks. That began a professional relationship and friendship that was to become very meaningful in my life and the basis for a second career in the think tank community.

In the meantime, after this brief but fruitful sojourn in Washington, I returned to Israel unable to change my job and stuck in the rut of covering defense issues. At least the defense minister was now Yitzhak Rabin, who got the job in the National Unity Government set up following the July 1984 elections, in which Shimon Peres and Yitzhak Shamir would hold the premiership for two years each. Rabin was to be defense minister for the entire four years.

I had always had a great deal of respect for Rabin, but one Friday evening in the last week of May 1985, I had the opportunity to get a real insight into what a special leader he was.

On May 21, Israel released 1,150 terrorists in exchange for three Israeli soldiers being held by Ahmed Jibril's Syrian-backed Popular Front for the Liberation of Palestine: Hezi Shai, 31, captured at Sultan Ya'acoub in June 1982; Nissim Salem, 21; and Yosef Groff, 22, captured in Bhamdoun in September 1982 under circumstances the chief of staff later described as "cowardly, disgraceful and worthy of a court-martial." Among those released were dozens of mass murderers, including Kozo Okamoto, who killed twenty-seven Peruvian pilgrims in the baggage hall of Lod Airport in 1972, the terrorists who committed the 1978 Coastal Road massacre that sparked off the Litani Operation, the killers of Danny Harran and his two small daughters in an attack in Nahariya in 1978 and the terrorist who killed the two Aroyo children in Gaza the same year when he set fire to the car they were riding in.

We were at the home of Nachman Shai, Rabin's spokesman, and Rabin was sitting alone on the couch nursing a whiskey in both hands. He was notorious for his dislike of small talk, but I approached him anyway.

"Why did you do it?" I asked quietly.

He looked me squarely in the eye. "We don't leave soldiers in the field," he said, "no matter what. If I had been bringing back three heroes would the public not now be singing my praises? Soldiers are soldiers. If there are disciplinary measures to be taken, we will take them. These men have committed no crime that deserves a death sentence, which is what leaving them in Jibril's hands indefinitely would have meant."

"But won't this encourage terrorism?" I persisted.

"As if terrorism needs this to be encouraged," he answered with disdain, taking a deep drink of scotch, lighting up yet another cigarette and making it absolutely clear that the conversation was over. I was just about to stand up and leave when he looked over and, with that lopsided grin that was more a wince of embarrassment than a smile, said very softly and very simply: "Leadership is lonely." With that he got up and went to replenish his glass.

The prisoner exchange certainly did nothing to stymie terror. In October 1985, Ehud Barak, then head of Military Intelligence, and at 40 one of the youngest generals in Israel's history, said in a briefing that there had been six hundred terrorist attacks and attempted attacks in the previous fifteen months.

On October 10, together with Avi Hoffman, who was now working with me, I met Rabin for an interview over hot chocolate and cheesecake in the Jerusalem Hilton. He looked drawn, the lines on his face had gone deep, and the skin under his neck hung loosely.

In recent weeks Israeli planes had bombed PLO headquarters in Tunis and eight Israeli tourists had been killed by a lone Egyptian gunman while holidaying on the beach at Ras Burka in the Sinai, as were three more while on their yacht in the port of Larnaca in Cyprus. An Italian cruise ship, the *Achille Lauro,* had been hijacked and an American Jewish tourist, Leon Klinghoffer, who was disabled and confined to a wheelchair, had been killed.

"Where would it end?" we asked. Arafat, Rabin said, had made a strategic decision eighteen months before to step up the terror, so Israel was now systematically going after its leadership. I gave him a look as if to say, "Where have I heard this before?"

In reply he spread out his hands, palms upward, sighed, sucked on a cigarette, and said, "It's hard to be a Jew."

It was going to become even harder. On November 21, the FBI arrested Jonathan Pollard, an analyst with U.S. Naval Intelligence, on charges that he had spied for Israel. Pollard had been refused entry into the Israel embassy compound when he arrived at the gates that morning seeking asylum. Still, Israel could not hide that it had recruited an agent to spy on its most important friend. The consequences were devastating.

Pollard's handlers were Avihu Sella, a colonel in the Israeli air force serving as an attaché in the United States; Yosef Yagur and Ilan Ravid, both "scientific attachés" at the Israeli mission in New York; and Rafi Eitan, the former head of Mossad Operations and now leading a super-secret unit in the Defense Ministry that worked on scientific espionage. Pollard had provided them with mounds of material.

Unfortunately for the American intelligence community, this contained not only information about Arab capabilities, but also the names of American agents and the layout of entire spy networks and raw material. While there was some consolation that this damaging material was in the hands of friends, a senior American intelligence official explained to me at the time, Israel's own intelligence community was penetrated by spies and who knew where Pollard's secrets could ultimately end up? Because of this, he explained, Pollard would probably never again see the light of day.

There was another spy incident a year later in which I was to find myself playing a role: the Vanunu affair. I had started working as a stringer for the *Sunday Times* in the late 1970s when my old mentor, Asher Wallfish, heard they needed someone in Israel and recommended me—a job I was glad to do in order to augment my salary from the *Post*. In the last week of September 1986 I received a call from the foreign editor at the *Sunday Times*, Peter Wilshire, an owl-like little man with a perpetual sneer on his face who always managed to get the best out of his correspondents. In snipped sentences he told me that on Sunday the paper was going to publish a major investigative scoop based on firsthand reports by Mordechai Vanunu, an Israeli who had worked at the top-secret Dimona nuclear reactor. Vanunu, he said, had provided them with photographs of the facility, nuclear experts had examined and verified his story and it was assumed that Israel had up to two hundred nuclear warheads. They would like an Israeli government reaction, he said.

"Bullshit," I said instinctively. "I don't believe a word of it."

"I'm not asking you to," said Wilshire. "Get a reaction, that's all."

At first I was peeved that the *Sunday Times* had not included me in the investigation and then, almost instantly, I was relieved. It would have been a test of loyalty for me to choose between the news organization I had worked for for seven years, or my country. Wilshire must have known I would have told the authorities immediately. He was too wise to have placed me in that situation and I was grateful for his wisdom.

I phoned Nimrod Novick, the head of the Prime Minister's Bureau, and said I had to meet with him immediately. When I got there, one of Shimon Peres's aides, Yossi Beilin, was already in the room waiting. I told them what I knew and they thanked me. They asked me if I could intervene with the *Sunday Times* not to publish. I said that would be impossible.

Could I get them to hold publication "while we regroup and organize?" Novick asked. I said that would not be possible either. As I got up to leave, Novick ordered his secretary to phone about a dozen people. Clearly Israel had a crisis on its hands, though the official reaction I was given was essentially that it was beneath the government's dignity to respond to what was obviously a practical joke being pulled on one of the world's great newspapers. Novick went on to say that Vanunu had tried to peddle the same story in Australia and London before and was laughed out of the room. It was unbelievable the *Sunday Times* would fall into such a trap, he said, and he wondered off the record whether this had anything to do with the paper having recently been purchased by Rupert Murdoch and Murdoch's love for making splashy headlines.

Andrew Neil, the editor of the *Sunday Times,* phoned me later that afternoon and asked about the government's reaction. I told him and he suggested I come to London the next morning for a final editorial meeting on whether to print the story or not.

I left Israel on the 7 A.M. flight and arrived in London at about 11:30. A driver was waiting for me at the exit hall and led me to a dark blue Bentley, Neil's car. The night before I had met in Tel Aviv with three defense officials, including the head of Field Security, an officer I knew only by the name of "Fishy," trying to get a handle on the story. I also contacted a friend who had worked at Dimona.

It turned out that Vanunu was a known quantity to the intelligence community and that he had indeed tried to sell pictures and the story in

Australia, where he had converted to Christianity, and later to an English tabloid. The sources would not say whether he had worked in Dimona or not, though they did mention that he had had affairs with young Arab men, belonged to a radical group of "leftists" at Ben-Gurion University and had been photographed posing in front of the Palestinian flag. In other words, Vanunu was not exactly the type of person one would entrust with the country's top secrets.

As we neared Wapping, to where Murdoch had moved the *Times* and the *Sunday Times* from Fleet Street in order to circumvent the print unions that were blocking modernization, the driver said I should brace myself for "some unpleasantness." The "unpleasantness," it transpired, was a mob of print workers frothing at the mouth, holding signs condemning Murdoch to hell and screaming "Scab! Scab! Scab!" at me and the driver as we negotiated our way through a wall of private security guards.

It was horribly embarrassing driving though the sea of recently unemployed print workers in the backseat of a luxurious limo. I nearly let the window down to tell them the car was not mine, but the driver warned me firmly against doing so. "They'll beat you to pulp given half the chance sir. They're very angry," he said.

The new editorial offices of the *Sunday Times* were industrial, spartan and devoid of charm or glamour. Neil and the senior editorial staff were waiting in a conference room, a series of satellite pictures spread over the table. One of the editors briefed me quickly: Vanunu had been moved to a safe house. There were Mossad agents with video cameras mingling among the strikers at the gate waiting to pounce on him.

The Mossad desperately wanted Vanunu before he could give a post-publication press conference. Wilshire took over. They had established beyond any doubt that Vanunu had worked at the Dimona plant, that the pictures taken with a 35 mm Yashika camera were authentic, that he had accurately traced his path to and from work and described where the dining hall was and other known facilities at Dimona. He added that Vanunu's pictures and descriptions compared well with the satellite pictures on the table, and that scientific experts had no doubt that Vanunu's evidence was credible. He then told me to play the devil's advocate.

It was impossible, I said, for a man who would be under constant security surveillance to photograph, over a period of time, the inner sanctum, the holy of holies, Israel's nuclear reactor, including shots from the famous "Golda Balcony," a platform overlooking the nuclear production process, using a regular camera. Employee lockers are regularly searched at the facility, I said, quoting "Fishy," and there was no way Vanunu's camera, which he claims to have hidden in his locker, would have gone undiscovered for months on end.

Then there was Vanunu's ostentatious political behavior that he'd made no attempt to hide. I told them how a friend of mine, a former deputy head of military intelligence, was dismissed after being caught with a prostitute on the Tel Baruch beach. All people entrusted with state secrets are subject to random surveillance, so how is it possible that Vanunu, who posed with the Palestinian flag and did everything he could to broadcast his anti-Israel views on campus, was still employed in a top-secret nuclear facility? It made no sense, I argued. And why, I asked, had other publications turned him down?

I then said something that surprised even me. "Maybe he's a plant."

"Someone the authorities knew about and led on to 'reveal' massive Israeli power to the world that perhaps we don't have." For the first time I sensed a crack in the team's self-confidence.

After a long debate, and to the chagrin of the staff, Neil decided to postpone publication for a week. The paper had invested too much in the story to take even the slightest chance. Credibility was everything and every angle had to be rechecked. I came out of the meeting with a deep admiration for his leadership and judgment. Though some troublesome questions remained, it seemed as if the paper indeed had a massive scoop.

It was not careful enough with Vanunu, however. On September 30, Vanunu and a pretty young blond he had met in the park, called Cindy, were last seen aboard Flight British Airways 504 from London to Rome. In Rome he was drugged and smuggled aboard an Israeli naval vessel that brought him back to Israel.

Cindy took off her blond wig and became Mossad agent Cheryl Hanin, and the *Sunday Times* never got to have their press conference with Vanunu. It was a big story that made world headlines and resonated for years to come, but Vanunu paid a heavy price. He got eighteen years in solitary confinement and would continue to live with serious restrictions after his release in 2004. If the establishment took him seriously enough to imprison him under such harsh conditions for so long, perhaps I should have taken him more seriously at the time. The truth be told, though, I still have serious doubts about the true nature of the Vanunu affair. It seems impossible that the security would have been so lax. But then again, as I have seen so often in this country, the impossible often happens.

In October 1986, halfway through the Unity Government's four-year term, Begin's colleague Yitzhak Shamir became Israel's prime minister. Shamir replaced Shimon Peres, Moshe Arens replaced Shamir as foreign minister, Peres became finance minister and Rabin remained in defense.

On December 9, 1987, I was with Rabin in his suite on the seventh floor of the Grand Hotel in Washington when the first pictures of the Intifada appeared on the evening news. Though the riots seemed massive in scale, particularly in Gaza, Rabin remained impassive. Later he was reported as having said "We will break their bones," an unfortunate statement he didn't deny and that was to come back to haunt him, especially when a few weeks into the Intifada a CBS cameraman captured Israeli paratroopers breaking a young Palestinian stone thrower's arm with a rock.

Rabin had been in the United States for eleven days and critical issues hung in the balance, including an Israeli bid for the F-16, some $1 billion in additional aid for an anti-missile system and the strengthening of the Israeli-American security dialogue that had taken a nosedive when Sharon was defense minister. Later that same evening Rabin was due to meet Frank Carlucci, the secretary of defense, to put the final touches to a Memorandum of Understanding between the two countries that would have given Israel a similar status to NATO in terms of American security commitments.

Rabin watched the news, spoke with National Security Advisor Colin Powell, made a few calls to Israel and then gave me the answer I had been waiting for. Yes, he would speak at a Washington Institute for Near

East Policy breakfast the next morning, an event that had been in preparation for weeks. He had decided to stay put in the States. His aides in Israel, he said, had assured him these riots too would pass. A truck driver had accidentally killed seven Palestinians in Gaza. The outrage was natural, he said. For once he was wrong, very wrong.

The first Intifada was different from Palestinian demonstrations before it. This was not a strategic war in which modern weapons were used by the Palestinians, but a conflict motivated by a hatred that had been suppressed by Israeli bayonets for twenty years. It was fought by youngsters who had grown up knowing nothing other than occupation, who had seen their parents humiliated by Israeli soldiers, their homes demolished, fields ploughed under and lands confiscated.

They were a generation of Palestinians who had nothing to lose. Their cause had been essentially abandoned by the Arab world. Egypt had made peace with Israel, King Hussein of Jordan was known to have met every single Israeli leader, including Peres and Shamir, and seemed very much on his own track, Saddam in Iraq was far away and besieged by his own problems, and there was little hope of salvation from Arafat exiled in Tunis.

While the Intifada started off spontaneously enough, it soon became organized, and brilliantly so. Those guiding it understood the power of the press, particularly the needs of the newly developing 24-hour television news channels, and by skillfully portraying stone throwers against tanks, boys and girls against soldiers and, in areas closed to the press, providing videotapes taken by Palestinian cameramen of Israeli actions that generally looked brutal on the small screen, they managed to place the Palestinian issue back on the international agenda. Israel was at a loss in how to handle the situation.

"The army has met a new Palestinian," I wrote. "They have no fear, they wave the Palestinian flag proudly and they come, wave after wave of Palestinian youngsters, throwing rocks at the soldiers, leaving them profoundly unsure of how to react."

Things did not get better as the months passed by, and I watched the Israeli army slowly but surely begin to lose this war. I knew it when Amram Mitzna, then a brigade commander serving on the West Bank and later without doubt the most lackluster leader the Labor Party was ever to have, showed me with no small amount of pride a gravel-shooting cannon he had developed in response to the stone throwers. A year later in one of my last pieces for the *Jerusalem Post,* this one on the occasion of Israel's fortieth anniversary, I wrote that "The IDF's 40th anniversary parade will not wipe away the stain of these recent months. The dazzling display of weapons will not remove the specter of a gravel-shooting cannon and paratroops clubbing women in Jenin," which I had also witnessed on that visit to Mitzna's headquarters.

Now with this new round of violence upon us I was desperate to leave the *Post.* I was sick of writing about the same thing. Officers I knew as youngsters were now in key positions; getting the story was not much of a challenge anymore. When I interviewed them, or even Rabin, I felt I had asked the same questions and received the same answers before. Just the faces on the other side of the desk had changed.

There had also been management changes at the paper. David Landau was named News Editor with expanded responsibilities to the point where the paper's co-editors, Ari Rath and Erwin Frenkel, were not allowed in the newsroom, nor could they deal with news-related issues; they were restricted to the paper's comment and editorial sections.

David, who was incredibly talented and went on to become the Editor in Chief of Israel's premier paper, *Ha'aretz,* had been a distinguished diplomatic reporter for as long as I had covered the military beat. He had also been the first Israeli reporter to interview Anwar Sadat and had made an international name for himself as a commentator. But with David in charge and with Yehuda Litani, the Arab Affairs editor, and Benny Morris, then a night editor, the paper took a sharp swing to the left. I had always thought of myself as being on the left, prepared to give up every last inch of territory for peace and totally opposed to the occupation and what the army was doing, but there were two sides to every story; they wanted to only hear and print one.

I suppose I was also more than a little peeved at not having been included in the management reshuffle, so by the middle of 1988, thankful for the opportunities the paper had given me, we parted ways and I headed for Washington to the Institute for Near East Policy. There I spent a wonderful and productive year immersed in studying how policy is made and how interest groups try to influence it. I also wrote a book with my colleague W. Seth Carus, *The Future Battlefield and the Arab-Israeli Conflict,* published by Rutgers University Press, which I don't even think my late father bothered to read.

My next venture was born from a totally unexpected meeting that had occurred two years earlier. In April 1986, a month after I had turned forty and in the midst of an appropriate midlife crisis, I received a call from Sam Lipski, the former Washington correspondent of the *Jerusalem Post* and now the editor of the *Melbourne Jewish News.*

He said he was in Jerusalem and would like to meet for a cup of coffee and I agreed, thinking he wanted to discuss Israel and what was going on for a column he wanted to write. We arranged to meet at the Max Café on the corner of Ben Yehuda and King George Streets, opposite the former Frumin Biscuit Factory Building, the site of Israel's first Knesset.

We had not seen each other since 1982 when I was on a lecture tour in Australia, but I recognized him immediately, Sam being a large, corpulent man with a shock of unruly brown-gray hair and distinctive pouches under his eyes. He always had a smile on his face.

We spoke about mutual friends for a while and then he launched into it: The owner of the *Jewish News,* Richard Pratt, had been convinced by Sam to bid for the *Jerusalem Post* when it had come up for sale the year before. Pratt, he said, was one of the wealthiest men in Australia, having made his fortune in the paper and packaging industry, enjoyed owning the *News,* and wanted to be more involved in the mainstream international Jewish community.

But the bid failed, as did several others, including that of the Canadian Jewish philanthropist Charles Bronfman, because Hollinger, a Canadian publishing company headed by Conrad Black, not one of our brethren and not previously known for any interest in Israel at all, came in with the astounding bid of $22 million, over three times the estimated value of the paper. No one could believe it. I thought the Saudis were behind it, playing a joke on the Jewish people.

The *Post* now lost, Lipski said, Pratt was still determined to publish something out of Israel and wanted to know my thoughts. I told him there was no room for a second English daily in Israel as there was no advertising base to justify it and the audience of English readers in the country had shrunk alarmingly as the old German Jews died off and tourism dried up with the continuing Intifada. What there was a place for, I said, was an international Jewish magazine that would inform Jews about Jews wherever they may be. There were hundreds of local Jewish papers around the globe, and the *Post* put out a weekly international edition, but it was a cut-and-paste job of the previous six dailies, not a product carefully thought out to cater to the needs of the international community.

Thus was born *The Jerusalem Report,* but only after a difficult period of false starts, missteps and extraordinary effort. A few months into the project, in April 1989, Pratt went through a major financial crisis. The banks in Australia pressured him to consolidate his business affairs, which meant closing us down. I had already hired sixteen people, signed on major renovations to a building in downtown Jerusalem and had placed orders for tens of thousands of dollars worth of equipment, so I flew to Melbourne to reason with Pratt and his financial advisors.

He was not a pleasant man and neither was the meeting. Pratt, his wife Jeanne and son Anthony picked me up at noon from my hotel and took me out to a posh Italian restaurant for lunch. The owner almost scraped the floor when we walked in he bowed so low. Pratt, who had made his fortune in cardboard packaging and clever investments, was obviously a revered customer.

It all started out well enough as I showed them page proofs and pictures of the building, but then we got to the business plan. Anthony, who had arrived smelling of Scotch and had had several more through lunch, suddenly exploded.

"You fucken thief," he screamed at me. "You're trying to rob us," lunging across the table, the veins in his neck looking as if they were about to pop, his eyes as red as his hair. The entire restaurant was looking in our direction, knowing glances being exchanged between the diners. Apparently Anthony Pratt was not unknown in the city.

I arrived back at my hotel room in a deep depression. Anthony had calmed down toward the end of the meal and had mumbled an apology of sorts at his mother's urging, but his father remained determined to close the operation down. He told me to phone Israel that night and freeze all work, which I did, but I got an overnight extension from him on a final decision.

The next morning in his office on a very high floor of a Melbourne skyscraper, Pratt remained pugnacious. He told me I had "no balls" and was a "crybaby." All sorts of things get started and then canceled. He had lost hundreds of millions of dollars almost overnight, so what if I had to fire sixteen people back home and cut off paying creditors. He had just fired over a hundred people, he told me almost boastingly.

There was just the two of us in the room. I said it was easy to sit up here real close to the sky, the world at your feet, and issue orders firing people. I knew every one of the people I had hired away from secure jobs. I had placed my signature on contracts on his instructions and those of his senior management. My credibility was on the line. Instead of killing the project, let's find partners, I said. Charles Bronfman had also bid for the *Post*, I reminded him. Perhaps he would be interested, I suggested.

His response was bellicose. "I'm not crawling to anyone for money," he said.

"Then I'm going to make your name mud in the Jewish world. Don't fuck with me and don't fuck with my name," I said, amazed at the words coming out of my mouth, hardly believing it was me speaking. "As a journalist all I have going for me is my credibility and you are not going to take it away. I don't care how rich you are. You dirty my name and your name goes with it."

He looked at me with utter hatred, his huge, flat face about to explode under his bushy eyebrows. "Lipski will write the letter to Bronfman," he said. "Now get out of my office and out of my face," which I was more than happy to do.

"Give my love to Anthony," I said, and turned to leave, our relations to remain a shambles ever since.

I was lecturing in Los Angeles about a month later when I got a call that Bronfman was prepared to see me. Thankfully, meeting Charles was not only a totally different experience, but an exhilarating one as well.

Bronfman was a pixie of a man with twinkly eyes and a slight stoop, who was unpretentious, welcoming, warm and intelligent. I liked him immediately. Since then we and our families have become best friends and neighbors in Jerusalem. I showed him the dummy layouts we had prepared, presented the business plan and made a commitment to have the first edition out by the end of 1990 if I could secure financing. He listened politely, thought for a few moments and said that he was prepared to invest, but there was a condition: "An international Jewish magazine needs an international group of Jewish owners." We needed at least five owners, he said. "That will allow us to spread the losses and you to keep your editorial independence."

With Bronfman on board, finding additional investors became doable and within two months we had our group of five: Pratt from Australia, Bronfman from Canada, Daniel Abrahams—"Mr. SlimFast"—from New York, Stephen Floersheimer, an investment banker from Zurich, and, in Israel, Jonathan Kolber, then head of Claridge, a Bronfman investment firm in which he had a partnership. The first issue appeared in October 1990, initially as a weekly and later a biweekly. By the time I handed over the editorship in 1998 when it was sold to, ironically, the *Jerusalem Post*, *The Report* had a circulation of 56,000 in over seventy countries and had placed many an important issue on the international Jewish agenda, as it continues to do today.

In the meantime Yitzhak Shamir, chin always thrust forward in defiance, was becoming known as "Mr. Nyet" given his habit of saying "No" to every single initiative to try to end the Intifada. This brought Israel's relations with the United States to their lowest point ever. Then, after seven months of shuttle diplomacy by U.S. Secretary of State James Baker, Shamir finally agreed in October 1991 to allow Israel to attend the Madrid Conference, where Israel and its Arab neighbors, including official Palestinian representatives, albeit as part of the Jordanian delegation, sat face-to-face for the first time since the 1949 Rhodes Armistice Talks.

Other than keeping Israel out of the first Gulf War, though the country was attacked with thirty-nine Iraqi missiles, which caused mass panic, cost millions in civil defense procedures, but inflicted no casualties, Shamir's accomplishments in office were unremarkable. It was only because he was known for his right-wing obduracy that he could resist the pressure from his generals, particularly Ehud Barak, then chief of staff, to retaliate. The George Bush administration had made it clear that Israeli retaliation would not be appreciated as the administration was determined that the war not be perceived as an American war against the Arabs but rather an international response to Saddam Hussein and the tyrant's decision to invade Kuwait. Had Israel intervened, the Americans feared, it would have lost its Arab coalition partners, particularly the Syrians, and the war would have taken on an entirely different tone.

Then on a balmy summer day in July 1992 the Israeli electorate said "Nyet" to Shamir and the Likud, and voted Yitzhak Rabin and Labor in with 44 seats to the Likud's 32. Meretz, the leftist socialist pro-peace party, came in with 12 seats and Shas, a relatively new political phenomenon comprising ultra-Orthodox Sephardic voters, with 6. This gave Rabin a coalition for a major restructuring of national priorities. Shas was, at the time, pro-peace and had no sentimental attachment to settlements, especially if the funds diverted from settlements went into their causes.

Over 1,200 Palestinians had died in the Intifada that Rabin as Defense Minister had earlier dismissed as just another demonstration, almost a hundred of them under the age of 18. Israel had over 14,000 Palestinians in make-shift jails like Ketziot in the Negev and around 2,000 homes had been demolished in punitive actions. Rabin knew it had to end.

Rabin appointed his archrival within the party Shimon Peres, a dove, as foreign minister as a signal that he was serious about peace. And with the skilled pen of Eitan Haber, whom Rabin named head of the prime minister's office, Rabin's first Knesset speech was eloquent and left no doubt as to which direction he intended to take the country.

From the same Knesset podium where the late Anwar Sadat had made his plea for peace between the nations of the region, Rabin now invited the joint Palestinian-Jordanian delegation to the Madrid talks to come to Jerusalem "not to speak of a peace process, but to make peace." He promised the country's youth "that the day will come when there will be peace, there will be a better future, *she yom yavo*—the day will come." It seemed that Israel, finally, was emerging from the darkness, that the forty years of intermittent fighting to maintain our nationhood were coming to an end. There was a sense of optimism and hope, a feeling that the country had the right leadership in place.

Rabin had an agenda and he intended to implement it. Immigrants from the former Soviet Union were flooding into the country. These immigrants needed jobs. Investment would not come as long as there was instability and conflict with the Palestinians. Peace was therefore necessary if Israel were to absorb the blessing arriving on its doorstep; it desperately needed economic development. At the same time the country's infrastructure needed to be revolutionized, resources had to be redirected from settlements to education, health and absorption.

Things moved very quickly. In September 1992 Rabin went to Cairo for the first visit to Egypt by an Israeli prime minister in six years. Talks between Israeli academics Yair Hirschfield and Ron Pundak and the senior PLO official Abu Ala and his assistants in Oslo developed into secret negotiations led by Uri Savir, Peres's trusted aide and the director-general of the Foreign Ministry, and Abu Ala, with the full knowledge of both Rabin and Arafat, but with the Americans being kept out of the loop.

After stubbornly refusing to negotiate directly with the PLO or Arafat for years, thinking he could deal instead with the local Palestinian leadership in the West Bank and Gaza, or through the Jordanians, Rabin understood by the middle of 1993 that he had no choice. In September he signed a Declaration of Principles, the Oslo Accords, on the White House lawn with a beaming President Bill Clinton looking on. Rabin and Arafat, after some hesitation, shook hands. The look on Rabin's face was one of pure agony.

For the Israeli right Rabin was a traitor. He had agreed to the principle of a Palestinian state in *Eretz Yisrael*, he had shaken the hand of a terrorist, a man who had slaughtered innocent men, women and children for years, and he was going to uproot settlements built in the name of God. Rabin further inflamed things by dismissively calling the settlers *"kugelagers,"* or ball bearings, and mockingly referring to the West Bank towns of Ariel and Immanuel as *"Shmariel"* and *"Shmanuel."*

He said his intention was to leave isolated settlements outside settlement blocs to "dry up on the vine." At times he was so abusive to the settlers that even I, a Rabin admirer ever since we met in the Sinai in the Six Day War, started questioning his style. "Rabin has led us into the Oslo process. Now he has to lead us through it. Leadership is not cursing and demeaning those who do not agree with you," I wrote in *The Jerusalem Report.*

In the same column, "The Enemy Within," published in the November 2, 1995, issue of the magazine just days before Rabin's assassination, I wrote: "Israelis have a new enemy. Themselves. The political divide has grown deep and wide, and hysteria and hatred have replaced debate. Friends who think differently are shouting at each other and a culture of violence has permeated the atmosphere. The nation's leaders are being physically and verbally attacked wherever they go and rational voices on the right are being shouted down."

It did not take a prophet to predict what this future held. *The Report*'s offices at the time were in downtown Jerusalem, the scene of many right-wing demonstrations where Rabin was often depicted on posters dressed in Arafat's *kaffiya,* or with his face in the center of a bull's-eye, the word "Traitor" painted across it in blood red. Black coffins carrying Rabin effigies were paraded through the streets and a group of extreme right-wingers led by Avigdor Eskin recited the dreaded *Pulsa Dinora,* a prayer condemning someone to eternal damnation, outside his Jerusalem residence. He was even jostled and cursed at what was supposed to be a civilized English-type picnic organized by the Anglo-Saxon community at a sports club near Netanya.

I interviewed Rabin in his Jerusalem office for *The Report* in late October. We met at lunchtime on a busy day when members of his own party were threatening to bolt and demand an early election. Uri Dromi, the head of the Government Press Office, and Cathy Rath, a talented photographer specially chosen for the assignment by the magazine's art department, were the only people in the room other than the prime minister. A waitress came in with two bottles of Goldstar beer and one glass and placed them next to Rabin. We were not even offered coffee. He was wearing a dark suit, a blue silk tie with a checkered pattern on it and a light blue shirt that matched his eyes. His hair was thin, white and combed back and he sat comfortably at the edge of a gray chair, an

Israeli flag in the background, always in arm's reach of his cigarettes and ashtray.

I asked him about his brewing political troubles and he told me to cut the small talk. I asked him about the vociferousness of the demonstrations against him and he said that he had told me to cut the small talk. Instead it was straight to business, in which he outlined his conditions for peace with the Syrians, saying that the depth of Israel's withdrawal from the Golan would be the same as the depth of peace. If the Syrians wanted full normal commercial and diplomatic relations, then full withdrawal was possible.

As I was leaving he asked me if I had noticed that the entire road from Tel Aviv to Jerusalem had been illuminated with electric lights. He was very proud of the achievement. I then said I thought it would be a good idea if he gave *The Report* another interview in time for the upcoming Council of Jewish Federations' General Assembly in Boston in late November. His relations with the American Jewish community had been strained and I said this would be a good way to level the field in advance of his speech. He nodded to Uri and told him to schedule the meeting, which was set for Monday, November 7, in the late afternoon.

In the Prologue to a book later put out jointly by *The Report*'s staff I recounted how several years before he had explained to me while we were waiting in a side room at the Jerusalem Laromme Hotel, now the Inbal, that as a general one sent people into battle. In peace, as in war, those you lead will not always fully understand what they are being asked to do and peace, like war, will have its casualties, he said. Little did he know, or perhaps he did know, that he would be added to the list on Saturday night, November 5, 1995, when he was shot and killed by Yigal Amir minutes after awkwardly singing the "Song of Peace" together with a crowd of tens of thousands who had gathered in the square outside Tel Aviv's city hall to call for an end to violence and the beginnings of peace. *"Yom Yavo"*—The day will come, he told them.

PART FIVE

CONQUEST
AND
CONSEQUENCES

13

SHAI

*Young Shai and myself on the morning he was inducted into
the Israeli army, February 13, 1989, for the start of a
miserable three years in a unit specially formed to fight
the Intifada, the first Palestinian uprising.*

ONE FRIDAY EVENING IN THE THIRD WEEK of January 1991, when the first Gulf War was at its height, I drove out to the Christian Palestinian town of Beit Jalla near Bethlehem, where my son Shai was stationed doing the third and last year of his compulsory military service. At the time of his induction he had said that he was prepared to do anything the army required of him other than serving in the occupied territories.

The officer at the intake center listened politely and answered that if good, sensitive boys like Shai refused to serve in the territories who would the army send? Animals? So Shai did what they told him to and agreed to join a new unit, one of two the army established to deal specifically with the Intifada. The idea was that these men would be stationed in one area for almost the entire duration of their service, get to know the locals, the streets, nooks and crannies and thus be better able to deal with the uprising.

He was billeted in the Panorama Hotel at the top of a hill, past the furniture dealers whose shops were now shuttered, their walls painted thick with ever-changing Intifada graffiti and the houses built of Jerusalem stone with twisted Eiffel Towers of television antennae atop their red roofs.

We had often taken Shai and his sister Maya to the Panorama as children, usually on a Saturday for lunch after visiting the nearby monastery of Cremisan, where we bought wine from red-nosed French monks, or Bethlehem with its great markets, antique stores, money changers, non-kosher butchers and incredible sense of history. The Panorama had been a happy place. It had a little park with swings, a merry-go-round and a seesaw within sight of the tables so the adults could eat while the children played. The service was friendly and efficient and the food always delicious.

Now the swings were rusty, the seesaw broken and the once welcoming entrance piled high with sandbags and guarded by two suspicious soldiers in full battle gear. The courtyard, once alive with geraniums in locally made earthen pots, was home to a roaring generator, also protected by sandbags. The lobby had been converted into a dining room with a long wooden table and wooden benches on a muddy floor, and the reception area was a buzzing communications center with khaki-colored radio receivers piled atop each other.

Shai's room was on the third floor. He was fast asleep between two coarse blankets, his clothes still on, snoring heavily. One of his friends who had just come out of the shower said Shai had come in from eighteen hours of straight work. His friend did not know the details, just another raid he presumed, knocking down doors in the early hours of the morning looking for suspects the security services wanted to question, dragging men away from their families as women and children screamed and cursed and spat at the soldiers. As Shai told me later, he had actually spent the night making men in their fifties and sixties wash anti-occupation graffiti off walls with toothbrushes while their children, the force behind the Intifada and the authors of the hastily sprayed slogans, watched their fathers and grandfathers be humiliated.

His clothes were dank with sweat and his socks had that particular army smell. He looked so innocent. My heart went out to him. He so much did not want to be here, but being a "good boy" he had gone where they sent him and slowly but surely formed into the soldier the army wanted. Peer pressure, relentless training, the same sense of brotherhood I had felt with my comrades soon overshadowed all, and he managed to justify his duties by convincing himself that what he did saved lives. They knew the territory and they knew the people. Soldiers unfamiliar with the topography, with the narrow winding alleys, would overreact and use their weapons at every threat.

That is what Shai believed while in uniform. Immediately after he finished his military service in 1991 he left for India. He traveled the country extensively, spending the summers in the high hills at Manali and the winters on the beach in Goa, and his fascination with India grew as his stay extended from one year to two to three.

One November night in 1993 over dinner in Vienna, where he was selling posters on the pavement outside the main railway station earning money for yet another stay in India, I asked him why he did not come home to Israel for a while, study, be with family and friends. "I can't Daddy," he replied. "I am too angry. I will never forgive the country for what it made me do."

His eyes flashed defiantly. So this was why he preferred the beach in Goa to the lecture halls of Hebrew University, the heights of Manali to the reserves, pot to his mother's cooking and scruffy friends to his family. Not laziness but white hot anger and disgust with his people, what he had done in their name and what he had done to himself.

I had been there when the occupation was sown and Shai had eaten its bitter fruits. After the initial fighting in 1967, while the spoils of war were being assessed, our unit was billeted at the looted though still opulent El Arish Officer's Club located in a majestic palm grove on the Mediterranean. The Club had a very British feel to it with a squash court, overstuffed leather chairs in the billiard room, silver cutlery and delicate crockery in the mess, marble in the bathrooms. Six of us were allotted a room with a sea view, given boxes of emergency rations and told to cook for ourselves. We were to be at parade each morning at seven, when we would be assigned our duties, which turned out to be patrolling El Arish and securing its key installations such as the railway station, power supply, military airport, water plant and bridges.

Unlike the Palestinians in Gaza, where the hatred for Israelis was palpable, the people of El Arish seemed quite happy to see us, offering us bottles of Seven Up, papayas and oranges as we drove through the streets and patrolled the markets. It took a while to understand that the smiles were smiles of fear and the food offerings not of hospitality but supplication. They were used to being occupied. The Turks, British and countless others had been there before us, but they had yet to figure the Israelis out.

There was power in being an occupier, swaggering through the streets, submachine guns slung over our shoulders, red berets perched on our heads. There was also a tacit assumption that some rules were made to be broken. Thus, almost inexorably, as if by some de facto sanction, each of us started showing up with dubiously earned acquisitions. Finnie arrived with four mattresses that he claimed he had swapped for two camels he had found wandering around near the airport. Ziegler came in with a gas ring and a set of pots he had "found." I happened to "find" some plates and a few books in one of the houses we had

searched for suspects. Moyal came in with a magnificent crystal chande-
lier that we hung from the ceiling though we had no electricity.

And then, more and more, we found ourselves being dispatched to
operations in Gaza where the scene was totally different. Its population
of 600,000 was primarily refugees who had left homes in Jaffa, Ramle,
Lod and dozens of other towns and villages during the 1948 war. The
relative safety of Egyptian-controlled Gaza had offered a refuge. Now,
twenty years later, they were still refugees being fed and educated by the
United Nations and living in abject misery in refugee camps that reminded me, I could not help it, of the Black Locations like Soweto and
Alexandria back in Johannesburg.

In the refugee camps the hatred was intense and danger omnipresent.
The alleys were narrow and the shadows dark. There were pockets of
armed Palestinian resistance. There were no smiles, no offerings of pa-
paya or Seven Up, but a wall of resentment, of young people bred in misery, told stories of their former homes just over the sand dunes, stolen
and destroyed by the Jews. They were a people, to paraphrase the Israeli
diplomat Abba Eban, with only more tunnel at the end of the light.

I watched our behavior change as the scene got uglier and more
threatening. When Ariel Sharon and his hit team were assigned to clean
up the viper's nest that Gaza had become, we cleaned up after them by
imposing curfews while people were taken in for questioning.

Once, and again in Sidon during another war, I happened to stumble
into a school courtyard that had been taken over by the military interrogation unit. "The Monkey," as informers were nicknamed, was sitting in
the back of a jeep, his head covered by a burlap sack with two holes for
his eyes cut in the rough cloth. Men were brought before him one at a
time and he signaled with his index finger, the only part of his body visible, whether the person should go to the left or the right. To the left
waited freedom. To the right was to be lined up for questioning, made to
sit in the sun, hands bound from behind with plastic ties, tightly blindfolded with the cloth one uses to clean a rifle, DDT powder sprinkled
on their heads to humiliate them, forced to do their needs where they
sat, waiting to be questioned. When summoned they were brought to

the entrance of what was once a classroom. There the blindfold was removed just in time to see two Israeli soldiers dragging a corpse out of the room. The man up for questioning could not know that the same corpse was used in this exercise over and over. Once discovered I was quickly herded out of the schoolyard. It remained with me forever.

There was another scene that has always stayed in my mind. In 1967 saboteurs had been laying mines on the railway out of Sinai. The railway line was crucial for bringing the weapons left behind by the fleeing Egyptian army to depots in Israel where they would be integrated into the Israeli army, cannibalized or sold to a third party.

Increasingly frustrated by the delays, our commanders ordered the tracks patrolled in advance of the trains and ambushes set at points from where attacks were anticipated. Both tactics failed as we did not have enough manpower to be all places all of the time. Then it was decided to have two flatbed railway cars loaded with sandbags and barrels of water placed ahead of the engine to absorb the shock of the mines. This saved the engines, but still caused delays while derailed cars were moved from the tracks.

Then someone had an idea: One day while we were eating lunch, Nehemiah, our sergeant, strode into the mess and designated about ten of us to follow him. We split into four jeeps, drove to the Khan Yunis railway station, then into the center of the adjacent refugee camp and, using loudspeakers, declared a curfew. We then ordered all men between the ages of 15 and 25 out of their houses promising them no harm. About twenty men walked out, their hands above their heads. Their relatives could be heard wailing and crying, praying to Allah, through the thin doors of the shack dwellings, this hell on earth these people called home.

The two flatbed trucks had been cleared of their water barrels and, our guns at the ready, we ordered the young men to start filling sandbags and placing two rows of them around. It was for their protection, we explained, and then ordered them to climb aboard for the journey from Khan Yunis to El Arish and back. They were to serve as human shields against attack from their own people.

The *Fedayeen* stopped planting the mines, but I remember being deeply troubled performing a roundup in a refugee camp, barking orders into a microphone, separating young men from the old, women from husbands, children from fathers, brothers from sisters, marching people at gunpoint onto a train, fear, loathing, hatred, pride, defiance all reflected in wide-open eyes.

Sitting with Shai in Vienna, all those days came back to me. Though heady with victory at the time and awed at visiting the Old City of Jerusalem, touching the Western Wall, driving to the Dead Sea and visiting Jericho, going to Abraham's tomb in Hebron and Rachel's tomb in Bethlehem, seeing the Garden of Gethsemane, the Church of the Holy Sepulcher, the absolute beauty of Samaria and the hills around Jenin, it quickly became clear to me that the occupation was a curse that would consume us from within.

But occupation and conquest were not generally on peoples' minds in the immediate wake of the 1967 war. That would come later. On June 16, just days after the guns fell silent, Israel forwarded an offer through the Americans to Egypt and Syria to return the territories conquered with some minor border adjustments in return for peace. In November, UN Resolution 242 was passed, which was built on the principle of territory in return for peace, Israel agreeing to the resolution only after the word "all" was removed from its place in front of the word "territory." Israel continued to plan for minor border modifications to address specific Israeli military concerns, not perpetual conquest.

At the heart of articulating Israel's policies in the territories was then defense minister Moshe Dayan. Dayan was born and raised in Palestine, drank tea with the Bedouin as a small boy, knew every nook and cranny of the land, was deeply attached to its history and spoke Arabic. He respected the Arabs and their customs and knew of their attachment to their land. In the hope of pacifying the situation until a diplomatic solution could be found, his first order to General Chaim Herzog, the first military governor appointed in the territories and later Israeli president, which then filtered down to us, was clear: Let the people govern themselves; stay out of their lives; have a military presence only where absolutely necessary; work with existing institutions such as hospitals and UN agencies to maintain normal life in the territories; and do everything possible not to become a conquering force. Predicting that Israel would be in the territories for two to four years, Dayan explained to Herzog and the army that Israel should arrange matters so that an Arab could be born, live and die in the West Bank without ever seeing an Israeli official.

Despite his enormous arrogance, Dayan was treated like a prophet in his time, but it is now clear that he was so blinded by his own sense of invincibility that he did not understand the consequences of what had happened in 1967. His assumption that Israel's stay in the territories would be short-lived was horrendously off the mark, as was his understanding of the Arab world he professed to know so well. He did not understand that the issue had become one of grievously wounded pride, that the Arabs had been soundly humbled, and as everything in their life experience, their education and even their sense of manhood evolved around pride, this humiliation would prove intolerable. A coalition of great Arab nations armed to the teeth had been ignobly defeated by three million Jews defending a precariously positioned country with indefensible borders, and they had accomplished this during an arms embargo imposed by its principal ally and supplier, France. Dayan assumed that the neighboring Arab countries would be quick to make peace in return for the territories. But the defeated Arab countries did not want territory in return for peace—they wanted revenge, to correct the imbalance, to regain the pride.

The June 16 offer disappeared into the trash bin of history. Instead, Egypt immediately started preparing for the next round. Nasser, who had resigned in disgrace, was now brought back by popular demand, his generals and defense minister left to take the rap for the defeat of 1967. On September 1, at Egypt's instigation, the Khartoum Arab Summit issued its historic resolution: "No peace. No negotiation. No recognition."

In October, using newly acquired missiles from the Soviet Union, the Egyptians sank an Israeli naval destroyer, the Eilat, 20 kilometers off Port Said on the Mediterranean coast. The incident took place outside Egyptian territorial waters, killing 47. Israel responded with a massive bombardment of Egyptian positions along the Suez Canal. The refineries at Suez City were totally destroyed and Ismailia was evacuated. We were rushed from Gaza to the Suez Canal and back to Gaza and then down to the Jordanian border over which *Fedayeen* attacks into Israel were multiplying in intensity. Clearly Israel's wars with the Arabs were far from over.

The areas taken in the war took on a new significance, cards for peace became vital strategic assets. The 1948 cease-fire lines at the end of the War of Independence had left Israel with a border that looked like an elongated kidney. At one point, the state was only 9 kilometers wide between the Mediterranean and the Jordanian border. In the north the country narrowed to a sliver between Lebanon and Syria like a finger thrust between them, with the Syrians atop the Golan Heights being able to shoot into the Galilee below at will and controlling Israel's water sources. Israel's borders with Egypt and Jordan were long, vulnerable and porous. In 1967 the Egyptians had planned to cut Israel in half by rushing through the undefended Negev to the Jordanian border. They were foiled by a brilliant Israeli deception that included loudspeakers creating enough noise to be a division on the move at night.

Israel was now atop the Golan Heights within striking distance of Damascus. Syrian gunners could no longer shell towns and settlements in the Galilee. Israel was now in total control of all of the Kinneret, the Sea of Galilee, Israel's principal water resource, so Syria could no longer divert the water as it had done in the 1960s. If Syria's answer to the June 16 proposal was "the three no's of Khartoum," better to be on the Golan than at Syria's mercy at its foothills. Better to be atop Mount Hermon with early warning stations that could look and listen into every corner of Syria than in the Galilee from where one could see nothing. If there were to be a future war it would be fought on Syrian territory.

And if there were to be another war with Egypt, better it take place in the desert, with the Suez Canal as a hurdle to Egyptian armor. In a war, control of Sharm el Sheikh on the southern tip of Sinai would become critical for Israel's southern supply route. For some pragmatists, the territories provided strategic depth and bargaining cards for the future when the Arabs finally came to understand that one Holocaust was enough and three million Jews were not going to swim away. But the territories were also seen literally as a godsend by the emerging national religious movements, later to be at the forefront of the ideological settler movement.

The original Land of Israel Movement ideologues who in August 1967 demanded that Israel never give away the newly acquired biblical heartland were not nationalists but romantics. They called the West Bank Judea and Samaria. The Jewish people got their name from Judea. This is where Abraham, Isaac and Jacob had walked and lived. Abraham was buried in Hebron. This was the land Joshua had entered and conquered, that King Solomon had consolidated. This was a land where every knoll, road and hilltop could be found in the Bible just as you could find them on any contemporary map. For them this was the real Land of Israel, the land of milk and honey Moses had pointed to from Mount Nebo. This, not the beaches of Tel Aviv or the steaming markets of Jaffa, the Port of Ashdod or Arab Lod and Ramle, was the true biblical home of the Jewish people. The founder of the movement, Moshe Tabenkin, was from the Achdut Avoda party, slightly right of Ben-Gurion's Mapai but still well left on the Israeli political spectrum. The poet Haim Guri, the songwriter Naomi Shemer and Moshe Shamir, the writer and poet, were far from the ideological right.

It would not be too long, however, before the Land of Israel Movement, comprising mainly liberal socialists who would have shuddered at the thought of placing Palestinians under curfew, destroying homes as a collective punishment or making middle-aged men scrub graffiti off walls with toothbrushes, saw its ideas hijacked, distorted, transformed into nationalistic fervor and, ultimately, turned into a new religion that professed to speak in God's name. Gush Emunim, the Bloc of the Faithful, was founded in the same year Shai was born, 1971. It preached the Oneness of the land of Israel. At its spiritual helm was Rabbi Zvi Yehuda Kook, son of the former Chief Rabbi of Israel, Avraham Isaac Kook, who had preached as early as the 1930s that the Jewish return to *Eretz Yisrael,* the Land of Israel, was divinely ordained, that the link between the people of Israel and the Land of Israel was inviolate, and that to give up this land would be sacrilege.

The secular Land of Israel Movement, the messianic Gush Movement, the powerful Herut Party headed by Menachem Begin that saw a greater Israel on both sides of the Jordan, and strategists insisting on territorial depth were all to converge in the early 1970s into a powerful force that today has created a situation where separation between Israel and Palestine is almost impossible. Back then no one seemed too concerned about the 1.2 million Palestinians living on the West Bank and Gaza. It was as if they were a non-people, only a civil administration problem.

It was the same for me then. I was so proud of Israel's victory that I decided to change my name, like all pilots and diplomats were required to do, into Hebrew. After much consultation with my Ulpan teacher Moshe and several friends, I settled on Yetiv (from *tov,* which means good) for Goodman. Hirsh (which means a deer in Yiddish) would now be Tzvi (deer in Hebrew). Tzvi Yetiv, the new Hirshie Goodman. I thought my father would be proud. After all he was a Hebrew teacher, a proponent of reviving Hebrew as a living language and an ardent Zionist. When he received my letter with the news he wrote back saying simply that the name was certainly a good translation, but that when Mr. Yetiv walked into his lawyer's office to hear his will, his lawyer, unfortunately, would have no idea who this Yetiv was.

Now I was sitting in Vienna with Shai, who could not bring himself to come home.

14

PARADISE IN HELL

*In April 1982, Israeli bulldozers, under orders from then defense minister
Ariel Sharon, razed the northwestern Israeli town of Yamit to the ground
in the context of a peace agreement with Sinai. It now seems that
Israel's settlements in the Gaza Strip face the same future.*
(Copyright Joel Kantor)

BACK IN EARLY NOVEMBER OF 1972, on my first official magazine assignment, I left home in Jerusalem before dawn and headed for Kfar Darom in the southern Gaza Strip. Kfar Darom was a kibbutz lost to the Egyptians in the 1948 war and was now being reestablished by soldiers from the Nahal Brigade. An aide to Israel Galili, the minister in charge of settlement in Golda Meir's government and, many suspected, the real power behind it, had phoned a few days before and said that the minister would like to invite a few members of the press on a tour of Gaza so that he could "explain the strategic importance of Gaza and Israel's plans for its future." We were to meet at Kfar Darom at 10 A.M.

As always when I drive through Israel, the trip to Kfar Darom reminded me what a beautiful country this is. The forests of the Jerusalem hills, down to the Latrun Plain with its majestic Trappist monastery, where one of the pilots who dropped the atomic bomb on Hiroshima was rumored to live as a monk, landscapes of wheatfields and vineyards, the branches of the barren vines covered in early morning dew.

And then, traveling west toward the Mediterranean coast and south to Gaza, miles upon miles of rich farmland, orchards of oranges, pecan nuts, pears, plums, the trees planted as neatly as soldiers on parade. Onward past Kibbutz Yad Mordechai, named after Mordechai Anielewicz, the hero who led the Warsaw Ghetto uprising against the Nazis, and that, unlike Kfar Darom, stood its ground against the Egyptians despite being heavily outgunned in the 1948 war. Shortly beyond the kibbutz lay the Erez checkpoint, the gateway to hell.

Once inside Gaza, the road immediately deteriorated into more potholes than tar. Tanks, armored personnel carriers and military jeeps darted along, narrowly avoiding the ubiquitous Palestinian donkey carts. At almost every turn vendors were trying to sell oranges or whatever else was seasonal, competition being fierce given that nearly everyone seemed to be selling the same thing. This was the sole source of income for many Palestinians. The poverty was palpable.

Then I came upon the refugee camps that string Gaza City. First I drove through Jabaliya, a hapless, hopeless, mud-covered place. The school was built with mud-covered cinder blocks. Its playground, with two thin wooden goalposts painted white, was all mud. The houses that lined the mud roads were also made of cinder blocks and fortified with corrugated tin sheets. Again I thought of Alexandria and Soweto and the other Black townships of my boyhood. No lights, no water, no sanitation, muddy in the winter and hellish hot in the summer, a breeding ground for despair and hatred that could only deepen with each year of continued occupation.

Kfar Darom, as its name suggests (*darom* meaning "south" in Hebrew), was at the southern end of the Strip, just before the barren dunes of Rafiah and, as fate would have it, exactly where the UN camp had been where we had found all those tins of pineapple five years earlier in the opening days of the Six Day War. It seemed surreal that I was on my way to hear about Israel's settlement plans for the region. Why would any Israeli want to settle here? It was one of the more miserable places on earth and arguably harbored the greatest concentration of anti-Israel sentiment on the planet. Already Gaza had one of the highest population densities in the world and one of the fastest-growing populations. Kfar Darom was situated at the point where the heavily populated Palestinian towns and refugee camps of Nusseirat, Muazi, El Burej and Dir el Balah converge. It would be a Jewish settlement of less than a hundred young religious men and women soldiers from the Bnei Akiva youth movement in a sea of Palestinians more than a thousand times their number.

What reason could there possibly be for Israel to undertake responsibility for the 660,000 local people, a good proportion of whom subsisted totally or partially on international aid? Why settle Gaza when the Negev was empty? Why build a home in a sea of enmity?

But who was I to ask. I had only been on the job for three months, had been hired by default and knew nothing of the geostrategic complexities that ministers and war heroes such as Moshe Dayan and Yigal Allon and others around the cabinet table had weighed so carefully before drafting government policy. Or so we all assumed.

I arrived at Kfar Darom at about nine in the morning. On passing through its gates, the world of mud and misery I had just driven through disappeared. The settlement consisted of several prefabricated concrete buildings placed around a quadrangle within a fenced compound. A neat lawn surrounded by rose beds and a path marked by two parallel rows of freshly whitewashed stones formed the centerpiece around which the settlement's buildings had been placed. A freshly painted white flagpole stood in the center, the Israeli flag fluttering in the brisk morning breeze.

At the far end of the quadrangle, to the side of the dining hall, was an area shaded by camouflage netting. There chairs were placed in front of a long table covered with a starched white cloth with four clusters of small Israeli flags placed equidistant on it and jugs of orange juice placed between them. At the other end of the netting was a second table laden with fruit, cans of red juice, biscuits, *burekas,* coffee, and tiny savories of sliced hard-boiled eggs and black olives, salmon and cream cheese. No sense of poverty here.

I struck up a conversation with a few of the young soldier-settlers. With great pride they told me how they had managed despite all odds to plant a hundred *dunam,* twenty-five acres, of assorted vegetables in land thought to be barren. They then took me to see the local industry. About twenty young women soldiers were working in a shed under the sharp eye of an old man with white hair nicknamed Saba, grandpa, cutting leather according to cardboard patterns for what would eventually be the upper part of paratrooper boots, later to be joined to soles imported from Italy. Lots of civilians, they told me, were expected to arrive soon to take over from the army. They pointed me in the direction of four caravan homes the Jewish Agency's settlement department had trucked in a few days before.

Galili and his entourage arrived on time, the minister himself being driven in a large gray Chevrolet with a bevy of Jewish Agency officials and two or three army officers, presumably from the local military administration, in tow. A flustered young aide quickly set up a row of easels and placed on them a series of large aerial photographs and maps with blue, red and green lines scrawled wildly across them. He laid a long wooden pointing stick on the table and disappeared into the crowd.

The guests now numbered about forty, half being members of the press: military correspondents to report the strategic importance of what was said; agricultural reporters who were expected to fill tomorrow's papers with stories of new technologies that would benefit all the people of the region; political reporters to ensure that Mapai, the governing party, got its mileage for carrying on Ben-Gurion's dream of making the desert bloom (although this desert was in Gaza and not Ben-Gurion's beloved Negev) and a few columnists who would no doubt have much to pontificate on in the coming days.

Galili was a diminutive man, dressed in gray trousers and an open-neck white shirt. He not only looked like Ben-Gurion with the same crown of unruly white hair, but spoke like him as well—the same staccato voice, using the same measured Hebrew, the words coming out like bullets, one at a time, the vision being described crystal clear.

Using the stick to point to the maps and aerial photos, Galili introduced us to what later became known as the "Five Finger Plan": Five corridors of Jewish settlement would be placed through the Strip to ensure that if another war broke out between Israel and Egypt there "will be barriers of defense between us." Galili reminded us that he had told the Knesset in March 1971 that "the Gaza Strip will never be separated from Israel, even after peace is achieved." There "is no contradiction," he argued, "between settlement and negotiation with the Arabs."

He then went on to note the tremendous benefits Israeli settlement in Gaza would bring to the local population. Jobs would be created, Israeli advanced technologies shared, tourism developed, Gaza City's markets and local producers would thrive and, to top it all, Israel's security needs would be served in the most fundamental way. There would be a wedge of settlement along the Egyptian border to ensure that the Egyptians and Gazans would not be able to join up in an attack against Israel; there would be a finger of settlement in the north, cutting off Gaza from Israel proper, and there would be three more fingers going through Gaza from east to west so that if there was ever an uprising against Israel, the Strip could be immediately cut into four segments, which would make the situation more manageable.

Then came the question and answer period. The first questions were asked by people whose names I had only known until then as senior by-lines in the Hebrew press, and I felt somewhat awed in their company. They asked how much this would all cost and what the projected time frame was and what did the minister envision when he spoke of tourism.

There were penetrating questions about the new agricultural techniques revealed by the minister and, as one would expect from a columnist from the lefty Mapam Party newspaper *Al Ha'Mishmar* (On Guard), questions as to whether Arab lands were being expropriated for Jewish settlement. (Galili claimed they were not.)

But no one seemed to question the basic soundness of the concept itself. Why push fingers of Jewish settlement into this already overtaxed piece of unhappy real estate? Why place civilians at risk doing duties the military was supposed to carry out?

I decided to use my mouth for the purpose of eating those delicious little savories rather than to embarrass myself and my newspaper by asking questions no experienced reporter, like those in attendance, with their sources in government and knowledge of what was going on behind the scenes, would even think of asking. Instead we all bought the picture of idyllic beaches, ever-so-clever Israeli technologies turning the dunes of Rafiah into fertile soil and good neighborly relations with the people of Gaza, who had nothing but advancement and prosperity to expect. Paradise on earth or, as I scribbled in my notebook at the time, "paradise in hell????"—a thought I remember sharing with Michael Arnon, the former cabinet secretary, when we drove home together that evening.

A return visit to Kfar Darom in the summer of 2003 was just as surreal. In three decades things had deteriorated for the Palestinians almost beyond belief. The second Intifada that erupted after Ariel Sharon's visit to Temple Mount in September 2000 would soon enter its fourth year. In an attempt to control terror, Gaza's cities had been pummeled by hundreds of Israeli attacks from helicopters, armor and infantry.

The Gush Katif (Harvest Bloc) Regional Council, as envisioned by the Five Finger Plan, now had 6,000 people living on twenty-one settlements. The Jewish population of Gaza was growing all the time, but living in a near-constant state of terror. Over 2,100 mortars and rockets had landed on their homes and fields since the conflict started. Mines had been laid on the roads. People had been shot and killed in their fields or their cars. For many of the Jews, living out Galili's dream had become a nightmare. Either economically or ideologically, they were trapped in a situation that even the most optimistic observers concede is untenable.

To get to the bulk of the Jewish settlements concentrated mainly in the Strip's southwest corner, I entered Gaza via the Kissufim crossing point at the southern end of the Strip, thus negating the need to traverse it from north to south as I did back in 1972. Like Erez, this was now a military checkpoint with buildings protected behind stone walls and massive concrete blocks. A policeman in a flak jacket guarded by a tank on one side and an army machine gun position on the other waved me through after a cursory check that I was not a Palestinian. Past the crossing, the road becomes Jews-only. When the security situation allows, the Palestinians have their own road that runs under a hastily constructed American bridge. This ensures that drivers from either side never meet. If the security situation does not allow free movement, Galili's Five Fingers snap into place, cutting the Strip into sectors sealed off from each other.

Once comfortably on the Jewish road I was greeted by a huge billboard of the Lubavitcher Rebbe bringing the message that the Messiah is on the way. A kilometer or so on, a rustic wooden sign with arrows in various directions pointed to hotels, beaches, restaurants and the offices of the local regional council.

The sign belied a reality far removed from hotels and beaches. Wide areas on both sides of the road had literally been shaved. Olive trees, fruit orchards and buildings had been bulldozed and leveled to the ground, this after the Palestinians kept successfully laying mines and booby traps along the road, killing both soldiers and settlers. By clearing the road's margins, it was hoped, terrorists infiltrating from Gaza would be seen before they could lay their mines. What the Israelis did not take into account was that the terrorists they were fighting did not mind dying for their cause. Indeed, many positively desired to die as a *Shahid* and thus be guaranteed a place in heaven. So instead of crawling through the orchards to lay their mines as they once did, they now sprinted across the cleared margins, throwing themselves against Israeli vehicles in the hope of killing as many Jews as possible.

In desperation the army had then put down row upon row of viciously spiked coils of barbed wire along the entire length of the road; it also erected specially designed concrete pillboxes covered with camouflage nets every few hundred meters and mounted special monitoring cameras on tall poles, enabling it to watch every minute of the day and send pictures back to the various military commands in the area. Extra-bright floodlights had been installed to illuminate every meter of the road at night; tanks and armored personnel carriers were positioned on every hill and machine gun posts were set up on the roofs of the few Palestinian homes that had been allowed to survive. This was probably the most expensive per capita security outlay anywhere in the world.

I did not come to Gush Katif with an open mind. I had thought settlement was crazy thirty years ago, and consider Galili a fine specimen of Israel's post-1967 arrogance. Since the start of the second Intifada, I thought that anyone who continued to live there with their children was either a fanatic or a fool.

I had arranged to meet Anita and Stuart Toker, whose son Amichai is married to my wife's cousin. The Tokers were one of the first seven civilian families to move into Kfar Darom. Together with their three children, they had been in one of the new caravans pointed out to me by the soldier the day of Galili's visit. They now live just a few minutes' drive away at Netzer Hazani, the first civilian settlement built in Gaza after Kfar Darom. The Tokers have two married sons living at Netzer Hazani, each with two children, who are now third-generation Israeli settlers in Gaza. They know no other home.

Ironically the Tokers had never considered living in Gaza as part of their plans. They had arrived as new immigrants from the United States in 1969. She was from Brooklyn, he from Cleveland, he was a teacher of biology and she of geology, both religious. On arrival in Israel they were directed toward Beersheba, an ancient city and the traditional gateway to the Negev, where many new immigrants had been settled and where there was a serious need for teachers.

After five years there, they went to visit friends who had recently moved to a religious *moshav,* a semicollective agricultural community. Unlike a kibbutz, where everything was owned by the collective, on a *moshav* each family retains its integrity and owns its property but shares items such as farm implements and other utilities. For the Tokers this way of life seemed idyllic. While the community was essentially agricultural in nature, a *moshav*'s members were free to hold jobs outside the settlement, which suited Stuart, who wanted to continue teaching. The Tokers thought *moshav* life would be open and healthy and good for the children, that it would offer a higher quality of life and, at the same time, give one the satisfaction of growing their own crops. A sort of suburbia down by the farm was what they had in mind.

But the government of Yitzhak Rabin, who was prime minister at the time, had another vision for their future: Galili's Five Fingers. At the ministry of agriculture, where applications to join an agricultural settlement were made, the Tokers were told that all new applications were being diverted to the national effort to settle Gaza and, fortunately for them, a pioneering new settlement, Kfar Darom, was now accepting members. Not enthralled with the idea of taking three young children to settle Gaza, they approached the settlement department of the Jewish Agency in the hope of being made a better offer as recent immigrants. Like the Agriculture Ministry, the Agency's bureaucrats were categorical: If you want to live on a religious collective agricultural settlement the only thing on offer was Gush Katif. It was, they were told, the Zionist thing to do.

So they did it. They lived in the caravan at Kfar Darom for a little over a year, waking up each morning to a new day on their tiny island in the middle of a hostile Palestinian sea, Stuart traveling to Beersheba to teach and Anita growing more and more interested in agriculture. They then moved to Netzer Hazani with thirteen other families, all Sephardim from nearby development towns. For these people the government-provided homes and hothouses on the dunes of Gaza seemed to promise a better future than jobs in the state-subsidized textile mills.

Reaching Netzer Hazani, I was struck by the sight of a Chinese man driving a lawn-mowing tractor in concentric circles, cutting the round of lawn with a cluster of palm trees in the middle with the same care one would apply to a putting green at some prestigious golf course. Two bored reservists guarded the gate. Once inside the settlement there was a general feeling of neatness, order and harmony. Some seventy families comprising over 500 souls now live in Netzer Hazani (which says something about the birth rate here and on the other Jewish settlements in Gaza). Many, like the youngest Tokers, are third-generation settlers.

Though Netzer Hazani's residents hail from eighteen different countries and backgrounds, they share one synagogue—a rare, possibly even unique phenomenon in the Jewish world. As the world was delighted to note when an Israeli reporter finally made it to Kabul, Afghanistan, after the Taliban fled in 2002, he found that the city's last two Jews were not speaking to each other and prayed at separate synagogues.

The Toker home, like most of the houses at Netzer Hazani, is large without being ostentatious. Anita is an ample woman with a big presence; Stuart is quiet and withdrawn. She invited me to sit down for breakfast at the family's dining room table. The wood-paneled room and inner calm of the place seemed incongruous with the journey I had just taken to get there and the dangers with which they live.

Anita suggested we take a ride in her pickup truck, which, by her own admission, was an incredible mess. Her driving was erratic and jerky as we hurtled through row after row of hothouses, she talking the whole time. Workers from China and Thailand were everywhere, brought in to replace the Palestinians, who could no longer be trusted now that several, even those cleared by the security authorities as "kosher," had killed their bosses in the fields.

"It's a tragedy," Anita told me with absolute sincerity. "When we first got here the *mukhtar* of Dir el Balah, the neighboring town, greeted us with bread and salt, the traditional way one welcomes new neighbors. There was nothing here. Nothing but dunes and dunes and dunes. Not even flies. "For years, until only recently, we worked with the Arabs. They earned a living, were thankful for the work and learned new technologies from us which we happily shared."

Anita grows celery, tons of it in pots in computer-controlled hothouses. Two smiling Thai workers, who she says drink too much, hitched a wagon containing that morning's crop to her truck and we made off for the central packing plant at Kfar Darom. As we drove through the settlement she pointed to house after house where a family member had either been killed, wounded or narrowly escaped death from incoming mortars and rockets, attacks on the roads or other acts of terror. There had been dozens of mortar and rocket attacks in or around the settlement in recent months.

We arrived at the central packing house at Kfar Darom, the place I thought had no future thirty-one years ago. Another Chinese worker was mowing the quadrangle of lawn. The white flagpole was still there, as were some of the original buildings. Behind a twenty-foot-high wall of concrete is Palestinian Dir el Balah, which has probably doubled in population. Kfar Darom by now had sixty families, or a population of about 300 souls, with twenty-two new families registered to join as soon as the houses being built in the shadow of the concrete wall were completed.

The families were all Orthodox, the fathers all students studying at the *Kollel,* a yeshiva for married students. As Anita explained, if you have six or seven children and you are a professional divinity student, Kfar Darom, with its almost free housing, heavy subsidies and excellent educational system tailored to suit your beliefs, becomes quite an attractive proposition, even with all its drawbacks—legions of soldiers (approximately six for each settler) in the front garden, tanks, jeeps, armored cars, artillery pieces, watchtowers and regular barrages of Palestinian homemade mortars and rockets.

The packing plant is privately owned, buys all its produce from farmers in the Gush and operates under the strictest rabbinical supervision to ensure that all its products are kosher. What could be not kosher about celery, one could ask. Plenty, Anita says. There could be bugs in the vegetables, which even if cooked to death remain not kosher, and then, of course, one-tenth of the crop must be set aside for the traditional Temple offering, even though the last Temple was destroyed over 2,000 years ago, but a custom still adhered to by the strictly Orthodox.

When we arrived the trailer was unhitched and unloaded by two smiling Chinese. Eleven random heads of celery were removed and delivered to a battery of bug inspectors, all of whom looked like rabbis, who peered through magnifying glasses to ensure that the crop was indeed bug-free. The ten percent for the Temple was taken and thrown onto a garbage heap. Why don't they give it to the poor, I asked Anita. There was some problem with that, she explained, but was not quite sure what it was, something to do with a Temple offering not being meant for consumption by mere mortals.

The packing plant is somewhat of a mystery. Its owners are anonymous and don't want any publicity. It was built with state money by Natan Sharansky, the famous Prisoner of Zion in the former Soviet Union who became an Israeli politician, when he was minister of trade and industry in Benjamin Netanyahu's government. Sharansky liked to spend his vacations at the Palm Beach Hotel in Gush Katif and apparently had a soft spot for the settlers there. Aside from the Thai and Chinese minions, the plant employs Israeli workers from nearby development towns in Israel proper, where unemployment is high, and from the Gush settlements themselves.

The plant also provides work for the army of bug inspectors and *kashrut* supervisors who might otherwise be unemployed. So for the first time, thanks to the unique growing methods in the sands of Gaza, even the strictest ultra-Orthodox and Orthodox Jews can eat lettuce, cabbage, celery, parsley, carrots, turnips, herbs and dozens of other vegetables without fear of contamination. Since the kosher market is worldwide and the plant's owners have developed a method of ensuring that the washed and bagged veggies stay fresh for at least eleven days, they are exported the world over, bringing in many millions of dollars a year. The plant, however, being in Gush Katif, a region defined as having "high national priority" status, gets generous tax breaks and, initially, large investment subsidies.

I left Anita chatting with two Bedouin women harvesting herbs in a neighbor's hothouse and drove south to Neve Dekalim, a town of 2,500 inhabitants, including fifty new families from the Bnei Menashe tribe recently discovered living with strong Jewish traditions in villages somewhere in northeast India by the same rabbi who found the Shingling Jews in China and a lost Jewish tribe in Peru. While they will still have to undergo some form of conversion process to get them as kosher as Anita's celery, the Bnei Menashe seemed delighted to be at the forefront of Zionism and are said to have integrated extremely well into the community.

The journey to Neve Dekalim is relatively fast and safe. Again there is one road for the Jews, well maintained and tarred, and a parallel road for Palestinians with special permits or for members of the Bedouin Mawasi tribe, which, for whatever reason, is considered "nonhostile" by the security authorities. Neve Dekalim, or Oasis of Palm Trees, which indeed it is, on the surface anyway, was established in 1983 after the evacuation of the town of Yamit in the northern Sinai as all the Egyptian territories captured by Israel in 1967 were gradually returned. Some of the Yamit evacuees were Neve Dekalim's founders.

Like Galili, Ariel Sharon, the defense minister at the time, reasoned that if peace broke down, he wouldn't want a large Egyptian civilian population living over the border in Yamit. He thus decided to destroy the entire town rather than hand it over to the Egyptians intact.

The decision led to horrific scenes of soldiers removing Israelis from their homes. One picture in particular became etched in the national consciousness, a symbol of the potential consequences to Israeli society of settlement. This photograph showed soldiers in cages lifted by cranes trying to haul protesters off the top of Yamit's water tower, doused in the white paint being thrown at them.

Neve Dekalim's avenues are broad. Palm trees, true to the place's name, have been carefully planted along them. There is a neat shopping center, a gas station with cheerful attendants and a building that houses the local council. Quite a large number of the five hundred families here are French, uniformly Orthodox, many of North African origin, and extremely right-wing and militant in their views. In the summer of 2003, twenty new homes were being built and there was a long waiting list of families ready to move in, mainly more immigrants from France. A facility for the aged and a new youth center were also under construction. New roads were being laid and additional telephone and electricity lines were being installed. A sheltered workshop for the handicapped had recently been completed, along with a new wing for the regional religious girl's high school. There was nothing about the place or the national resources being spent there indicating that anyone in Israel's government considered the place anything but permanent.

Over six hundred mortars and rockets had fallen on Neve Dekalim in three years of war with the Palestinians. There had been dozens of attacks of one form or another against both the town and its residents, with many casualties. Adjacent to Neve Dekalim's small industrial area is Khan Yunis. It was no accident that the town's planners had placed the settlement's industrial zone next to the Palestinian town since the intention had been for Palestinians to work there, earn a good wage and be good neighbors.

Instead, dividing the industrial area from Khan Yunis was one of the most remarkable walls I have ever seen. Its thick base of twenty-foot-high concrete slabs served to block the Palestinians from directing drive-by shootings against their Jewish neighbors. Then another thinner level of concrete was added because snipers were firing from some of the taller buildings in town. Then, because the snipers began using the minarets of mosques, yet another level of an even thinner material was added, making the entire structure grotesque and, finally, relatively effective against snipers. That was when the Palestinians started using mortars.

I found the house of Estie Lillienthal, Anita's sister, who was just as feisty. Estie moved out here twelve years ago when her son and daughter-in-law had triplets and needed some help. Estie and her husband had lived in Pardes Hanna, near Hadera, where she was active in local politics and served as deputy mayor. It is wrong, she said, to consider the Gush settlers right-wing religious fanatics. Rather, most of the people here, she insisted, were modern Orthodox, had professions, served in the army and were just like any other average religious Israelis.

What she loved about the place was the quality of life, the proximity of the sea, where there were family beaches and separate beaches for men and women available for the extremely religious. There was a similar arrangement at the regional pool. People were moderate politically and religiously. The education system was good, the air clean, the people polite and considerate.

But things were beginning to change, she noted. Three years of Palestinian violence had damaged the moderation that may have once characterized the Gush's residents. The original Orthodox settlers were being overtaken by the ultra-Orthodox. The influx of angry, radical and vocal French immigrants added yet more shrillness to local debate. Many children of the first generation and even yeshiva students with new families could not afford to live in town.

When discussing Israeli and Palestinian demographics, those who have decided to make the Gaza Strip their home usually turn their eyes heavenward and say it's all in the hands of God. But this is not entirely true. Estie's son and his wife had nine children by now, and lived on nearby Atzmona, where televisions are prohibited and members live a strictly ultra-Orthodox way of life. Altogether, Estie had seven grand-children living in close proximity to her home, another nine on Atzmona and twelve more on other settlements in the Gush and elsewhere. And the production line was far from closed.

"People are becoming more messianic the more we can't see solutions and the more we feel threatened," Estie said, echoing what her sister had told me a few hours before. Later that day a young man with a surfboard on the beach at Kfar Yam would say the same thing.

I heard this sentiment twice more, once from a settler and once from a soldier, while waiting for an armored bus with steel-plated floors that would be escorted by a convoy of assorted military vehicles, now the mandatory mode of transport from Kissufim to the settlement of Net-zarim—Galili's fourth finger on the right hand. Since we had time before the bus came, the settler, a newly ultra-Orthodox son of modern Ortho-dox parents, defined the word "messianic" for me. The settlers' mission now, he explained, is in the name of God, not the government or the set-tlement arm of the Jewish Agency. So if, heaven forbid, there came a time when any government would try to remove the Gaza settlements, the set-tlers would have to choose between God and government, not an easy choice to make.

When Galili told the Knesset on March 28, 1971, that "the Gaza Strip will not be separated from Israel even after peace has been achieved," not even he was thinking in divine terms. The ties between Gaza and the Bible are indeed tenuous. A glossy brochure put out by the Gaza Coast Regional Council can only weakly claim that "Abraham and Isaac were active here and after them came the mighty Samson who uprooted the gates of the city." That's it. Two out of our three forefathers "were active here," like passing through, and Samson tore down the city's gates, an event of total religious irrelevance.

The whole place is sad. Sadness permeates every inch of ground and every conversation. From Gush Katif one can only view the Palestinian side by climbing atop hills and watchtowers to catch a glimpse of the misery, misery and sadness at least as pathetic and hopeless as what I encountered on that November morning so many years ago. While the Jewish settlements have flourished agriculturally and the Gush has brought to the world the kosher cabbage, a dangerous and untenable situation has been created by Galili's Five Fingers, just as I suspected in 1972 but was too afraid to ask. People's lives continue to be risked to support concepts that have not withstood the test of time.

Galili invested massive fortunes in Jewish settlement in the Gaza Strip because Israel was at war with Egypt. Then Sharon destroyed Yamit because of peace with Egypt. All the polls consistently say that most Israelis would gladly give up the Gaza Strip in return for peace, or even without it, and on June 6, 2004, Ariel Sharon's cabinet approved a plan for unilateral disengagement from Gaza in 2005. Those who oppose the notion of unilateral withdrawal, which they call "a gift to the terrorists," are determined and well-organized. They see the uprooting of settlements in Gaza as a precursor for taking them down on the West Bank and are prepared to fight against it using all means, including violence.

Despite this, in the last week of October 2004, Sharon, as wily as ever, took the issue to the Knesset, where he knew he was assured of the support of the Left, making opposition within his own party meaningless. Indeed, he won the vote 67 to 45, an absolute majority of the 120-member house. The following month, in early November, a similar Knesset majority voted into law reparation agreements for those who would be losing their homes. It seemed that, finally, the settler movement that had managed to dictate the national agenda since the early 1970s had been defeated and that Sharon, of all people, was about to break the mythology that settlements cannot be removed. Anita and Stuart, their children and grandchildren could imminently be losing their homes.

"If I knew there was a chance of real peace, that me not leaving my home was the only thing preventing real peace, then I would pack up and go happily," said Anita. "But there can never be real peace. We came here to live together, to grow together and all we have seen, starting with Yamit, then Oslo and now this war, with each concession we have made, has been a deepening of hatred for us as Jews, not Israelis, but as Jews and that makes me a very determined person."

Determined but, I suspect, behind the glint of her dark sparkling eyes, deeply troubled. The dream has been clouded. There has been too much death, too many people wounded, too much punishment inflicted on the Palestinians, too much sadness to go around for anyone to be happy.

15

THE GORDIAN KNOT

On the road to Hebron, old crenulated olive trees that have seen it all,
except what they symbolize: peace.

BY WHAT MUST HAVE BEEN no one's design or intentions, it was Jimmy Carter's Camp David summit that irrevocably tied Israel's fate to the West Bank and Gaza. It was clear to Carter in early September of 1978 that the Israeli-Egyptian peace accord—stuck in neutral for over six months—was in danger, that Israel and Syria could be on the verge of war, and that unless he acted quickly and forcefully, all could be lost. Sadat wanted to link the treaty to a return of territories taken in 1967 to the Palestinians, while Begin was only making peace with Egypt and giving up the Sinai in order to keep those territories. This was the main sticking point.

Carter took the high-profile and risky move of inviting both sides to Camp David, the presidential retreat, where, for thirteen days and nights, they tackled the issues one by one. At times it looked as if the talks would collapse, but by skillful, ingenious diplomacy the participants rounded off the various corners. For example: On the issue of Jerusalem, Begin and Sadat wrote two entirely different letters as appendices to the main agreements. Begin's letter said the city would be Israel's undivided capital for eternity; Sadat's said it was indivisible from the West Bank and should be returned to Arab sovereignty.

The Palestinian issue was danced around in a similar way. Sadat and Begin did not sign a peace agreement but rather "A Framework for Peace in the Middle East." This allowed Sadat to claim that Camp David comprised the first of what would be several steps toward a comprehensive peace—including with the Palestinians—in the region, while Begin could claim that while Camp David was an important first step, there was no understanding that future agreements with any parties would necessarily entail territorial compromise. Sadat had taken his first step and Begin had taken his last.

In what seemed to be a concession to the Palestinians, the document specified that within five years the Palestinian issue should be resolved in a way that took into account "the legitimate rights of the Palestinian people and their just requirements." Illustrating again that diplomatic language always exists in the ear of the listener, for Begin "legitimate rights" meant the Palestinians would be provided with some autonomy and economic well-being and a choice of becoming citizens of either

Jordan or the Jewish State in *Eretz Yisrael*. Sadat and Carter heard "legitimate rights" and envisioned an independent Palestinian State on the West Bank and Gaza.

Obtuse language may be good for diplomacy but is sometimes bad for history, as it was in this case. Though the Framework accord placed a sort of cap on the Middle East conflict for a while, Egypt, being the dominant country in the Arab world, understood that the Palestinian issue could never be simply hidden under a rock and expected to disappear.

The result: The war between Israel and the Palestinians continues. Thousands have been killed on both sides, many thousands more injured. Palestinian suicide bombings have brought the battlefield to Israel's malls and supermarkets, buses and city centers, placing its women and children on the front line. Hundreds of people have been shot and killed on the roads. Tourism is dead and the economy at its lowest point since the early 1950s. For the first time since the Holocaust, entire families have been wiped out, sometimes three generations at once. Fear is everywhere. Parents pray that children return home safe from birthday parties and get nervous when parked next to a bus at a red light. Hatred has reached new heights, despair new lows, and the terror is relentless.

The Palestinian experience is one of abject misery. Israel's response to the terror has had devastating effects. Cities are encircled and cut off from each other. Freedom of movement, even for ambulances trying to take the ill and injured to the hospital, has been curtailed. Tanks and armored vehicles enter the hearts of Palestinian cities and refugee camps. Entire neighborhoods have been demolished. Attack helicopters and on occasion F-16s have been deployed against targets in the middle of Palestinian population centers. Curfews have been imposed, sometimes for months at a time. Unemployment is above sixty percent.

Ultimately Begin did not believe that *Eretz Yisrael* was his to give up. He would have handed over the Golan Heights in exchange for a genuine peace agreement with the Syrians, but not Judea or Samaria and not even Gaza. And though Begin was, other flaws aside, a true democrat, he did not feel the Jewish Democratic State was threatened by Palestinian demography, there being slightly over three million Jews in

Israel at the time and 1.1 million Palestinians in the territories. The recent opening of the Soviet Union's gates to Jewish emigrants gave him confidence the Jews would always be a majority in their own land. Little did he envision that by 2004 the Palestinian population in Israel and the territories would total 4.7 million and be growing at almost six percent per year, fast closing in on Israel's 5.6 million Jews with a growth rate of only 1.9 percent and dropping. Perhaps he would not have been so quick to offer the Palestinians the choice of Israeli citizenship or, perhaps, to settle the territories. Both, he would have realized, would existentially threaten the Jewish Democratic State he held so highly.

After Camp David it still took the sides over two hundred days to arrange for Israel's subsequent withdrawal from all of Sinai. The Palestinian issue was referred to committee, where it remained. Much more time was spent on a dispute over several dozen *dunams* at Taba south of Eilat, also eventually resolved by clever use of language. The Palestinian issue was left to fester, to bubble and boil. Today it is so complicated that even Solomon would not be able to sort it out.

One only has to take a drive to Hebron to understand why. The city is only 30 kilometers from Jerusalem, but the journey takes one back centuries. Olive trees, crenulated and ancient, stand on the roadsides. The rocky terraced hills planted with vines and fruit trees evoke a different time. Shepherds, some looking as worn and bent as the olive trees, mind their flocks. It is like driving through a living Bible.

And then on the way out of Jerusalem, as one crosses the 1967 border to the left, in what used to be no-man's-land between Israel and Jordan, is Har Homa, a new Jewish neighborhood designed for an eventual 15,000 families. To the right is Giloh, a huge Jerusalem suburb, built on land taken in 1967. Past Giloh is the Tunnel Road, a massive engineering project of mountain underpasses and bridges built to allow settlers to bypass Bethlehem on their way to Jerusalem and back. Beyond the Tunnel Road is Beitar Ilit, a fast-growing ultra-Orthodox city of 35,000. (Settler families have on the average five children, as opposed to two in Israel proper.) And then continuing south, sitting atop the hilltops, their red-tiled roofs looking incongruous against the rough ancient landscape, the settlements of Neve Daniel, Rosh Tsurim, Elazar, Alon Shvut,

Efrat, Kfar Etzion, Bat Aiyin, Migdal Oz, Karmei Tsur, over 180 of them on the West Bank alone.

Kiryat Arba, the biblical name for Hebron, a Jewish settlement of 7,000, was built by Levy Eshkol's Labor government in 1968 as part of a compromise with Gush Emunim, the messianic settler movement led by Rabbi Moshe Levinger. Levinger and ten families posing as Swedish tourists had checked into the Park Hotel in Hebron over Passover in April 1968 and refused to leave, a tactic used effectively by the settler movement ever after.

Levinger had demanded that the ancient Jewish community of He-bron be revived, that Jewish property when the city fell into Arab hands be returned and that Israel gain sovereignty and control over *Ma'arat Hamachpela,* the burial place of the Patriarchs and Matriarchs Abraham and Sarah, Isaac and Rebecca and Jacob and Leah, holy to Jews and Muslims, and referred to by the latter as the Ibrahimi Mosque. Levinger and the families stayed at the Park Hotel for over a month until they agreed to move into caravans at a nearby army base with a government promise that Kiryat Arba would be built nearby.

The road to Hebron is eerily empty and despite the clear blue skies the few Palestinians waiting for buses or taxis seem dejected, their heads down, having already negotiated by foot mounds of rubble and sand put down as barricades by the army. The glass shops that used to sell the distinctive blue and green Hebron goblets and baubles to tourists and Israelis are closed, and at frequent strategic points Israeli soldiers stand guard in round watchtowers with machine gun posts. There are jeeps and military vehicles at most major junctions. This security is designed to prevent drive-by shootings and the infiltration of suicide bombers into Israel.

The civilian guard sitting behind the bulletproof glass and concrete booth at the entrance to Kiryat Arba waves me in through the massive yellow steel gate. Above it a banner flutters, welcoming Honorary Kiryat Arba Citizen Natan Sharansky, Minister of Diaspora Affairs.

Driving through those gates is not unlike driving into a gulag. A giant electric fence surrounds an area that seems almost empty until one reaches Ramat Mamre Junction. There an arrow points to several sad rows of houses on a hill to the left and another to a large communal center built by the National Lottery to the right. Further down the road, opposite an army camp, a cluster of Arab houses has somehow been placed inside another fence with a corridor leading to their vineyards and fields. Perhaps in irony, the windows of one house facing the army camp are made out of red heart-shaped glass, only the second hopeful sign I have seen all day, other than the Love and Peace Nursery just past the Palestinian town of Halhoul.

Arriving in the heart of Kiryat Arba, I am surprised by the neatly tended gardens and lawns. A big sign announces a new neighborhood of 210 apartments with staggered balconies so that each one is open to the sky, an important feature for an observant Jew who builds a *succah* on the Feast of the Tabernacles.

I drive through the town and pull up at a small shopping center. Other than Elitsur's Pizza and a minimarket, most of the shops are deserted. I chat with the owner of the minimarket, who tells me that he lived here for seventeen years but has now moved to Jerusalem, commuting each day to work. He tells me that half the population is religious, and that about a third of the residents are new immigrants from the former Soviet Union and Ethiopia. There is no industry other than one carpentry shop that employs twenty people. As on other settlements, the biggest employer is the local council, which enjoys heavy subsidies and provides a fairly high level of services. If it were not for the cheap vodka sold in massive quantities, soldiers who come in and buy a pack of smokes and a Coke and people visiting the grave of Baruch Goldstein, he would be broke.

The grave of Goldstein is at the end of a park and bordered by alcoves with benches in them. In the center, framing parallel paths, are bushes of lilac and beds of roses. Goldstein, a medical doctor, thought to have been a gentle soul, had come to Israel from America and lived in Kiryat Arba. On February 25, 1994, he entered the *Machpela* where Abraham is buried that now serves as both a synagogue and mosque, during the hour assigned to Muslim morning prayers, and with his submachine gun killed twenty-nine people and injured dozens more while they were supplicated in prayer. He would have killed more had he not been beaten to death by the enraged survivors. I was in Montreal that day and had to file my column for *The Jerusalem Report* from my hotel room. "I wonder how many Jews Baruch Goldstein killed today," I started.

At Goldstein's grave an enormous stone is engraved with his full name, Baruch Kappel Goldstein, and underneath the legend *"Naki Lelo Revav"*—"Pure and Without a Flaw." Two reserve duty soldiers are standing by the grave when I arrive. They are passing time before transportation to their position inside Hebron. Both are married with children and self-employed. They are in Hebron because of "fucking maniacs like this one," one says as he spits at the foot of the grave.

I find a young Yemenite man waiting by my car. He is dressed in his Sabbath best with a spotless white embroidered *kippa* on his head, the four corners of his *tallith* protruding from under his white starched shirt and black jacket. Am I going to the *Machpelah?* he asks. Another youngster wearing sandals and only a shirt with rolled-up sleeves despite the cold, a knitted *kippa* on his head, asks if I'm heading toward Avraham Avinu, the Jewish neighborhood in the center of Hebron a few minutes' drive away. I say I am going to both, happy for the company.

Yossi the Yemenite is from Jerusalem, where he is a yeshiva student and silversmith. He comes to pray at the burial site of Abraham when he has special things on his mind, as he does now. Personal problems to do with fertility, he says. His wife has gone to pray at Rachel's Tomb on the edge of Bethlehem. Yes, they are seeing a doctor as well. And Hanan, from Petah Tikva, is studying at the Shavei Hebron ("Return to Hebron") yeshiva with about two hundred other youngsters who have completed school and deferred their military service in order to fortify themselves spiritually before going into the army.

Those areas of the city of Hebron between the exit of Kiryat Arba and the Jewish quarter in Hebron is a city deserted, as if some evil spirit has come to rest on it. Rubble and destroyed houses lie on either side of the narrow, winding, potholed road. In the old casbah, row after row of shops are closed with steel shutters painted blue. On them Jewish settlers have painted graffiti in Hebrew and English. Particularly popular is *"mavet Le'Aravim"*—"Death to the Arabs." Now and then a Palestinian child scampers through the alleys, but 30,000 local Palestinians have been under regular curfew for years so that the five hundred Jews who have decided to live here, most of them transients like the yeshiva student, can move around with relative safety in the two city blocks they occupy.

Beit Hadassah, the Jewish hospital abandoned in 1936 and the base of Levinger's renewed campaign to have Jews move into Hebron once Kiryat Arba became a reality, now houses a museum of the August 1929 massacre when sixty-seven Jews were raped, slaughtered and mutilated by Arab mobs. The building next to it is called Beit Hashisha, the House of the Six, dedicated to the memory of six yeshiva students killed there in 1980. Barbed wire and fences surround the buildings now inhabited by Jews. Soldiers in a jeep stand guard outside Beit Schneerson, an apartment building, while dozens of children play in the small playground erected in memory of Shalhevet Pas, a baby killed in her stroller by a Palestinian sniper two years before. The litany of tragedies is endless.

After the Goldstein massacre there was public pressure on then Prime Minister Rabin to use the incident as an opportunity to get Levinger and his several hundred extremist supporters out of the heart of Hebron, a city of 120,000 Palestinians, the second largest on the West Bank. Even Rabin, one of the most powerful and forceful prime ministers Israel had ever seen, could not. Like Sadat before him, Rabin was assassinated for making peace. The hotbed of fanaticism Levinger created lives on. Worse, it has spread to an entire young generation of settlers who have been taught in the name of God to hate Arabs with the same passion as to love *Eretz Yisrael,* and to fight Israeli police and security forces sent to evacuate settlements as if they were a mortal enemy. If a civil war ever breaks out in Israel over the future of the settlements, its seeds will have been sown in Hebron.

With this thought deep in mind, I drive back alone to Jerusalem, having avoided the young yeshiva students with their thumbs out looking for a lift. I do not want to have people in my car who think it is O.K. to fight Israeli soldiers and to keep 30,000 Palestinians under curfew so that they can reclaim six houses in Hebron. And I feel ashamed. There is something fundamentally wrong, I think to myself, with a society that would tolerate such arrangements.

16

TAKING STOCK

*Outside 27 Yeo Street, Yeoville Johannesburg, the house I grew up in,
on election day April 1994, the day Apartheid ended in South Africa.
Just a block away, in the field I used to play in as a child, a line many
miles long of black South Africans waited patiently to vote in the
community center that until that day had been closed to them.*

IT IS MARCH 2004, almost six decades since my mother was pulled away from Aunt Rosie's bridge table in Port Elizabeth, South Africa, to give birth to me. I have been in Israel for thirty-nine years, one month and two days, but who's counting? Uncle Felix and Aunty Feiga, who came to greet me at the airport on my arrival, are both long dead. They left Israel for the United States in 1969 with Felix in a rage after he was accused of using Post Office materials, labor and vehicles to run a private television antenna company. The charges were true, of course.

Both my cousins, Haim and Ya'acov, whose clothes I first wore with such agony, live in the States, where they have done very well. My sister Rochie and her husband Monty, who arrived from South Africa on the eve of the Yom Kippur War, remain here, as do their four children and twelve grandchildren. Beulah, my former wife, lives in Tel Aviv, as does Maya, our daughter, who is a senior producer for Channel Two News. She speaks fast, thinks fast and lives fast.

Twice Maya has been within inches of losing her life in a terror attack, once at Dizengoff Center in March 1996, a few days before my 50th birthday, when a suicide bomber detonated himself at a busy intersection, and again exactly a year later while meeting her landlord at the Apropo Café in Tel Aviv. The bomb went off in the crowded center of the restaurant just where Maya's landlord had been sitting moments before he got up to greet her at the entrance. A woman, a young mother, was killed with two others. Her baby, dressed as a little clown for Purim, survived.

I was in Helsinki that Friday morning at a behind-closed-doors meeting with Palestinians, Iranians, Egyptians, Jordanians and others from the region when I was called to the front desk to take an urgent call. When I came back into the room and word got out why I had been called away everyone was shocked and came up to express their sympathy, even the Iranian delegates who had up to that point ignored me.

Two senior members of the PLO who were at the meeting, including the brother of Abu Jihad, who Israel had assassinated in Tunis in April 1988, insisted on taking me to the airport later that afternoon and, of all things, helped me get through security and immigration quickly on the strength of their diplomatic papers.

Shai lives in a paradise. He manages the Mateya Safari Lodge in the Madikwe game reserve on the South Africa–Botswana border. He has established a reputation as a gifted ranger and his lodge is as close to nature as one can get. He remains an Israeli, visits twice a year, has his best friends here, pines for humus despite the gastronomic excellence at Mateya, loves to read in Hebrew, loves Israeli music and, when he is ready, will come back to Israel to make a difference. In the meantime he revels in the New South Africa, and is an active participant in the effort to remove the stain of Apartheid by developing ecotourism and jobs in what used to be the poorest of all the Bantustans, Bophuthatswana.

My sister Sorelle and her husband Eric died tragically in 1997. Other than Shai, my only close family in South Africa is my nephew, Anthony, now a well-known architect. Johnny, his older brother and a doctor, like so many other South African Jews, moved to Australia, where there are now probably five times as many graduates of South Africa's Zionist youth movements as in Israel. David, the third brother, lives in New York with his family.

As for myself, Beulah and I sat down on a winter's evening in 1990 in the dining room of our quaint little house overlooking the Jerusalem Botanical Gardens. Both kids were in their late teens, Shai was in the army, Maya hardly ever home. We had a frank, open and honest discussion about how the glue between us had worn thin; that the kids were old enough not to be hurt and we were young enough to start new lives. We parted friends and remain so.

I rented a great apartment overlooking the Valley of the Cross, where, according to legend, the tree from which Jesus' cross was hewn was cut down and where today a Greek Orthodox monastery stands. I also had a view of the Knesset and the Israel Museum with its distinctive architecture, especially beautiful when lit up at night. At the entrance to the museum, like a white inverted ice cream cone, is the Shrine of the Book, home of the Dead Sea Scrolls. The sunsets from the west-facing floor-to-ceiling window in the lounge were spectacular and I looked forward to the bachelorhood I had been thinking of for years. I started cooking, listening to music, reading, not making my bed, leaving the dishes for the maid, sleeping in on Saturdays, drinking and playing poker with my friends and generally doing what bachelors do, much to the chagrin of my Orthodox neighbors.

Two months later, however, I met Ehud Ya'ari, the Middle East editor of *The Jerusalem Report,* and his assistant Isabel Kershner for dinner at a small Italian restaurant in the heart of Jerusalem. Sitting outside in the yard of the beautiful old building under budding grape vines on a clear crisp evening, drinking grappa and red wine, I fell hopelessly in love. Despite my commitment to the joys of bachelorhood, Isabel and I soon moved in together and about a year later, in April 1992, we were married on the balcony of the King David Hotel overlooking the Old City walls and the Tower of David.

We now have two great little guys, Gavriel, ten, and my little late lamb Lev, seven. Their relationship with Shai and Maya is wonderful. I mean, what little fellows wouldn't want a ranger "in the jungles of Africa" for an older brother and a sister who works with the top television stars in the country and who loves nothing more than parading them around the studio.

Gavs is named for my mom, Ginda, who, like him, was an angel. We also chose the name because of its message. Gavriel is the angel charged by God with making it possible for good people to do good things. He is also the only angel common to all three of Jerusalem's religions, whether pronounced Gavriel, Gabriel or Jibril. Lev is named after my late dad, Leib, who committed suicide a month before he was born. Meaning heart in Hebrew and lion in Russian, it combines compassion and strength, which is our hope for him.

The four of us live in a lovely house in the Talbiya suburb of Jerusalem, just a few blocks from great vantage points overlooking the Old City, Mount Zion and the Judean Desert all the way down to the Dead Sea. Sometimes, on a clear night one can see the twinkling lights of Amman and Madaba in Jordan. It was from Madaba that Moses looked into the Promised Land after forty years in the desert, but was forbidden from entering it. Some say he was lucky.

Most of my friends have left Jerusalem over the years. It's a poor city and some call it dingy. Maya, after spending a week here looking after her two small brothers while Isabel and I were abroad, said it reminded her of a "soup kitchen," the people being so drab compared to her set of smart Tel Avivians. It's a city of civil servants, professors at the university, yeshiva students, small-time businessmen and loud-mouthed politicians. Very few regular, secular youngsters stay. One evening in 2003 we gave a dinner for Shai's friends when he came for a visit. Of the twenty-two young people there only one, Rafi, who works at the Israel Museum, had remained in Jerusalem. All the rest had moved down to Tel Aviv to jobs in advertising, television, theatre, architecture or running chic restaurants, to a lifestyle they all said they couldn't find here.

I love Jerusalem and have from my early years in the city as a student in 1965. It has an energy I find nowhere else other than, strangely, in the African bush. In both places I feel close to God. In the bush it's the openness, the proximity to nature; here it's the intensity. In the African bush there is an incredible spirituality pulsing through the endless blue skies, the closeness of the stars at night, the fierceness of the lightning; in Jerusalem there is the same feeling on Friday afternoon when the Muslims end their prayers on Haram al-Sharif and the Jews make their final preparations for the Sabbath. The same happens at sunset when the hard stone from which the city is built softens into a golden hue. There is magic in the air.

But now there is also danger and it is everywhere since the current war with the Palestinians started in September 2000. There have been thirty-one suicide bombings in Jerusalem alone in the space of three years, killing dozens and injuring hundreds more, some of them by the nails, nuts, bolts and glass shards that pack the suicide vests. Even the woodcut of the sad clown in my favorite bar-restaurant, Finks, has a ball bearing embedded near his right shoulder.

What happened to dash the hopes of the Oslo Accords of 1993, the plan that envisioned the creation of an independent Palestinian state living in peace side-by-side with Israel? Those heady days when Rabin and Arafat shook hands, gave brave speeches about brave partners in peace? When committees and subcommittees were working on protocols for trade, water-sharing, transport regulations, cooperation in agriculture, medicine, culture? When Palestinian cars with their green license plates were almost as numerous on Israel's highways as Israeli vehicles? When Israeli forces were withdrawing from the West Bank and Gaza and Palestinian youngsters were waving olive branches for the television cameras?

The Oslo Accords, like all agreements, were imperfect, yet despite their shortfalls, by the time the second Intifada erupted, Israel had withdrawn from all the major Palestinian cities and towns; Arafat and the Palestinian Authority were in control of over 95 percent of the Palestinian population; Palestinian institutions were in place and foreign donor money was flowing in. Tourism was booming in Israel and the territories, as were new tourist projects. The Casino in Jericho was doing so well with Israeli clients that a glatt kosher restaurant was opened in the refugee camp across the road. An American president, Bill Clinton, had paid a state visit to Gaza. A spanking new airport paid for by the Saudis had just been opened in Gaza and a Palestinian national airline created. Slowly but surely the slums of Gaza were being improved, sewerage, electricity, clean water all being installed, parks being built.

The truth is we arrived at this war through a litany of sad events longer than the mind cares to contemplate. Rabin, a strong, forceful, direct and honest leader who understood what was best for his people and had the courage and conviction to do what had to be done, even if it meant shaking Arafat's hand, was assassinated. Rabin knew of the anger his political course was creating and was aware of the danger to his own life, but I think he, like the rest of the country, never believed for a moment that a Jew would kill a Jew over politics. Yet horrific rhetoric from ultra-nationalist rabbis, Levinger's disciples, warped Yigal Amir's mind until he believed he was killing Rabin in the name of God.

Though Shimon Peres, also from the peace camp, replaced Rabin, the peace effort never regained its footing. I suspect Arafat did not have the same respect for Peres that he did for Rabin. Peres had never served in uniform, while Rabin had been a soldier; Rabin spoke straight while Peres dreamed and spoke of a New Middle East with no borders, with railway lines and highways creating a kind of Europe in the region. But what must have worried Arafat most of all about Peres was that while Rabin had been studious and slow, Peres wanted full peace now. As we would learn a few years later when Ehud Barak became prime minister,

Arafat had his own agenda and full peace with Israel was not on it. From his exile in Tunis, Arafat had used Oslo to get a foothold back in Palestine, but that was as far as he was prepared to legitimize Israel at that point. Full peace was not in the cards.

Another fateful turning point came in early February 1996 when the Israeli secret service assassinated Yehiya Ayyash, dubbed "the engineer" by the Israelis and thought to be the leading supplier, recruiter and bomb maker of Hammas, the radical Islamic group opposed to any compromise with Israel and the Oslo Accords. They managed to track him down after years of hard work and killed him by paying one of his cousins to place a tiny but highly explosive charge in his cell phone. It was his last "hello."

The Palestinian reaction to Ayyash's assassination was three suicide bombers in late February and early March of 1996 in Jerusalem and Tel Aviv, one about a block away from my office. The attacks came as a tremendous blow to Peres, who was facing a serious electoral challenge from the Likud's young, articulate, energetic, smart young candidate, Benjamin Netanyahu. A fierce critic of Oslo, Netanyahu could rightly claim in his campaign that whereas before Oslo there had been one suicide bombing in Israel, on April 16, 1993, at Mehola in the Jordan Valley, since Arafat shook Rabin's hand on the White House lawn there had been twenty-one more, killing and injuring hundreds. His message that Oslo was only Arafat's first step to Jaffa and Haifa seemed credible as pictures of Peres surveying the horribly burned remains of the three bombed buses filled the TV screens on the evening news.

There were other reasons for Peres's downfall. There was a low turnout of the Arab vote—almost 20 percent of the population that would have backed Labor's candidate for prime minister—because of Operation Grapes of Wrath. Peres had ordered the operation against Hizballah bases in Lebanon after incessant shelling over the northern border. During the campaign an errant artillery shell slammed into a building in a UN compound in the village of Kana used as a refuge by Lebanese civilians. Over a hundred people died and dozens more were injured.

Moreover, whereas the Israeli public had perceived Rabin as a careful man and hard-nosed negotiator, Peres was seen as someone who would give the store away, as overanxious to placate the Palestinians and Europeans, not to mention the Americans.

And fatefully for Peres, a few weeks before the election, Habad Lubavitch, the religious messianic group that commanded a significant voting bloc, came out in full force for Netanyahu with an ad campaign and slogan that "Bibi is Good for the Jews." The Habad campaign was paid for by Australian millionaire Joe Gutnik, who became religious after the Lubavitcher Rebbe told him where he would find gold in Australia, which he did.

Netanyahu won by the slimmest of margins, 50.4 percent to Peres's 49.5 percent. At midnight when the voting party at our Rehavia apartment began to disperse, it had seemed that Peres was well on his way to victory. Ed Abington, then the American Consul General in Jerusalem and the administration's point man in contacts with the Palestinians, wailed to me the next morning that "I had gone to sleep with a princess and have woken up with an ugly duckling." He then predicted a dire future for the peace process.

An ugly duckling he was not, but Netanyahu had the double misfortune of being politically inexperienced and wedded to an international agreement, Oslo, guaranteed by the United States, that he intellectually, ideologically and politically opposed. Elected because of his opposition to Oslo, as prime minister he had to carry it out.

Netanyahu's short term was disastrous for Israel and the Palestinians and for Israel's relations with the United States. Under his tenure the economy was characterized by stagflation and record unemployment rates. He crossed the Rubicon when after extended wrangling with the Americans and the Palestinians he withdrew from part of Hebron, the first time a Likud leader had withdrawn from an inch of the West Bank, let alone Abraham's city. But then he almost caused a war when he "balanced" this by building the highly controversial Jerusalem suburb of Har Homa on the northern slopes bordering Bethlehem and then agreeing to open a tunnel to tourists under Temple Mount, the plot the Jews revere as the site of Solomon's Temple and that now houses the Al Aksa Mosque, Islam's third holiest site after Mecca and Medina. The act committed at night and without consultation with the Wakf, the Islamic

Trust that administers the Muslim holy sites, was portrayed by the Trust as an Israeli attempt to collapse the Mosque by subterfuge, a ridiculous claim but enough to spark violent riots in the territories and Muslim protest across the world.

Netanyahu is no fool. He holds a degree from MIT in architecture and one in politics from Harvard and was a brilliant spokesman for Israel at the United Nations. Like Rabin in his first term, however, he just could not get a handle on power or politics. Having been elected directly by the public and not the Likud Party, he operated under the illusion that he could get things done without having to work with the party, and from day one antagonized some of his greatest supporters. He initially left Ariel Sharon out of his cabinet after Sharon had worked hard for Netanyahu's victory, and then put him in because the party demanded it. Instead of a friend at the cabinet table, he now had an enemy, and a bad one at that. He did the same with a series of other ministers, notably Benny Begin, Menachem Begin's son, and Dan Meridor, the scion of an old and established Herut movement family. Like he was to do so often in his stint at the helm, he cut off his legs before he could walk and ended up virtually crawling out of office.

Netanyahu received an unprecedented trouncing at the polls in 1998 by Ehud Barak, who had taken over leadership of the Labor Party from Peres. Barak's popularity at the time he took office was similarly unprecedented. He was seen by many as Rabin's successor and, indeed, he had been carefully groomed for the job by Rabin, who first made him interior minister and then foreign minister. His military background as chief of staff and head of Military Intelligence, the fact that he was Israel's most decorated soldier and his experience in government all combined to make him the perfect candidate. It was not to be. When he resigned at 9:23 P.M. on December 9, 2000, he had served seventeen months and five days of his four-year term, even less than Netanyahu.

Barak was perfect in every way except his personality. He was arrogant and impatient, behaving as if he was still in the army where one could order people about instead of schmoozing, as one has to do to get things done in parliament, the party and government bureaucracies. He was suspicious in the extreme, distancing even his most loyal aides who, to a person, would leave and turn against him. He often assigned two aides with the same task and gave neither the full picture. The result was chaos. Gilead Sher, Barak's chief of staff and supposedly close to him, would arrive for secret talks with Arafat only to discover to his great embarrassment that someone else from Barak's bureau had been there on the same mission just several hours before.

Barak had advisers but never took advice. In September 2000 he was told over and over again by Palestinian officials, his advisers, the intelligence community and the Israeli think tanks not to push Arafat into a hasty summit with a lame duck President Clinton. Arafat had said emphatically that he was not ready for the "end of conflict" treaty Barak was demanding, that there was a need to consolidate the Oslo process first.

Barak was also told not to push for quick resolutions of thorny issues like the refugee problem and Jerusalem, but Barak insisted on going for all or nothing. In the end this led to Israel getting worse than nothing: a full-scale war.

Barak had all the right ideas. It was in the execution that things fell apart. He almost made peace with Syria but then backed out at the last minute. He said he was for Oslo and permanent peace with the Palestinians, yet built more homes in settlements during his short tenure than any prime minister since Menachem Begin. As for domestic issues like state and religion, military service for yeshiva students, local governance, unemployment, not one remedy featured in his campaign promises came to fruition. He did finally withdraw Israeli forces from Lebanon after eighteen long and bloody years and there was increased economic growth, but that was attributed more to the era's high-tech bubble than to cogent government policy.

Perhaps the most unfortunate thing about Barak is that in addition to not listening, he does not learn. About a year after he left office Isabel and I were at a small dinner party given by a mutual friend in honor of a departing ambassador. There were two tables very close to each other in the lounge and dining room of the apartment and Barak sat at one with eight other people. Waving his hands in the air, thumping the table with his fist, his voice at full pitch, he lectured those around him as if addressing an audience of several hundred.

He had unmasked Arafat at Camp David, he said, unclothed him, let the world see him for what he was. He did no wrong, could do no wrong. The whole collapse of Oslo and the summit had been a brilliant exercise in exposing Arafat, not an abject failure of diplomacy. Not one ounce of contrition. Not a moment of self-doubt. Apparently not a thought given to the devastation, conflict and casualties that resulted, to the political turmoil created, to the destruction of the Labor Party and the hopes and ideology of those who believed in swapping territory for peace.

Barak needed the agreement with Arafat to try to save his crumbling coalition, once the broadest in Israel's history, 75 Knesset seats out of 120, now down to 59 and diminishing rapidly. He thought that if he could get an "end of conflict" agreement with Arafat he would be able to call an early election to have the public ratify the peace deal, which would be his platform. He was sure he would win, as all the polls were indicating that a healthy majority of Israelis wanted the deal, even if it meant giving up parts of Jerusalem. And Clinton wanted to claim this major foreign policy achievement before leaving office in less than four months. He also reportedly coveted the Nobel Peace Prize and considered this his best bet. Arafat, who already had his Nobel, was apparently in no hurry. Patience has always been a Palestinian trait.

What went on at the Camp David summit is still open to interpretation, as is what Barak actually offered Arafat. There is, however, a consensus among those who participated that the Israeli offer included returning 92 percent of the West Bank, all of Gaza, all of non-Jewish Jerusalem other than the Armenian Quarter of the Old City, control but not sovereignty over Temple Mount and a partial land swap to compensate for the four to six percent of the West Bank that would remain in Israel's hands. It was an offer that broke every taboo in the country's political history. No mainstream politician, let alone a prime minister, had ever spoken of redividing Jerusalem. It was unthinkable, as was the idea of giving up parts of Israel. Arafat rejected it. He also rejected a subsequent offer of 96 percent of the territories and sovereignty over Temple Mount made by Clinton with Barak's approval.

Why Arafat turned it down remains an enigma. The simplest answer is that Barak was trying to do the wrong deal with the wrong man at the wrong time. Perhaps Arafat, like the Revisionists led by Vladimir Jabotinsky of the early Zionist movement, who wanted both sides of the Jordan, wanted all of Palestine. After all he had devoted over four decades of his life to fighting for this.

Arafat was not going to be the Palestinian leader to legitimize the Jewish State on what he considered to be 78 percent of historic Palestine. He was also not going to sign an agreement that annulled the right of return for five million Palestinian refugees, many of them, particularly in Lebanon and Jordan, still living in refugee camps. Fatah, the movement he created, is dedicated to the refugee issue and represents their interests. Thousands of people have given their lives for its cause. There was no way he could be expected to leave the refugees waving the keys to homes they abandoned almost six decades ago, keys that are passed on from generation to generation, with no hope of ever returning to them.

Barak should have understood this and lowered his sights. Instead of an "end of conflict agreement," he should have tried to move the Oslo process along or go for the Begin-Sadat model in which a peace accord was signed and thorny issues referred to committee. And Arafat should never have been singled out as he was by Clinton for the failure. Clinton's anger and frustration with the Palestinian leader overshadowed diplomacy.

Arafat emerged as a humiliated and isolated leader of a hopeless people. They had tried to bring him to make peace on his knees, with key issues remaining unresolved and no real homework having been done on even so sensitive an issue as Temple Mount. The Palestinian delegation was truly surprised that the Jews had any territorial claim to it and some genuinely had no idea that it had been the site of Solomon's Temple. The Americans, Europeans, Egyptians and Jordanians were all furious with Arafat, as were many within the Palestinian camp who, for the first time in over thirty years, saw a possible end to military occupation, particularly the pragmatic young generation who fought the first Intifada, have grown up alongside Israel and understand that Israel is here to stay.

Arafat's only way out: war. What he needed was a reason and that was supplied in late September 2000 by none other than Ariel Sharon, his old antagonist from Beirut.

I was in Istanbul with Isabel at the time, at another of those conferences with participants, mainly journalists, from Israel and most of the Arab world. On the morning news I saw images of Sharon and what seemed to be an army of men with machine guns and rifles, some policemen, some secret service, pouring through the narrow gate that leads onto Temple Mount or, as the Muslims call it, Haram al-Sharif.

"Holy shit," I yelled through the bathroom door at Isabel, "it looks like Sharon's conquering Temple Mount," which is exactly the way the Islamic world from Cairo to Cape Town and Jakarta to Bombay saw it.

That was on Thursday morning, September 28. It was clear that Barak's government was on its last legs, his coalition having dissipated at an alarming rate. In preparation for the inevitable election, Sharon was fighting Netanyahu for the leadership of the Likud, which Netanyahu seemed almost certain to win.

To outflank Netanyahu from the right, reminding everyone that it had been Netanyahu who had given up Israeli control of some of Hebron, Sharon decided to make a statement in Jerusalem: a demonstrative visit to Temple Mount with the message that the site was and would remain under Israeli sovereignty, part of Israel's undivided capital.

Barak did not stop Sharon from paying the visit despite advice to the contrary from the intelligence services and his own security advisors. Shlomo Ben Ami, who was minister of both Foreign Affairs and Internal Security at the time—almost a contradiction in terms and another example of Barak's curious leadership style—is adamant that Jibril Rajoub, then head of Preventive Security on the West Bank, had led him to understand there would be no problem with the visit. Muhammed Dahlan, Rajoub's counterpart in Gaza at the time, was equally adamant in telling me later that he had given Ben Ami exactly the opposite prognosis: "I told him there would be blood in the streets."

Whatever, Arafat had his excuse. The following day, Friday, tens of thousands came to pray on the Mount. The police were out in full force and, against logic and standing practice, came armed with live ammunition rather than rubber bullets and other crowd control measures, even though it was absolutely clear to them in advance that there would be trouble.

And, as expected, following prayers that afternoon the riots began, and before the evening when Sabbath descended on the city seven people, all East Jerusalem Palestinians, were dead and dozens more were wounded. Fury in the Muslim world reached new heights. In Cape Town, Muslim crowds paraded through the city's main streets chanting "one bullet one Jew," and in Israel riots broke out on a scale never seen before among its usually quiescent Arab population.

By October 2, thirteen Israeli Arabs, most of them youngsters, were dead, killed by armed policemen serving what was supposed to be the most left-wing, peace-seeking government in Israel's history. Ehud Barak got into office in no small part because of Israeli Arab support for his candidacy. Arab voters had turned out in unprecedented numbers for him. Shlomo Ben Ami, the minister who should have made sure that the nightmare experience of the previous Friday had never occurred, and that the police did not use live ammunition against unarmed protesters, was a lead negotiator, and one of the most forthcoming, with the Palestinians. Yossi Beilin, one of the foremost doves in Israeli politics, was justice minister.

The riots passed, but the government's relations with its 1.2 million Arab citizens remain an even larger accident waiting to happen. For five decades they have heard promises that have not been kept. Budgetary discrimination is rife at every level—education, health, land allocation, investment in infrastructure.

Every government since that of Menachem Begin has said it recognizes the gravity of Israeli-Arab issues and has vowed to address them. Not a single one has. Even so basic a problem as that of the internally displaced, or the "Present Absentees" as the official bureaucracy calls them, has yet to be resolved. There are now over 300,000 people whose parents and grandparents fled from the coastal cities and other battle zones during the 1948 War of Independence for the relative safety of the Galilee and have never been allowed to return home; people who are now refugees in their own land. The Negev Bedouin, the fastest-growing population on earth, live in appalling conditions.

Resentment among the Israeli Arabs runs high, and four years of war with the Palestinians has brought them to a point of serious self-examination. The politics of the eight Arab Knesset members has changed from affiliation with mixed Arab-Jewish parties like the Communists, and even Zionist parties like Mapam, to being vociferously anti-Israel. Increasingly, they no longer want just their share of the national pie, equality and integration, but official recognition as a national minority and a redefinition of Israel from being a Jewish State to a state of all of its citizens.

As the pictures on television continue streaming in of Israeli tanks and bulldozers leveling Palestinian homes in Gaza and on the West Bank, the language the Arab Knesset members use to make their arguments is often hate-filled and pugnacious, and at times borders on sedition. Their hostility to Zionism and all it represents is no longer subliminal or muted, but emphatic and uncompromising. They are, naturally, unequivocal in their support for the Palestinian cause, and have refused to specifically condemn suicide bombing, saying rather that all the violence has got to stop. So closely have they become identified with the Palestinian cause that one veteran parliamentarian, Dr. Ahmed Tibi, has openly served as one of Arafat's key advisers on how best to maneuver against the Jewish State.

Yet Israeli Arabs are neither a security nor a demographic threat to Israel. While a few tumbleweeds have drifted over to the path of armed resistance, others to the extremes of Islam, most are loyal citizens who like being here. Every poll conducted has over 70 percent of them preferring to continue living in Israel even after the creation of an independent Palestinian state. The Arab minority constitutes less than 20 percent of the population, like the ultra-Orthodox, and has roughly the same birth rate as the ultra-Orthodox, so that the two "cancel each other out." The real threat to Israel stems not from its own Arab population but from holding onto the territories. If it continues to retain them, and the almost four million Palestinians who live in them, it will be faced with a fundamental challenge to the democratic nature of the state, and with impossible choices. Within a decade there will be more Arabs than Jews between the Jordan River and the Mediterranean Sea. What happens then?

I ask these questions of my relatives who live on settlements in the West Bank and Gaza. One-on-one they are truly good people and I am in awe of their belief, dedication and pioneering zeal. But it is impossible to have a rational political discussion with them. Their belief in God is so deep and genuine that they have blindly placed their futures entirely in His hands. For them Jordan is Palestine and the West Bank is Judea and Samaria. They even claim a biblical right to Gaza. There is no question in their minds that not one inch can be given up and if the price is Israeli democracy and moral decency so be it. Democracy, they note, had not even been thought of when God mapped out the future Israel to Moses in the desert and when his spies came back with news of the Promised Land. It's all in God's hands they say.

These are the parents speaking. Their children, a new generation of settlers, have grown up in a bubble, cut off from the secular world and realpolitik, taught to take every word in the Bible literally, and to believe that the commandments given to Joshua about cleansing the Land of its enemies three millennia ago are still a divine mission today. They see no place in Greater Israel for anyone but Jews and advocate the transfer of the Palestinian population, whether by incentive or force, to Jordan.

It was this generation of settlers and some of their rabbis who produced Rabin's killer, and it is this generation of settlers who have taken to the hilltops of the West Bank, creating more "facts on the ground," cutting down thousands of Palestinians' olive trees to keep them off land they have lived on for centuries. They do not hesitate to physically attack, sometimes brutally, the soldiers and police sent in the name of the law to evacuate them. This is a wild generation that has to be curtailed, not given weapons by the state ostensibly to defend themselves.

In August 2002 my family flew to Durban, South Africa, on holiday. We chose Durban because we were both exhausted from covering and living with the then two-year war between Israel and the Palestinians and decided to go somewhere where there was little chance of meeting Israelis or Palestinians; we needed to clear our heads. Instead we walked into a city festooned with banners declaring Israel the Apartheid state and denouncing Zionism as racism. These and similar messages were carried on thousands of T-shirts being worn by local youngsters thankful for the free gift. Comparisons of Israel to the hated, oppressive Apartheid regime were present on every corner, at every turn.

We had not known back in March that a UN international conference on racism and discrimination had been scheduled for August, the same month we had chosen for our vacation. It was to have dealt with slavery, the plight of women, genocide in Africa, ethnic cleansing in the Balkans. Instead the agenda was hijacked by the Palestinians and their allies, who had been working for months on the project. They used it to launch what has now become the cornerstone of a Palestinian strategy to demonize Israel by hammering home the comparison of Israel's occupation to Apartheid, hoping to isolate Israel, bring about international sanctions like those that brought Apartheid South Africa to its knees and, ultimately, led to a change of regime. The tactic was repeated when a Palestinian delegation went to the UN International Court of Justice in The Hague in early 2004 to argue against the "Apartheid Wall," as they called Israel's security barrier, though only about eight percent of the barrier is an actual wall and it is not being built to separate Israelis and Palestinians, but as a last-ditch attempt to stop the never-ending wave of suicide bombers terrorizing life in Israel.

Israel is not a racist society. I know, as I came from one. In Apartheid South Africa there was no independent legislature, no free press, no open and accountable government, no equal representation. There was no independent judiciary, so strong in Israel. There was total economic exploitation. It was a world where some two million Whites dominated, enslaved, abused and systematically discriminated against people ten times more numerous than them under the guise of the law. It was a dark place where people disappeared into the night without recourse to legal representation, where more judicial hangings were carried out, even for menial crimes, than any other place on earth. There was no public dialogue; free thinkers were treated brutally if they strayed beyond the permissible. Israel's declaration of independence could not be clearer in stipulating tolerance for all citizens regardless of race, creed, color or religion. The South Africa I grew up in was not the healthy, open, critical, vibrant society I live in today in Israel. There was no universal suffrage, no tolerance or freedom of expression. To compare the two demonstrates ignorance or malevolence. Apartheid South Africa was unique and should be remembered as such lest it be repeated.

But there are racist elements in Israeli society, including one-time cabinet ministers like Avigdor Lieberman and Benny Eilon of the right-wing National Union Party and Effi Eitam of the National Religious Party, who openly advocate the transfer of Palestinians, and others whose hatred of the Arabs knows no bounds. These people consider the Israeli High Court an impediment to their goals. They build on fear, not hope, and believe in power, not conciliation. They complain that the press is too liberal and its freedom should be curbed. Though still a minority, they are adroit at manipulating the political system and have managed to infiltrate the ruling party, the Likud, with the goal of blocking any attempt to uproot settlements or return one inch of land. Even Natan Sharansky, the former Prisoner of Zion and most associated with human rights, is for the occupation, all of it including Gaza, despite the moral costs involved.

They are a force to be reckoned with and one, if successful, that could fundamentally change the future face of Israel. They could turn it into a pariah state in which "security considerations" transpose all else, where might is right, and morality and democracy the words and values of sissies, not "true Zionists." If they succeed the country will inexorably be drawn to the precipice of a moral black hole from which there is no simple return; into a daily routine of continuing to subject tens of thousands of Palestinians to restrictions, roadblocks, body searches and humiliation; of encircling cities and imposing curfews; of creating two societies in one country, one with all the privileges the other with none.

Because of the occupation, discrimination has already started to infiltrate our lives. The Gaza I drove into had two sets of roads, one for Israelis, and the other for Palestinians. Dozens of similar roads (the Palestinians call them Apartheid roads) are now being built in the West Bank so that Jewish settlers can drive to and from home in relative safety. Instead of the road in Gaza being a unique and temporary feature, as it was described to me at the time by one of the Jewish residents of Gush Katif, it has become a model to be emulated: one road for Jews, the other for Palestinians.

In 2004 an emergency regulation was passed at the request of the Interior Ministry, then in the hands of a so-called "enlightened" political party, Shinui, banning Israelis who had married Palestinians from the

West Bank or Gaza from taking up joint residency in Israel. The Israelis, if they wanted, could go live in the territories but Palestinian spouses were barred from living in Israel. Explaining the "temporary" emergency regulation then Interior Minister Avraham Poraz said that Palestinian terrorists were found to be taking advantage of their Israeli residency papers. He admitted that this had only happened in less than a dozen cases out of thousands of marriages but Israel, he said, could not afford to take risks. This emergency regulation was extended, almost without public notice or protest in December 2004. There are dozens of similar examples of the temporary and the threatening becoming permanent, and unremarkable.

These are insidious and dangerous trends to Israel democracy, horribly familiar to me from another life in another place. When I listen to those in Israeli politics who want to keep the territories and believe that power can resolve all, I am reminded of how the Afrikaners put a lot of energy into creating a nuclear weapon that was supposed to have guaranteed their staying in power forever. The problem with their weapon of survival, however, was that it was useless against the real threat to their regime, the challenge from within, those who demanded justice.

The Israeli military could probably rule the territories forever and it certainly has the power to do so. But, as this war has shown us, there are costs involved and the world will not sit idly by as entire Palestinian neighborhoods are reduced to rubble by Israeli bulldozers and tanks trying to hunt down terrorists or get those responsible for firing mortars and rockets at Israeli settlements and towns. Already close allies and former fast friends have accused Israel of "war crimes" and "disproportionate use of force" in its war against the Palestinians.

There is now a strong anti-colonialist sentiment in Europe, perhaps because of its own bloody past in this endeavor. Ethnic cleansing in the Balkans and the genocide in Rwanda have given international justice a new importance. The Geneva Conventions, specifically those clauses pertaining to occupied territory, are being pulled off dusty shelves and reexamined. If their course for Israel's future is followed, there is no doubt that Israel will face isolation and sanctions and be delegitimized as a democracy. The warning bells could not be louder.

Despite this, or maybe because of this, support for the settlers is beginning to diminish and Israelis are eager to see a resolution to the conflict. The polls consistently say that over 70 percent want peace and
would be happy to make a deal with a Palestinian partner they could
trust. The same number says that Israel should unilaterally disengage
from the Palestinians if no agreement is possible. At the heart of this shift
is the ongoing war with the Palestinians that has in four bloody years
claimed the lives of just over a thousand Israelis and three times as many
Palestinians, and left thousands more injured and maimed, some for life.
And what sweet irony that the man now leading the effort to get Israel
out of the territories, or at least some of them, is Ariel Sharon, the great
settlement builder.

In January 2001 he became prime minister, just as Uri Dan predicted,
and Shimon Peres the head of the opposition. Later, the two would join
forces in a national unity government. Together they have a combined
age of over 150, over eighty of them in politics. After Netanyahu and
Barak, the electorate obviously felt it was time for experienced, not ex-
perimental, leadership. They wanted to feel a sturdy hand on the wheel,
not have a prime minister whose feet couldn't reach the pedals.

People wonder how the man most associated with building Israel's
settlements in the occupied territories could now be prepared to tear
some of them down, as he is determined to do in Gaza. They forget that
Sharon, as defense minister under Menachem Begin, bulldozed Yamit
into the ground and oversaw the evacuation of all the Sinai settlements
as part of the peace treaty with Egypt. He is a pragmatist who built the
West Bank settlements because he saw a security threat to Israel from the
east—Iraq, Jordan and Syria. With the Iraqi army destroyed in two suc-
cessive Gulf wars, Israel's peace treaty with Jordan and the Syrians now
isolated and weak, that threat no longer exists. The territories have gone
from being a shield to being a burden.

There are those who argue, probably correctly, that Sharon wants to
get out of Gaza in order to keep most of the West Bank. As he has been
saying for years, he is not prepared to come to a final settlement with the
Palestinians, but is prepared to allow for the creation of an independent
Palestinian State with provisional borders, their final status to be agreed

upon at some later date. In the interim a cease-fire would be observed, trust between the sides rebuilt and, eventually, a final peace treaty signed.

While the Palestinians, understandably, do not want a state with provisional borders and do not want issues like Jerusalem and the return of refugees swept under the rug and referred to committee in perpetuity, there is merit to Sharon's plan. It would formally lead to the establishment of an independent state, begin the process of Israeli withdrawal from Palestinian territories and facilitate the creation of Palestinian institutions capable of enforcing law, order, civil government and an end to terror, nurturing a new environment in which final status issues could be resolved permanently.

Meanwhile, the lack of a viable Palestinian partner as long as Arafat was alive led Israel into unilateralism. The Israelis did not trust Arafat and would not accept his signature on any agreement. He had signed too many bad checks since Oslo. The two most striking aspects of Israel's new unilateralism are the withdrawal from the Gaza settlements and the security barrier now going up like a colossal scar in the land separating Israel from the West Bank, the single most expensive infrastructure project in Israel's history. It is primarily seen as a barrier against terror, not the delineation of Israel's future border, but all understand the political implications. By building the barrier, a border in every respect, with patrol roads, sensors, obstacles, and barbed wire, Israel is drawing a new line in the sand as the de facto boundary until a Palestinian partner comes forth to challenge this country not with war but with peace.

Arafat, as he has proved, was not immortal and in the wings are erudite, intelligent and pragmatic people, many of whom I have had the honor to meet. While they despise Israel for its occupation, they admire it for its democracy, tenacity, strength and will. And better than others they understand that this Six Million are not going to disappear; that at the end of the day we have to live together.

In April 1994 Isabel and I were in South Africa for the first election that signaled the end of Apartheid. The field next to our house at 27 Yeo Street in Yeoville, where Jerry used to call me a fucking Jew, had a line for miles of Blacks waiting to vote for the first time. They cast their ballot in the community center that once had a sign on the door saying "No Blacks Allowed."

At nine o'clock that night, we stood on the steps of the Johannesburg Civic Center just behind Winnie Mandela as the old South African flag came down and the new flag went up. We sang *"Nkosi Sikelel' i Afrika,"* "God Bless Africa," the new national anthem and the song we used to sing surreptitiously in Habonim in defiance of the regime.

I have seen the end of Apartheid and witnessed modern Israel rising from the ashes of the Holocaust. Don't tell me miracles can't happen.

SELECTED BIBLIOGRAPHY

Some Documents and Books Consulted in the Course of Writing.

SOUTHERN AFRICA AND THE JEWS

The Jews of South Africa: An Illustrated History to 1953, by Gustav Saron, edited by Naomi Musiker. Scarecrow Books, Metuchen, N.J., 2001; published in association with the South African Board of Deputies.

Founders and Followers: Johannesburg Jewry 1887–1915, edited by Mendel Kaplan and Marian Robertson. Vlaerg Publishers, Cape Town, 1991.

Zion in Africa: The Jews of Zambia, by Hugh Macmillan and Frank Shapiro. I.B. Tauris, London/New York, 1999; published in association with the Council for Zambia Jewry.

Rivonia's Children: Three Families and the Cost of Conscience in White South Africa, by Glenn Frankel. Farrar, Straus & Giroux, New York, 1999.

The Mind of South Africa: The Story of the Rise and Fall of Apartheid, by Allister Sparks. William Heinemann Ltd., London, 1990.

Jews and Zionism: The South African Experience 1910–1967, by Gideon Shimoni. Oxford University Press, Cape Town, 1980.

Community and Conscience: The Jews and Apartheid South Africa, by Gideon Shimoni. University Press of New England, Hanover, N.H., 2003.

ISRAEL

General

The Dairies of Theodor Herzl. Victor Gollancz Ltd., London, 1958.

Israel: A History, by Martin Gilbert. William Morrow & Company, New York, 1998.

A History of the Israeli-Palestinian Conflict, by Mark Tessler. Indiana University Press, Bloomington/Indianapolis, 1994.

Israel Now: Portrait of a Troubled Land, by Lawrence Meyer. Delacorte Press, New York, 1982.

Israel, Army and Defence: A Dictionary, edited by Zeev Schiff and Eitan Haber. Zmora-Bitan-Modan Publishers, Herzlia, Israel, 1976 (in Hebrew).

Justice in Jerusalem, by Gideon Hausner. Harper & Row, New York, 1966.

The Arab-Israel Wars: War and Peace in the Middle East from the War of Independence Through Lebanon, by Chaim Herzog. Random House, New York, 1982.

The Making of Modern Zionism: The Intellectual Origins of the Jewish State, by Shlomo Avineri. Basic Books, New York, 1981.

Biographies/Autobiographies

Ben Gurion, State-Builder: Principles and Pragmatism, 1948–1963, by Avraham Avi-hai. John Wiley & Sons, New York/Toronto, and Israel Universities Press, Jerusalem, 1974.

Chaim Weizmann: The Making of a Statesman, by Jehuda Reinharz. Oxford University Press, New York/Oxford, 1993.

Eshkol: The Man and the Nation, by Terrence Prittie. Pitman Publishing, New York/Toronto/London/Tel Aviv, 1969.

Golda Meir: The Romantic Years, by Ralph G. Martin. Piatkus Books, London, 1988.

The Story of My Life, by Moshe Dayan. Edanim Publishers, Jerusalem, 1976; published in collaboration with Dvir Publishing House, Tel Aviv, Yediot Aharonot Edition (in Hebrew).

Abba Eban: An Autobiography, by Abba Eban. Random House, New York, 1977.

The New Diplomacy: International Affairs in the Modern Age, by Abba Eban. Weidenfeld & Nicolson, London, 1983.

The Life and Times of Menachem Begin, by Amos Perlmutter. Doubleday & Company, Garden City, N.Y., 1987.

To Win or To Die: A Personal Portrait of Menachem Begin, by Ned Temko. William Morrow & Company, New York, 1987.

On Eagles' Wings: The Personal Story of the Leading Commander of the Israeli Air Force, by Ezer Weizman. Weidenfeld & Nicolson, London, 1976.

Raful (Rafael Eitan): Story of a Soldier, by Rafael Eitan with Dov Goldstein. Ma'ariv, Tel Aviv, 1985 (in Hebrew).

The New Middle East, by Shimon Peres. Henry Holt & Company, New York, 1986.

A Place Among the Nations: Israel and the World, by Benjamin Netanyahu. Bantam Books, New York, 1993.

Warrior: An Autobiography, by Ariel Sharon with David Chanoff. Macdonald, London, and Simon & Schuster, New York, 1989.

Shalom, Friend: The Life and Legacy of Yitzhak Rabin, by The Jerusalem Report Staff, edited by David Horovitz with prologue by Hirsh Goodman. Newmarket Press, New York, 1996.

War

Diary of the Sinai Campaign, by Major-General Moshe Dayan. Steimatzky's Agency Limited, Jerusalem/Tel Aviv/Haifa, 1965; English edition, Weidenfeld & Nicolson, 1966.

The Battle for Jerusalem: June 5–7, 1967, by Abraham Rabinovich. The Jewish Publication Society, Philadelphia/New York/Jerusalem, 1987.

Six Days of War: June 1967 and the Making of the Modern Middle East, by Michael B. Oren. Oxford University Press, New York/Oxford, 2002.

The Liberty Incident: The 1967 Israeli Attack on the U.S. Navy Spy Ship, by A. Jay Cristol. Brassey's Inc., Washington, D.C., 2002.

The Boats of Cherbourg: The Secret Israeli Operation That Revolutionized Naval Warfare, by Abraham Rabinovich. Seaver Books, Henry Holt & Company, New York, 1988.

"Today War Will Break Out": The Reminiscences of Brig. Gen. Israel Lior, Aide-de-Camp to Prime Ministers Levi Eshkol and Golda Meir, by Eitan Haber. Edanim Publishers, Jerusalem, Yediot Aharonot Edition, 1987.

Earthquake in October: The Yom-Kippur War, by Zeev Schiff. Zmora-Bitan-Modan Publishers, Herzlia, Israel, 1974.

Yom Kippur War Lexicon, by Eitan Haber and Zeev Schiff. Zmora-Bitan-Dvir Publishers, Or Yehuda, Israel, 2003 (in Hebrew).

Dado, 48 Years and 20 Days: The Full Story of the Yom Kippur War and of the Man Who Led Israel's Army, by Hanoch Bartov. Ma'ariv Book Guild, Tel Aviv, 1981.

Israel's Lebanon War, by Zeev Schiff and Ehud Ya'ari. Counterpoint, London, and Unwin Paperbacks, Boston/Sydney, 1986.

Going All the Way: Christian Warlords, Israeli Adventurers, and the War in Lebanon, by Jonathan C. Randal. Viking Press, New York, 1983.

Fatah, by Ehud Ya'ari. A. Levin-Epstein Ltd., Publishers, Tel Aviv, 1970 (in Hebrew).

Intifada: The Palestinian Uprising—Israel's Third Front, by Zeev Schiff and Ehud Ya'ari. Simon & Schuster, New York, 1989.

Peace/Price of Peace

The Year of the Dove, by E. Ya'ari and Zeev Schiff. Michaelmark Books, Zmora-Bitan-Modan Publishers, Tel Aviv, 1980 (in Hebrew).

The Battle for Peace, by Ezer Weizman. Bantam Books, New York, 1981.

Murder in the Name of God: The Plot to Kill Yitzhak Rabin, by Michael Karpin and Ina Friedman. Metropolitan Books, Henry Holt & Company, New York, 1998.

Harakiri: Ehud Barak: The Failure, by Raviv Druker. Miskal, Yedioth Ahronoth Books and Chemed Books, Tel Aviv, 2002 (in Hebrew).

Just Beyond Reach: The Israel-Palestinian Peace Negotiations 1999–2001, by Gilead Sher. Miskal, Yedioth Ahronoth Books and Chemed Books, Tel Aviv, 2001 (in Hebrew).

Internal Israel

Piety and Power: The World of Jewish Fundamentalism, by David Landau. Secker & Warburg, London, 1993.

The Palestinian-Arab Minority in Israel 1948–2000: A Political Study, by As'ad Ghanem. State University of New York Press, Albany, 2001.

The Annual Statistical Survey. Government Office of Statistics, Jerusalem, 1948 to present.

Racism in Israel 2004: A Special Annual Report, edited by Fuoad Aza'ar. Mossawa Center, The Advocacy Center for Arab Citizens of Israel, Haifa, 2004.

Settlements

Theft of Land: Israel's Settlement Policy on the West Bank. B'Tselem, 2002. Ongoing Survey, Peace Now, Jerusalem.

Tearing Ourselves Apart: After 35 Years Israel Still Can't Decide Where It Wants to Settle, by Isabel Kershner. *The Jerusalem Report,* November 2002.

The Price of Settlement. Ha'aretz Special Report, September 2003.

Archives

Author's articles in *The Jerusalem Post* archives.

Author's articles in *The Jerusalem Report* archives.

Ha'aretz archives.

INDEX

PUBLICAFFAIRS is a publishing house founded in 1997. It is a tribute to the standards, values, and flair of three persons who have served as mentors to countless reporters, writers, editors, and book people of all kinds, including me.

I. F. STONE, proprietor of *I. F. Stone's Weekly,* combined a commitment to the First Amendment with entrepreneurial zeal and reporting skill and became one of the great independent journalists in American history. At the age of eighty, Izzy published *The Trial of Socrates,* which was a national bestseller. He wrote the book after he taught himself ancient Greek.

BENJAMIN C. BRADLEE was for nearly thirty years the charismatic editorial leader of *The Washington Post.* It was Ben who gave the *Post* the range and courage to pursue such historic issues as Watergate. He supported his reporters with a tenacity that made them fearless, and it is no accident that so many became authors of influential, best-selling books.

ROBERT L. BERNSTEIN, the chief executive of Random House for more than a quarter century, guided one of the nation's premier publishing houses. Bob was personally responsible for many books of political dissent and argument that challenged tyranny around the globe. He is also the founder and was the longtime chair of Human Rights Watch, one of the most respected human rights organizations in the world.

·   ·   ·

For fifty years, the banner of Public Affairs Press was carried by its owner, Morris B. Schnapper, who published Gandhi, Nasser, Toynbee, Truman, and about 1,500 other authors. In 1983 Schnapper was described by *The Washington Post* as "a redoubtable gadfly." His legacy will endure in the books to come.

Peter Osnos, *Publisher*